CHILTON'S
REPAIR & TUNE-UP GUIDE
PONTIAC FIERO
1984 to
1985

All U.S. and Canadian models of Pontiac Fiero

President LAWRENCE A. FORNASIERI
Vice President and General Manager JOHN P. KUSHNERICK
Executive Editor KERRY A. FREEMAN, S.A.E.
Senior Editor RICHARD J. RIVELE, S.A.E.
Editor MARTIN J. GUNTHER

CHILTON BOOK COMPANY
Radnor, Pennsylvania
19089

SAFETY NOTICE

Proper service and repair procedures are vital to the safe, reliable operation of all motor vehicles, as well as the personal safety of those performing repairs. This book outlines procedures for servicing and repairing vehicles using safe, effective methods. The procedures contain many NOTES, CAUTIONS and WARNINGS which should be followed along with standard safety procedures to eliminate the possibility of personal injury or improper service which could damage the vehicle or compromise its safety.

It is important to note that repair procedures and techniques, tools and parts for servicing motor vehicles, as well as the skill and experience of the individual performing the work vary widely. It is not possible to anticipate all of the conceivable ways or conditions under which vehicles may be serviced, or to provide cautions as to all of the possible hazards that may result. Standard and accepted safety precautions and equipment should be used when handling toxic or flammable fluids, and safety goggles or other protection should be used during cutting, grinding, chiseling, prying, or any other process that can cause material removal or projectiles.

Some procedures require the use of tools specially designed for a specific purpose. Before substituting another tool or procedure, you must be completely satisfied that neither your personal safety, nor the performance of the vehicle will be endangered.

Although information in this guide is based on industry sources and is as complete as possible at the time of publication, the possibility exists that the manufacturer made later changes which could not be included here. While striving for total accuracy, Chilton Book Company cannot assume responsibility for any errors, changes, or omissions that may occur in the compilation of this data.

PART NUMBERS

Part numbers listed in this reference are not recommendations by Chilton for any product by brand name. They are references that can be used with interchange manuals and aftermarket supplier catalogs to locate each brand supplier's discrete part number.

SPECIAL TOOLS

Special tools are recommended by the vehicle manufacturer to perform their specific job. Use has been kept to a minimum, but where absolutely necessary, they are referred to in the text by the part number of the tool manufacturer. These tools can be purchased, under the appropriate part number, from Service Tool Division, Kent-Moore Corporation, 29784, Little Mack Rd., Roseville, Michigan, 48066-2298—or an equivalent tool can be purchased locally from a tool supplier or parts outlet. Before substituting any tool for the one recommended, read the SAFETY NOTICE at the top of this page.

ACKNOWLEDGMENTS

The Chilton Book Company expresses its appreciation to the Pontiac Motor Division, General Motors Corporation for their generous assistance.

Manufactured in the United States of America
1234567890   4321098765

Chilton's Repair & Tune-Up Guide: Pontiac Fiero 1984–85
ISBN 0-8019-7571-9 pbk.
Library of Congress Catalog Card No. 84-45473

CONTENTS

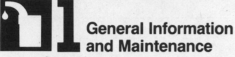

1 General Information and Maintenance

2 Tune-Up and Performance Maintenance

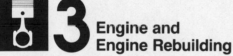

3 Engine and Engine Rebuilding

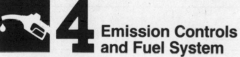

4 Emission Controls and Fuel System

5 Chassis Electrical

6 Clutch and Transaxle

7 Suspension and Steering

8 Brakes

9 Troubleshooting

Quick Reference
Specifications For Your Vehicle

Fill in this chart with the most commonly used specifications for your vehicle. Specifications can be found in Chapters 1 through 3 or on the tune-up decal under the hood of the vehicle.

 Tune-Up

Firing Order_____

Spark Plugs:

    Type_____

    Gap (in.)_____

Point Gap (in.)_____

Dwell Angle (°)_____

Ignition Timing (°)_____

    Vacuum (Connected/Disconnected)_____

Valve Clearance (in.)

    Intake_____   Exhaust_____

 Capacities

Engine Oil (qts)

    With Filter Change_____

    Without Filter Change_____

Cooling System (qts)_____

Manual Transmission (pts)_____

    Type_____

Automatic Transmission (pts)_____

    Type_____

Front Differential (pts)_____

    Type_____

Rear Differential (pts)_____

    Type_____

Transfer Case (pts)_____

    Type_____

FREQUENTLY REPLACED PARTS

Use these spaces to record the part numbers of frequently replaced parts.

PCV VALVE	OIL FILTER	AIR FILTER
Manufacturer_____	Manufacturer_____	Manufacturer_____
Part No._____	Part No._____	Part No._____

General Information and Maintenance

HOW TO USE THIS BOOK

Chilton's Repair and Tune-Up Guide for the Pontiac Fiero is intended to help you learn more about the inner workings of your vehicle and save you money on its upkeep and operation.

The first two chapters will be the most used, since they contain maintenance and tune-up information and procedures. Studies have shown that a properly tuned and maintained car can get at least 10% better gas mileage than an out-of-tune car. The other chapters deal with the more complex systems of your car. Operating systems from engine through brakes are covered to the extent that the average do-it-yourselfer becomes mechanically involved. This book will not explain such things as rebuilding the differential for the simple reason that the expertise required and the investment in special tools make this task uneconomical. It will give you the detailed instructions to help you change your own brake pads and shoes, replace points and plugs, and do many more jobs that will save you money, give you personal satisfaction, and help you avoid expensive problems.

A secondary purpose of this book is a reference for owners who want to understand their car and/or their mechanics better. In this case, no tools at all are required.

Before removing any bolts, read through the entire procedure. This will give you the overall view of what tools and supplies will be required. There is nothing more frustrating than having to walk to the bus stop on Monday morning because you were short one bolt on Sunday afternoon. So read ahead and plan ahead. Each operation should be approached logically and all procedures thoroughly understood before attempting any work.

All chapters contain adjustments, maintenance, removal and installation procedures, and repair and overhaul procedures. When repair is not considered practical, we tell you how to remove the part and then how to install the new or rebuilt replacement. In this way, you at least save the labor costs. Backyard repair of such components as the alternator is just not practical.

Two basic mechanic's rules should be mentioned here. First, whenever the left side of the car or engine is referred to, it is meant to specify the driver's side of the car. Conversely, the right side of the car means the passenger's side. Second, most screws and bolts are removed by turning counterclockwise, and tightened by turning clockwise.

Safety is always the most important rule. Constantly be aware of the dangers involved in working on an automobile and taking the proper precautions. (See the section in this chapter "Servicing Your Vehicle Safely" and the SAFETY NOTICE on the acknowledgments page)

Pay attention to the instructions provided. There are 3 common mistakes in mechanical work:

1. Incorrect order of assembly, disassembly or adjustment. When taking something apart or putting it together, doing things in the wrong order usually just costs you extra time, however it CAN break something. Read the entire procedure before beginning disassembly. Do everything in the order in which the instructions say you should do it, even if you can't immediately see a reason for it. When you're taking apart something that is very intricate (for example a carburetor), you might want to draw a picture of how it looks when assembled at one point in order to make sure you get everything back in its proper position (we will supply exploded views whenever possible). When making adjustments, especially tune-up adjustments, do them in order. Often one adjustment affects another, and you cannot expect even satisfactory results unless each adjust-

ment is made only when it cannot be changed by any other.

2. Overtorquing (or undertorquing). While it is more common for overtorquing to cause damage, undertorquing can cause a fastener to vibrate loose causing serious damage. Especially when dealing with aluminum parts, pay attention to torque specifications and utilize a torque wrench in assembly. If a torque figure is not available, remember that if you are using the right tool to do the job, you will probably not have to strain yourself to get a fastener tight enough. The pitch of most threads is so slight that the tension you put on the wrench will be multiplied many, many times in actual force on what you are tightening. A good example of how critical torque is can be seen in the case of spark plug installation, especially where you are putting the plug into an aluminum cylinder head. Too little torque can fail to crush the gasket, causing leakage of combustion gases and consequent overheating of the plug and engine parts. Too much torque can damage the threads, or distort the plug, which changes the spark gap.

There are many commercial products available for ensuring that fasteners won't come loose, even if they are not torqued just right (a very common brand is "Loctite"). If you're worried about getting something together tightly enough to hold, but loosely enough to avoid mechanical damage during assembly, one of these products might offer substantial insurance. Read the label on the package and make sure the product is compatible with the materials, fluids, etc. involved before choosing one.

3. Crossthreading. This occurs when a part such as a bolt is screwed into a nut or casting at the wrong angle and forced. Crossthreading is more likely to occur if access is difficult. It helps to clean and lubricate fasteners, and to start threading with the part to be installed going straight in. Then, start the bolt, spark plug, etc. with your fingers. If you encounter resistance, unscrew the part and start over again at a different angle until it can be inserted and turned several turns without much effort. Keep in mind that many parts, especially spark plugs, use tapered threads so that gentle turning will automatically bring the part you're threading to the proper angle if you don't force it or resist a change in angle. Don't put a wrench on the part until it's been turned a couple of turns by hand. If you suddenly encounter resistance, and the part has not seated fully, don't force it. Pull it back out and make sure it's clean and threading properly. Always take your time and be patient; once you have some experience, working on your car will become an enjoyable hobby.

TOOLS AND EQUIPMENT

Naturally, without the proper tools and equipment it is impossible to properly service your vehicle. It would be impossible to catalog each tool that you would need to perform each or every operation in this book. It would also be unwise for the amateur to rush out and buy an expensive set of tools on the theory that he may need one or more of them at sometime.

The best approach is to proceed slowly, gathering together a good quality set of those tools that are used most frequently. Don't be misled by the low cost of bargain tools. It is far better to spend a little more for better quality. Forged wrenches, 10 or 12 point sockets and fine tooth ratchets are by far preferable to their less expensive counterparts. As any good mechanic can tell you, there are few worse experiences than trying to work on a car or truck with bad tools. Your monetary savings will be far outweighed by frustration and mangled knuckles.

Begin accumulating those tools that are used most frequently; those associated with routine maintenance and tune-up.

In addition to the normal assortment of screwdrivers and pliers you should have the following tools for routine maintenance jobs (your Fiero uses both SAE and metric fasteners):

1. SAE/Metric wrenches, sockets and combination open end/box end wrenches in sizes from 1/8 in. to 3/4 in. and 3mm to 19mm; and a spark plug socket (5/8in.). If possible, buy various length socket drive extensions. One break in this department is that the metric sockets available in the U.S. will all fit the ratchet handles and extensions you may already have (1/4, 3/8, and 1/2 in. drive).

2. Jackstands for support
3. Oil filter wrench
4. Oil filter spout for pouring oil
5. Grease gun for chassis lubrication
6. Hydrometer for checking the battery
7. A container for draining oil
8. Many rags for wiping up the inevitable mess

In addition to the above items there are several others that are not absolutely necessary, but handy to have around. These include absorbant gravel, a transmission funnel and the usual supply of lubricants, antifreeze and fluids, although these can be purchased as needed. This is a basic list for routine maintenance. Only your personal needs and desires can accurately determine your list of tools.

The second list of tools is for tune-ups. While the tools involved here are slightly more sophisticated, they need not be outrageously expensive. There are several inexpensive tach/dwell meters on the market that are every bit as good for the average mechanic as a $100.00 professional model. Just be sure that it goes to at least 1200–1500 rpm on the tach scale and that it works on 4, 6 and 8 cylinder engines. A basic list of tune-up equipment could include:

1. Tach-dwell meter
2. Spark plug wrench
3. Timing light (a DC light that works from the car's battery is best, although an AC light that plugs into 110V house current will suffice at some sacrifice in brightness)
4. Wire spark plug gauge/adjusting tools
5. Set of feeler blades

Here again, be guided by your own needs. A feeler blade will set the point gap as easily as dwell meter will read dwell, but slightly less accurately. And since you will need a tachometer anyway.......well, make your own decision.

In addition to these basic tools, there are several other tools and gauges you may find useful. These include:

1. A compression gauge. The screw-in type is slower to use, but eliminates the possibility of a faulty reading due to escaping pressure
2. A manifold vacuum gauge
3. A test light
4. An induction meter. This is used for determining whether or not there is current in a wire. These are handy for use if a wire is broken somewhere in a wiring harness

As a final note, you will probably find a torque wrench necessary for all but the most basic work. The beam type models are perfectly adequate, although the newer click type are more precise.

Special Tools

Normally, the use of special factory tools is avoided for repair procedures, since these are not readily available for the do-it-yourself mechanic. When it is possible to perform the job with more commonly available tools, it will be pointed out, but occasionally, a special tool was designed to perform a specific function and should be used. Before substituting another tool, you should be convinced that neither your safety nor the performance of the vehicle will be compromised.

Some special tools are available commercially from major tool manufacturers. Others can be purchased from:

Service Tool Division, Kent-Moore Corporation, 29784, Little Mack Rd., Roseville, Michigan, 48066-2298

SERVICING YOUR VEHICLE SAFELY

It is virtually impossible to anticipate all of the hazards involved with automotive maintenance and service but care and common sense will prevent most accidents.

The rules of safety for mechanics range from "don't smoke around gasoline," to "use the proper tool for the job." The trick to avoiding injuries is to develop safe work habits and take every possible precaution.

Do's

• Do keep a fire extinguisher and first aid kit within easy reach.
• Do wear safety glasses or goggles when cutting, drilling or prying, even if you have 20-20 vision. If you wear glasses for the sake of vision, then they should be made of hardened glass that can serve also as safety glasses, or wear safety goggles over your regular glasses.
• Do shield your eyes whenever you work around the battery. Batteries contain sulphuric acid; in case of contact with the eyes or skin, flush the area with water or a mixture of water and baking soda and get medical attention immediately.
• Do use safety stands for any undercar service. Jacks are for raising vehicles; safety stands are for making sure the vehicle stays raised until you want it to come down. Whenever the vehicle is raised, block the wheels remaining on the ground and set the parking brake.
• Do use adequate ventilation when working with any chemicals. Asbestos dust resulting from brake lining wear is a suspected cancer causing agent.
• Do disconnect the negative battery cable when working on the electrical system. The primary ignition system can contain up to 40,000 volts.
• Do follow manufacturer's directions whenever working with potentially hazardous materials. Both brake fluid and antifreeze are poisonous if taken internally. Pets, especially cats and dogs seem to have an affinity for drinking ethylene glycol based antifreeze. It wouldn't take much to cause a fatal dose for a household pet. If any is spilled, wash it away. Never store antifreeze in an open container.
• Do properly maintain your tools. Loose hammerheads, mushroomed punches and chisels, frayed or poorly grounded electrical cords, excessively worn screwdrivers, spread wrenches (open end), cracked sockets, slipping ratchets, or faulty droplight sockets can cause accidents.

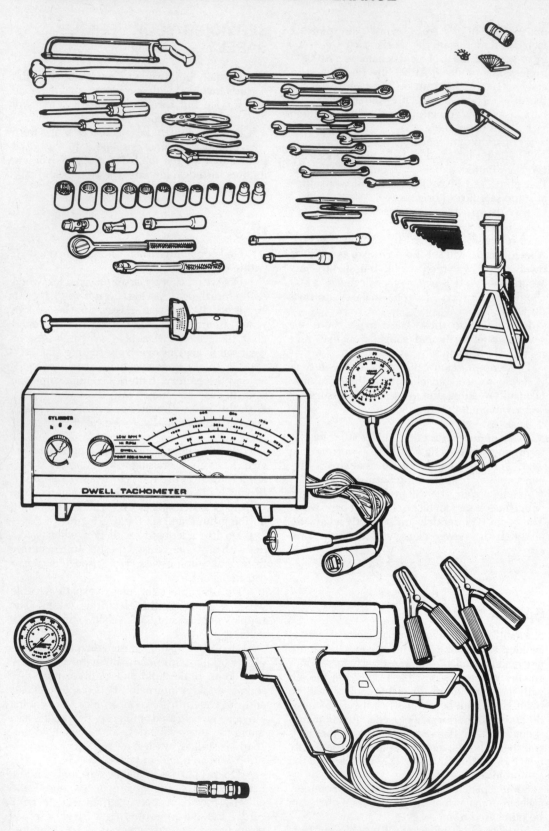

This basic collection of hand tools will handle most service needs

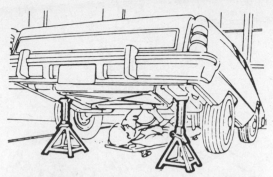

Always support the vehicle with jack stands when working underneath it

• Do use the proper size and type of tool for the job being done.

• Do when possible, pull on a wrench handle rather than push on it, and adjust your stance to prevent a fall.

• Do be sure that adjustable wrenches are tightly adjusted on the nut or bolt and pulled so that the face is on the side of the fixed jaw.

• Do select a wrench or socket that fits the nut or bolt. The wrench or socket should sit straight, not cocked.

• Do strike squarely with a hammer. Avoid glancing blows.

• Do set the parking brake and block the drive wheels if the work requires that the engine be running.

Don'ts

• Don't run an engine in a garage or anywhere else without proper ventilation—EVER! Carbon monoxide is poisonous; it takes a long time to leave the human body and you can build up a deadly supply of it in your system by simply breathing in a little every day. You may not realize you are slowly poisoning yourself. Always use power vents, windows, fans or open the garage doors.

• Don't work around moving parts while wearing a necktie or other loose clothing. Short sleeves are much safer than long, loose sleeves. Hard-toed shoes with neoprene soles protect your toes and give a better grip on slippery surfaces. Jewelry such as watches, fancy belt buckles, beads or body adornment of any kind is not safe working around a car. Long hair should be hidden under a hat or cap.

• Don't use pockets for toolboxes. A fall or bump can drive a screwdriver deep into you body. Even a wiping cloth hanging from the back pocket can wrap around a spinning shaft or fan.

• Don't smoke when working around gasoline, cleaning solvent or other flammable material.

• Don't smoke when working around the battery. When the battery is being charged, it gives off explosive hydrogen gas.

• Don't use gasoline to wash your hands; there are excellent soaps available. Gasoline may contain lead, and lead can enter the body through a cut, accumulating in the body until you are very ill. Gasoline also removes all the natural oils from the skin so that bone dry hands will suck up oil and grease.

• Don't service the air conditioning system unless you are equipped with the necessary tools and training. The refrigerant, R-12, is extremely cold and when exposed to the air, will instantly freeze any surface it comes in contact with, including your eyes. Although the refrigerant is normally non-toxic, R-12 becomes a deadly poisonous gas in the presence of an open flame. One good whiff of the vapors from burning refrigerant can be fatal.

SERIAL NUMBER IDENTIFICATION

It is important for servicing and ordering parts to be certain of the vehicle and engine identification. The VIN (Vehicle Identification Number) is a 17 digit number visible through the windshield on the drivers side of the dash. The 10th digit indicates the model year, and the 8th digit identifies the factory installed engine.

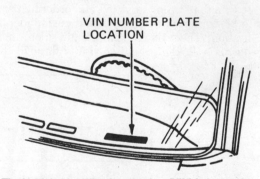

The Vehicle Identification number (VIN) is located on the driver's side of the dash

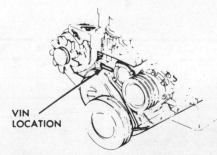

Four Cylinder- 151 engine code location

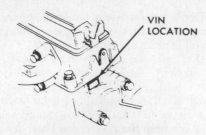

V6-173 engine code location

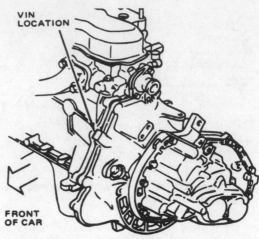

FRONT OF CAR

Four speed transmission code location

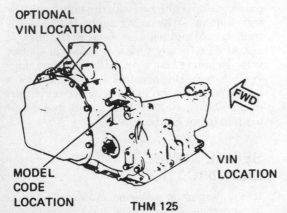

Automatic transmission code location

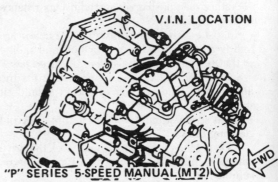

"P" SERIES 5-SPEED MANUAL (MT2)

Five speed transmission code location

VEHICLE IDENTIFICATION NUMBER (VIN)

It is important for servicing and ordering parts to be certain of the vehicle and engine identification. The VIN (vehicle identification number) is a 17 digit number visible through the windshield on the driver's side of the dash and contains the vehicle and engine identification codes. It can be interpreted as follows:

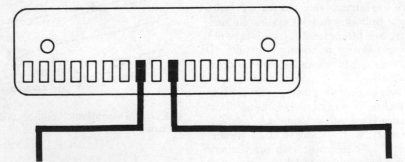

Engine Code

Code	Cu. In.	Liters	Cyl.	Carb	Eng. Mfg.
R	151	2.5	4	TBI	Pontiac
9	173	2.8	6	MFI	Chev.

Model Year Code

Code	Year
E	1984
F	1985

The seventeen digit Vehicle Identification Number can be used to determine engine application and model year. The 10th digit indicates the model year, and the 8th digit identifies the factory installed engine.
TBI (Throttle body injection)
MFI (Multi-port fuel injection)

ROUTINE MAINTENANCE

Air Filter And Crankcase Separator

REMOVAL AND INSTALLATION

Four Cylinder Engine

The air filter and crankcase separator should be replaced together periodically.

1. Remove the air cleaner cover by removing the two nuts on top of the air cleaner.

2. Remove the air filter from the air cleaner.

3. To remove the separator, lift up on the air cleaner assembly and move to one side without disconnecting any rubber tubing.

4. Remove the separator from the valve cover by pulling straight up

5. Installation is the reverse of removal. Tighten the cover nuts to 4 ft. lbs.

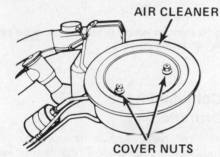

Air filter cover nuts - Four cyl. engine

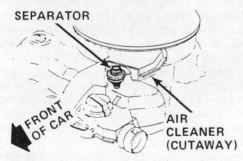

Crankcase separator - four cyl. engine

V6

The V6 uses a remotely mounted air cleaner canister, connected to the engine via a flexible duct. To replace the paper element, remove the nut securing the canister top, lift off the top and replace the element. Replace the top and tighten the nut

PCV Valve

REMOVAL AND INSTALLATION

1. With the hose attached, pull the valve out of the grommet with a twisting motion.

NOTE: *It may be necessary to roll the grommet back, in order to remove the PCV valve.*

2. Push the clip tabs in the opposite direction to open the clip which holds the rubber hose in place.

3. Separate the hose and the PCV valve with a twisting motion.

4. Before installing the PCV valve, coat the end to be inserted in the rubber hose with a small amount of oil.

NOTE: *For further information and illustrations, please refer to Chapter 4 under PCV Systems.*

Evaporative Emission Control Canister

NOTE: *For testing and removal and installation procedures for the evaporator canister, please refer to Chapter 4 under Evaporative Emission Control System.*

Battery

All Fieros are equipped with maintenance-free batteries, which do not require normal attention as far as fluid level checks are concerned. However, the terminals require periodic cleaning, which should be performed at least once a year.

The sealed top battery cannot be checked for charge in the normal manner, since there is no provision for access to the electrolyte. To check the condition of the battery:

FLUID LEVEL

1. If the indicator eye on top of the battery is dark, the battery has enough fluid. If the eye is light, the electrolyte level is too low and the battery must be replaced.

2. If the green dot appears in the middle of the eye, the battery is sufficiently charged. If no green dot is visible charge the battery at this rate.

Charging Rate Amps	Time
75	40 min
50	1 hr
25	2 hr
10	5 hr

CAUTION: *Do not charge the battery for more than 50 amp/hours. If the green dot appears, or if the electrolyte squirts out of the vent hole stop the charge.*

NOTE: *It may be necessary to tip the bat-*

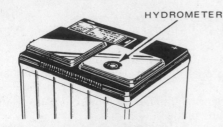

Indicator eye on the top of the battery

tery from side to side to get the green dot to appear after charging.

CABLES AND CLAMPS

At least twice a year, clean the side terminals and cable ends. Loosen the clamp bolts (you may have to brush off any corrosion with baking soda and water solution if they are really messy) and remove the cables, negative cable first. There is a special cleaning tool available for cleaning side terminal batteries. When using this tool, make sure you get the terminal and the cable ends clean and shiny. Any oxidation, corrosion or foreign material will prevent a sound electrical connection and inhibit either starting or charging.

Check the battery tray and wash it off with warm soapy water, rinse and dry. Any rust

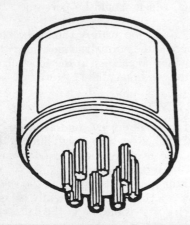

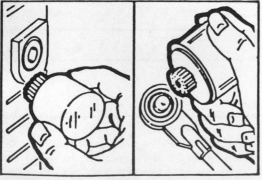

A special tool is available for cleaning the side terminals and clamps

should be sanded away, and the tray given at least two coats of a quality anti-rust paint.

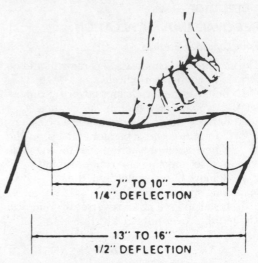

A gauge is recommended, but you can check the belt tension with thumb pressure.

Air Conditioning

PRECAUTIONS

There are two particular hazards associated with air conditioning systems and they both relate to refrigerant gas.

First, the refrigerant gas is an extremely cold substance. When exposed to air, it will instantly freeze any surface it comes in contact with, including your eyes. The other hazard relates to fire. Although normally non-toxic, refrigerant gas becomes highly poisonous in the presence of an open flame. One good whiff of the vapor formed by burning refrigerant can be fatal. Keep all forms of fire (including cigarettes) well clear of the air conditioning system.

Any repair work to an air conditioning system should be left to a professional. DO NOT, under any circumstances, attempt to loosen or tighten any fittings or perform any work other than that outlined here.

CHECKING FOR OIL LEAKS

Refrigerant leaks show up only as oily areas on the various components because the compressor oil is transported around the entire system along with the refrigerant. Look for oily spots on all the hoses and lines, and especially on hose and tube connections. If there are oily deposits, the system may have a leak, and you should have it checked by a qualified repairperson.

HOW TO SPOT WORN V-BELTS

V-Belts are vital to efficient engine operation—they drive the fan, water pump and other accessories. They require little maintenance (occasional tightening) but they will not last forever. Slipping or failure of the V-belt will lead to overheating. If your V-belt looks like any of these, it should be replaced.

This belt has deep cracks, which cause it to flex. Too much flexing leads to heat build-up and premature failure. These cracks can be caused by using the belt on a pulley that is too small. Notched belts are available for small diameter pulleys.

Cracking or weathering

Oil and grease on a belt can cause the belt's rubber compounds to soften and separate from the reinforcing cords that hold the belt together. The belt will first slip, then finally fail altogether.

Softening (grease and oil)

Glazing is caused by a belt that is slipping. A slipping belt can cause a run-down battery, erratic power steering, overheating or poor accessory performance. The more the belt slips, the more glazing will be built up on the surface of the belt. The more the belt is glazed, the more it will slip. If the glazing is light, tighten the belt.

Glazing

The cover of this belt is worn off and is peeling away. The reinforcing cords will begin to wear and the belt will shortly break. When the belt cover wears in spots or has a rough jagged appearance, check the pulley grooves for roughness.

Worn cover

This belt is on the verge of breaking and leaving you stranded. The layers of the belt are separating and the reinforcing cords are exposed. It's just a matter of time before it breaks completely.

Separation

HOW TO SPOT BAD HOSES

Both the upper and lower radiator hoses are called upon to perform difficult jobs in an inhospitable environment. They are subject to nearly 18 psi at under hood temperatures often over 280°F., and must circulate nearly 7500 gallons of coolant an hour—3 good reasons to have good hoses.

A good test for any hose is to feel it for soft or spongy spots. Frequently these will appear as swollen areas of the hose. The most likely cause is oil soaking. This hose could burst at any time, when hot or under pressure.

Swollen hose

Cracked hoses can usually be seen but feel the hoses to be sure they have not hardened; a prime cause of cracking. This hose has cracked down to the reinforcing cords and could split at any of the cracks.

Cracked hose

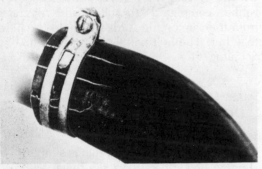

Weakened clamps frequently are the cause of hose and cooling system failure. The connection between the pipe and hose has deteriorated enough to allow coolant to escape when the engine is hot.

Frayed hose end (due to weak clamp)

Debris, rust and scale in the cooling system can cause the inside of a hose to weaken. This can usually be felt on the outside of the hose as soft or thinner areas.

Debris in cooling system

NOTE: *A small area of oil on the front of the compressor is normal and no cause for alarm.*

CHECK THE COMPRESSOR BELT

Refer to the section in this chapter on "Drive Belts".

KEEP THE CONDENSER CLEAR

Periodically inspect the front of the condenser for bent fins or foreign material (dirt, bugs, leaves, etc.) If any cooling fins are bent, straighten them carefully with needle nose pliers. You can remove any debris with a stiff bristle brush or hose.

OPERATE THE A/C SYSTEM PERIODICALLY

A lot of A/C problems can be avoided by simply running the air conditioner at least once a week, regardless of the season. Simply let the system run for at least 5 minutes a week (even in the winter), and you'll keep the internal parts lubricated as well as preventing the hoses from hardening.

REFRIGERANT LEVEL ChECK

The first order of business when checking the sight glass is to find the sight glass. It is located in the head of the receiver/drier. Once you've found it, wipe it clean and proceed as follows:

1. With the engine and the air conditioning system running, look for the flow of refrigerant through the sight glass. If the air conditioner is working properly, you'll be able to see a continuous flow of clear refrigerant through the sight glass, with perhaps an occasional bubble at very high temperatures.

2. Cycle the air conditioner on and off to make sure what you are seeing is clear refrigerant. Since the refrigerant is clear, it is possible to mistake a completely discharged system for one that is fully charged. Turn the system off and watch the sight glass. If there is refrigerant in the system, you'll see bubbles during the off cycle. If you observe no bubbles when the system is running, and the air flow from the unit in the car is delivering cold air, everything is OK.

3. If you observe bubbles in the sight glass while the system is operating, the system is low on refrigerant. Have it checked by a professional.

4. Oil streaks in the sight glass are an indication of trouble. Most of the time, if you see oil in the sight glass, it will appear as series of streaks, although occasionally it may be a solid stream of oil. In either case, it means that part of the charge has been lost.

Windshield Wipers

Intense heat from the sun, snow and ice, road oils and the chemicals used in windshield washer solvents combine to deteriorate the rubber wiper refills. The refills should be replaced about twice a year or whenever the blades begin to streak or chatter.

WIPER REFILL REPLACEMENT

Normally, if the wipers are not cleaning the windshield properly, only the refill has to be replaced. The blade and arm usually require replacement only in the event of damage. It is only necessary (except on Tridon refills) to remove the arm or the blade to replace the refill (rubber part), though you may have to position the arm higher on the glass. You can do this by turning the ignition switch on and operating the wipers. When they are positioned where they are accessible, turn the ignition switch off.

There are several types of refills and your vehicle could have any kind, since aftermarket blades and arms may not use exactly the same type refill as the original equipment.

The original equipment wiper elements can be replaced as follows:

1. Lift the wiper arm off the glass.
2. Depress the release lever on the center bridge and remove the blade from the arm.
3. Lift the tab and pinch the end bridge to release it from the center bridge.
4. Slide the end bridge from the wiper blade and the wiper blade from the opposite end bridge.
5. Install a new element and be sure the tab on the end bridge is down to lock the element in place. Check each release point for positive engagement.

Most Trico styles use a release button that is pushed down to allow the refill to slide out of the release jaws. The new refill slide in and locks in place. Some Trico refills are removed by locating where the metal backing strip or the refill is wider. Insert a small screwdriver blade between the frame and the metal backing strip. Press down to release the refill from the retaining tab.

The Anco style is unlocked at one end by squeezing 2 metal tabs, and the refill is slid out of the frame jaws. When the new refill is installed, the tabs will click into place, locking the refill.

The polycarbonate type is held in place by a locking lever that is pushed downward out of the groove in the arm to free the refill. When the new refill is installed, it will lock in place automatically.

The Tridon refill has a plastic backing strip with a notch about an inch from the end. Hold

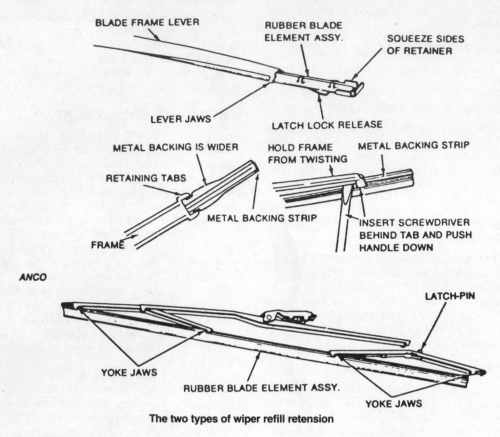

The two types of wiper refill retension

the blade (frame) on a hard surface so that the frame is tightly bowed. Grip the tip of the backing strip and pull up while twisting counterclockwise. The backing strip will snap out of the retaining tab. Do this for the remaining tabs until the refill is free of the arm. The length of these refills is molded into the end and they should be replaced with identical types.

No matter which type of refill you use, be sure that all of the frame claws engage the refill. Before operating the wipers, be sure that no part of the metal frame is contacting the windshield.

Tires

INFLATION PRESSURE

Tire inflation is the most ignored item of auto maintenance. Gasoline mileage can drop as much as 0.8% for every 1 pound per square inch (psi) of under inflation.

Two items should be a permanent fixture in every glove compartment: a tire pressure gauge and a tread depth gauge. Check the tire pressure (including the spare) regularly with a pocket type gauge. Kicking the tires won't tell you a thing, and the gauge on the service station air hose is notoriously inaccurate.

The tire pressures recommended for your car are usually found on the door post or in the owner's manual. Ideally, inflation pressure should be checked when the tires are cool. When the air becomes heated it expands and the pressure increases. Every 10° rise or drop in temperature means a difference of 1 psi, which also explains why the tire appears to lose air on a very cold night. When it is impossible to check the tires "cold," allow for pressure build-up due to heat. If the "hot" pressure exceeds the "cold" pressure by more than 15 psi, reduce your speed, load or both. Otherwise internal heat is created in the tire. When the heat approaches the temperature at which the tire was cured during manufacture, the tread can separate from the body.

CAUTION: *Never counteract excessive pressure build-up by bleeding off air pressure (letting some air out). This will only further raise the tire operating temperature.*

Before starting a long trip with lots of luggage, you can add about 2-4 psi to the tires to make them run cooler, but never exceed the maximum inflation pressure on the side of the tire.

TREAD DEPTH

All tires made since 1968, have 8 built-in tread wear indicator bars that show up as ½ in. wide smooth bands across the tire when 1/16 in. of tread remains. The appearance of tread wear indicators means that the tires should be replaced. In fact, many states have laws prohibiting the use of tires with less than 1/16 in. tread.

You can check your own tread depth with an inexpensive gauge or by using a Lincoln head penny. Slip the Lincoln penny into several tread grooves. If you can see the top of Lincoln's head in 2 adjacent grooves, the tires have less than 1/16 in. tread left and should be replaced. You can measure snow tires in the same manner by using the "tails" side of the Lincoln penny. If you can see the top of the Lincoln memorial, it's time to replace the snow tires.

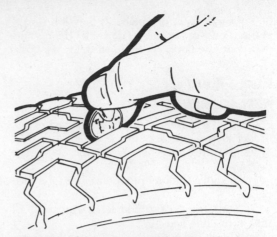

A Lincoln penny may be used to approximate tread depth. If the top of Lincoln's head is visible in two adjacent grooves, replace the tire.

TIRE ROTATION

Tire wear can be equalized by switching the position of the tires about every 6000 miles. Including a conventional spare in the rotation pattern can give up to 20% more tire life.

CAUTION: *Do not include the new "Spacesaver" spare tire in the rotation pattern.*

There are certain exceptions to tire rotation, however. Studded snow tires should not be rotated, and radials should be kept on the same side of the car (maintain the same direction of rotation). The belts on radial tires get set in a pattern. If the direction of rotation is reversed, it can cause rough ride and vibration.

NOTE: *When radials or studded snows are taken off the car, mark them, so you can maintain the same direction of rotation.*

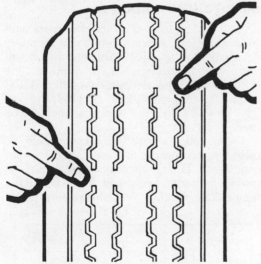

Since 1968, tread wear indicators have been built into the tire tread and appear as ½ inch wide bands when 1/16 inch tread remains

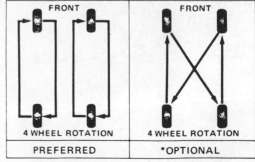

DO NOT INCLUDE "TEMPORARY USE ONLY" SPARE TIRE IN ROTATION.

* THE OPTIONAL 'X' ROTATION PATTERN FOR RADIALS IS ACCEPTABLE WHEN REQUIRED FOR MORE UNIFORM TIRE WEAR.

Tire rotation patterns

TIRE STORAGE

Store the tires at proper inflation pressure if they are mounted on wheels. All tires should

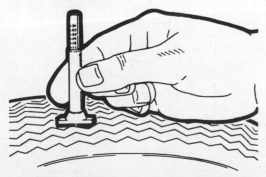

Check the tread depth with an inexpensive gauge

be kept in a cool, dry place. If they are stored in the garage or basement, do not let them stand on a concrete floor, set them on strips of wood.

Fuel Filter

REPLACEMENT

CAUTION: *Before opening any part of the fuel system, the pressure must be relieved.*
Follow the procedure below to relieve the pressure.
1. Remove the fuel pump fuse from the fuse panel.
2. Start the engine and let it run until all fuel in the line is used.
3. Crank the starter an additional three seconds to relieve any residual pressure.
4. Turn the ignition off and replace the fuse.
NOTE: *The fuel filter is an inline unit ahead of the TBI unit.*
5. With a cold engine, unclamp and remove the fuel hose, then unscrew the filter from the steel fuel line.
6. Installation is the reverse of removal.

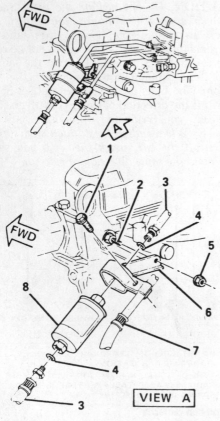

1. Bolt
2. Bolt/stud
3. Fuel feed pipe
4. "O-ring
5. Nut
6. Clamp assy.
7. Pipe assy.
8. Filter assy.

Fuel filter - four cyl. engine

FLUIDS AND LUBRICANTS

Fuel Recommendations

The Fiero engine is designed to use only unleaded gasoline, with an octane rating of at least 87.

Using leaded gasoline can damage the emission control system by decreasing the effectiveness of the catalyst in the catalytic converter and by damaging the oxygen sensor which is part of the "Computer Command Control System".

Do not use gasolines containing more than 5 percent methanol even if they contain cosolvents and corrosion inhibitors.

Although gasolines containing 5 percent or less methanol and appropriate cosolvents and inhibitors for methanol may be suitable for use in your car, Pontiac does not endorse their use, at this time.

Engine

OIL RECOMMENDATION

Engine oils are labeled on the containers with various API (American Petroleum Institute) designations of quality. Make sure the oil you use has the API designation "SF", either alone or shown with other designations such as SF/CC or SF/CD. Oils with a label on which the designation "SF" does not appear should not be used.

Engine oil viscosity (thickness) should be considered according to temperature weather conditions. Lower viscosity engine oils can provide better fuel economy, however, higher temperature weather conditions require higher

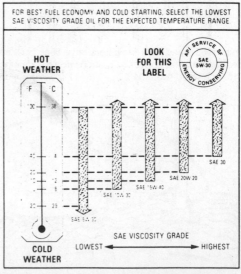

Manufacturers' recommended oil viscosities

Maintenance Intervals Chart

Intervals are for number of months or thousands of miles, whichever comes first.
NOTE: *Heavy-duty operation (trailer towing, prolonged idling, severe stop and start driving) should be accompanied by a 50% increase in maintenance. Cut the interval in half for these conditions.*

Item To Be Serviced	When To Perform (Months or Miles whichever comes first)
Chassis Lubrication	Every 12 mos. or 7,500 miles
Engine Oil Change	Every 7,500 miles ②
Oil Filter Change	Every Oil Change
Torque TBI Mounting Bolt	At first 7,500 miles
Flush and Refill Cooling System	Every 24 mos. or 30,000 miles
Repack Front Wheel Bearings	Every 30,000 miles
Change Transaxle Fluid and Filter	At 100,000 miles ①
Replace Spark Plugs	Every 30,000 miles
Inspect PCV Valve	Every 22,500
Inspect EGR System	Every 36 mos. or 30,000 miles
Air Cleaner and PCV Filter Replacement	Every 24 mos. or 22,500 miles ②
Check Engine Timing	Every 30,000 miles
Inspect Spark Plug Wires	Every 30,000 miles
Fuel Cap and Lines Inspection	Every 30,000 miles
Inspect Thermostatically Controlled Air Cleaner	Every 30,000 miles
Check Tire Inflation	Every Month

① Every 15,000 miles for Heavy Duty service
② Service more often when driven under severe or dusty conditions

viscosity engine oils for satisfactory lubrication. When selecting an oil viscosity, consider the range of temperature your car will be operated in before the next oil change. Pontiac recommends that if the outside temperatures are not expected to exceed 38°C (100°F) before your next oil change, SF quality, SAE 5W-30 Energy-Conserving engine oil is the preferred viscosity grade.

OIL LEVEL CHECK

At every fuel stop, check the engine oil in the following manner:

1. Park the car on a level area.
2. The engine oil may be either hot or cold when checking the oil level. However, if it is hot, wait a few minutes after the engine has been shut off to allow the oil to drain back into the oil pan. If the engine is cold, do not start it before checking the oil level.
3. Open the engine compartment and locate the dipstick. Pull the dipstick from its tube, wipe it clean and reinsert it.
NOTE: *Make sure the dipstick is fully seated when checking the oil level to assure accurate readings.*

Capacities

Year	V.I.N. Code	Engine Displacement Cu. In.	Eng. Mfg.	Crankcase Quarts	Transaxle Pints Manual 4 spd	Transaxle Pints Manual 5 spd	Transaxle Pints Auto	Gas Tank Gal	Cooling System Qts
'84–'85	R	151	Pont.	3 ①	6.0	—	8.0	10.5	②
'85	9	173	Chev.	4 ①	5.9	5.3	8.0	10.3	13.0

① With or without filter change
② Manual Trans. 13.8 qts.
  Auto Trans. 14.2 qts.

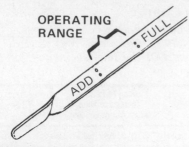

Oil dipstick

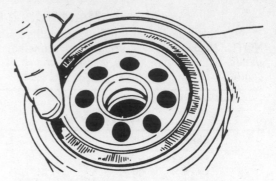

Coat the new oil filter gasket with clean oil

4. Pull the dipstick out again and while holding it horizontally, read the oil level. The oil level should be above the "ADD" line but not above the "FULL" line. Do not overfill.

OIL AND FILTER CHANGE

The milage figure given in the "Maintenance Intervals" chart are the Pontiac recommended intervals for oil and filter changes assuming average driving. If your Fiero is being driven under dusty, polluted, or off road conditions, cut the milage intervals in half. The same thing goes for cars driven in stop-and-go traffic or for only short distances.

Always drain the oil after the engine has been running long enough to bring it to operating temperature. Hot oil will flow easier and more contaminants will be removed along with the oil than if it were drained cold. You will need a large capacity drain pan which you can purchase at any auto store. Another necessity is

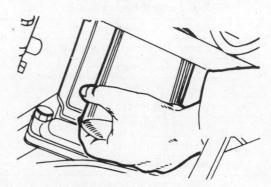

Install the new oil filter by hand

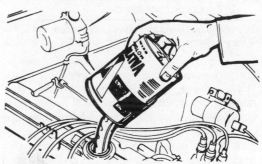

Add oil through the capped opening in the cylinder head cover

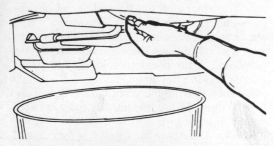

By keeping inward pressure on the plug as you unscrew it, oil wont escape past the threads

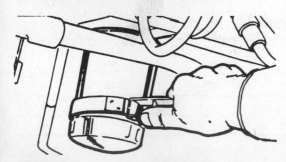

Remove the oil filter with a strap wrench

containers for used oil. You will find that plastic bottles such as those used for detergents, bleaches etc., make excellent storage jugs. One ecologically desirable solution to the used oil disposal problem is to find a cooperative gas station owner who will allow you to dump your used oil into his tank.

Pontiac recommends changing both the oil and filter during the first oil change and the filter every other oil change thereafter. For the small price of an oil filter, it's cheap insurance to replace the filter at every oil change. One of the larger filter manufacturers points out in its advertisements that not changing the filter leaves a quanity of dirty oil in the engine, which could be as much as a quart on some models. This claim is true and should be kept in mined when changing your oil. Change your oil as follows:

1. Run the engine until it reaches normal operating temperature.

2. Jack up the car and support it safely with jack stands.

3. Slide a drain pan under the oil pan.

4. Loosen the drain plug. Turn the plug out by hand. By keeping an inward pressure on the plug as you unscrew it, oil won't escape past the threads and you can remove it without being burnt with hot oil.

5. Allow the oil to drain completely and then install the drain plug. Be careful not to overtighten the plug and strip the threads in the oil pan.

6. Using a strap wrench, remove the oil filter. Keep in mind that it's holding dirty, hot oil.

7. Empty the old filter into the drain pan and dispose of the filter.

8. Using a clean rag, wipe off the filter adapter on the engine block. Be sure that the rag doesn't leave any lint which could clog an oil passage.

9. Coat the rubber gasket on the new filter with fresh oil. Spin it onto the engine by hand; when the gasket touches the adapter surface give it another ½–¾ turn. Do not overtighten or you may squash the gasket and cause it to leak.

10. Refill the engine with a correct amount of fresh oil.

11. Check the oil level on the dipstick. It is normal for the level to be a bit above the full mark. Start the engine and allow it to idle a few minutes.

CAUTION: *Do not run the engine above idle speed until it has built up oil pressure, indicated when the oil light goes out.*

12. Shut off the engine, allow the oil to drain for a minute, and check the oil level. Check around the filter and drain plug for any leaks, and correct as necessary.

Automatic Transaxle

FLUID RECOMMENDATION AND LEVEL CHECK

The automatic transaxle fluid level should be checked at each engine oil change. When adding or changing the automatic transaxle fluid use only fluid labeled Dexron®II.

1. Set the parking brake and start the engine with the transaxle in "P" (Park).

2. With the service brakes applied, move the shift lever through all the gear ranges, ending in "P" (Park).

NOTE: *The fluid level must be checked with*

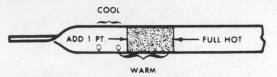

Automatic transmission dipstick marks; the proper level is in the shaded area

the engine running at slow idle, the car level and the fluid at least at room temperature. NOTE: *The correct fluid level cannot be read if you have just driven the car for a long time at high speed, city traffic in hot weather or if the car has been pulling a trailer. In these cases, wait at least 30 minutes for the fluid to cool down.*

3. Remove the dipstick located at the rear end of the engine compartment, wipe it clean, then push it back in until the cap seats.

4. Pull the dipstick out and read the fluid level. The level should be in the cross-hatched area of the dipstick.

5. Add fluid using a long plastic funnel in the dipstick tube. Keep in mind that it only takes one pint of fluid to raise the level from "ADD" to "FULL" with a hot transaxle.

DRAIN AND REFILL

Under normal operating conditions, the automatic transmission fluid only needs to be changed every 100,000 miles, according to Pontiac, unless one or more of the following driving conditions is encountered. In the following cases the fluid and filter should be changed every 15,000 miles:

a. Driving in heavy traffic when the outside temperature reaches 90°F.

b. Driving regularly in hilly or mountainous areas.

c. Towing a trailer.

d. Using a vehicle as a taxi or police car or for delivery purposes.

Remember, these are factory recommendations, and in this case are considered to be minimum. You must determine a change interval which fits your driving habits. If your vehicle is never subjected to these conditions, a 100,000 mile change interval is adequate. If you are a normal driver, a two-year/30,000 mile interval will be more than sufficient to maintain the long life for which your automatic transaxle was designed.

NOTE: *Use only fluid labeled Dexron®II. Use of other fluids could cause erratic shifting and transmission damage.*

1. Jack up your vehicle and support it safely with jackstands.

2. Remove the front and side pan bolts.

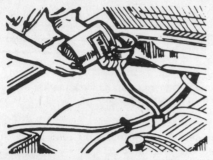

Add automatic transmission fluid through the dip-stick tube

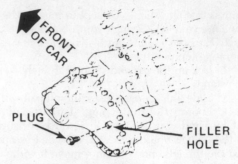

Manual transmission filler hole

3. Loosen the rear bolts about four turns.

4. Carefully pry the oil pan loose and allow the fluid to drain.

5. Remove the remaining bolts, the pan, and the gasket or RTV sealant. Discard the old gasket.

6. Clean the pan with solvent and dry it thoroughly, with compressed air.

7. Remove the strainer and O-ring seal.

8. Install a new strainer and O-ring seal, locating the strainer against the dipstick stop.

NOTE: *Always replace the filter with a new one. Do not attempt to clean the old one.*

9. Install a new gasket or RTV sealant then tighten the pan bolts to 12 ft. lbs.

10. Lower the car and add about 4 quarts of Dexron®II transmission fluid.

11. Start the engine; let it idle. Block the wheels and apply the parking brake.

12. Move the shift lever through the ranges. With the lever in Park, check the fluid level and add as necessary.

NOTE: *The transmission fluid currently being used may appear to be darker and have a strong odor. This is normal and not a sign of required maintenance or transmission failure.*

Manual Transaxle

FLUID RECOMMENDATION

Under normal conditions, the lubricant used in the manual transaxle does require periodic changing. The fluid level in the transaxle should be checked every 12 months or 7,500 miles, whichever comes first. The manual transaxle is designed to use SAE 5W-30 SF, SF/SC, or SF/CD engine oil as a lubricant.

LEVEL CHECK

1. Park the car on a level surface and turn off the engine.

2. The transaxle case must be cool to the touch. If the transaxle is hot, lubricant may flow from the filler hole when the plug is removed.

3. Remove the transaxle filler plug, which is located above the axle shaft on the driver's side of the case. When the lubricant is cool it should be level with the filler hole.

4. Lubricant can be added by inserting the end of a funnel into one end of a rubber tube, and inserting the other end of the rubber tube into the filler hole.

5. Reinstall the filler hole plug and torque to 24 ft. lbs.

Coolant

FLUID RECOMMENDATION AND LEVEL CHECK

A see-through plastic reservoir called a coolant recovery bottle, is located in the front compartment near the radiator assembly. This bottle is connected to the radiator by a hose. As the car is driven, the coolant is heated and expands, the portion of the fluid displaced by this expansion flows from the radiator into the recovery bottle. When the car is stopped and the coolant cools and contracts, the displaced coolant is drawn back into the radiator by vacuum. Thus, the radiator is kept filled with coolant to the desired level at all times. The coolant level should be between the "ADD" and "FULL" marks on the recovery bottle. If coolant is needed, add it to the recovery bottle not the radiator. The "ADD" and "FULL" marks on the recovery bottle are approximately one quart apart so that a 50/50 mixture can be added.(50% ethylene glycol antifreeze and 50% water).

CAUTION: *Do not remove the radiator cap or the thermostat housing cap while the engine and radiator are still hot. This also includes the recovery bottle cap if coolant in the recovery bottle is boiling. Scalding fluid and steam can be blown out under pressure if any cap is taken off too soon.*

CAUTION: *The engine cooling fan is electric and can come on whether or not the engine is running. The fan can start automatically in response to a heat sensor when the ignition is in "Run." Remember to keep hands, tools and clothing away from the cooling fan when working under the compartment lid.*

DRAIN AND REFILL

The cooling system should be drained and re-filled every 24 months or 30,000 miles. Please read the Cautions above then perform the following procedure:

1. When the engine is cool, open the rear engine compartment lid and turn the thermostat housing cap slowly counter-clockwise until it reaches a stop.

NOTE: *Do not press down while turning the cap.*

2. Wait until any remaining pressure is relieved, then press down on the cap and continue turning it counter-clockwise. Remove the cap.

3. Pull the thermostat straight out then install the cap. Run the engine at least one minute to circulate the coolant.

4. Stop the engine, then open the radiator drain valve and drain the coolant.

NOTE: *You may speed up drainage by removing the drain plugs in the engine block and in the left and right coolant pipes. The coolant pipes run underneath the car. The coolant pipe plugs are located at the rear of each pipe just ahead of the rear tires. The engine block drain plug is located on the front of the engine, on the driver's side, just above the starter.*

5. Run water through the thermostat opening until the drained liquid is nearly colorless.

6. Install all drain plugs and close the radiator drain valve.

7. Remove the radiator cap and add water through the thermostat housing until the water reaches the level of the radiator neck.

8. Install the radiator and thermostat housing caps.

NOTE: *Do not install the thermostat at this time.*

9. Tighten the thermostat housing cap to the first notch. At this point you should hear a clicking sound, and you will not be able to turn the cap counterclockwise without pushing it down.

10. Run the engine until the hose connected to the thermostat becomes hot. Drain the system again.

11. Install all drain plugs and close the radiator drain valve.

12. Remove, drain and clean the coolant recovery bottle, then install.

13. Add the correct amount of water and ethylene glycol antifreeze to provide the required cooling, freezing and corrosion protection. Use a solution that contains at least 50%

antifreeze but not more than 70% antifreeze.

14. With the engine off, remove the radiator cap. Add coolant through the thermostat housing until the coolant reaches the spill point of the radiator neck.

15. Install the radiator and thermostat housing caps, but do not install the thermostat at this time. Tighten the thermostat housing cap as in Step 9.

16. Add aproximately 3 qts. of coolant to the coolant reservoir bottle.

17. Run the engine at normal idle for 3 minutes, then at fast idle for 15 or 20 seconds. Turn the engine off.

18. Refer to Steps 1 and 2 and remove the thermostat housing cap. Add coolant to the thermostat housing until it reaches the housing cap seat.

19. Install the thermostat and cap. Make sure the thermostat is fully seated and the arrows on the cap line up with the coolant hose at the thermostat housing.

20. After driving the car for the first time after changing the fluid, let the engine cool then add coolant to the coolant recovery bottle as necessary to bring it to the proper level.

Clutch Master Cylinder

NOTE: *The clutch master cylinder is located under the front compartment lid, on the driver's side, next to the brake master cylinder.*

FLUID RECOMMENDATION AND LEVEL CHECK

The fluid level can be seen through the plastic wall of the clutch reservoir. Unscrew and remove the reservoir cover and add fluid as necessary. Use only Delco Supreme No. 11 or other DOT 3 specification brake fluid. Use of other fliuds may have an adverse affect on the operation of the hydraulic clutch.

CAUTION: *Do not allow anyone to depress the clutch pedal while the clutch fluid reser-*

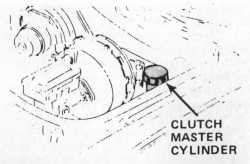

CLUTCH MASTER CYLINDER

The clutch master cylinder is located on the driver's side of the front compartment

voir cover is not in place. Also, brake fluid will remove paint. If spilled, flush the area immediately with water.

Brake Master Cylinder

NOTE: *The brake fluid reservoir is part of the brake master cylinder, and is located under the front engine compartment lid, on the driver's side of the car. Check the fluid level each time your engine oil is changed.*

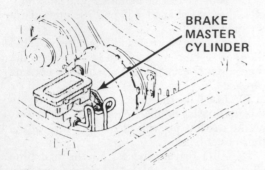

The brake master cylinder is located on the driver's side of the front compartment

FLUID RECOMMENDATION AND LEVEL CHECK

The fluid level can be seen through the plastic wall of the brake reservoir. The levels in both the front and rear chambers must be above the "MIN" lines. If it is necessary to add fluid, remove the cover by lifting up on the tabs on both sides of the cover. Use only Delco Supreme No. 11 or other DOT 3 specification brake fluid and add as necessary.

CAUTION: *Do not allow anyone to depress the brake pedal while the brake fluid reservoir cover is removed. Also, brake fluid will remove paint. If spilled, flush the area immediately with water.*

Chassis Greasing

Every 12 months or 24,000 miles Pontiac recommends lubrication of the suspension and steering pivot points.

1. There are 6 grease fittings (3 on each side) on the front suspension and 4 grease fittings (2 on each side) on the rear suspension. Wipe each one with a clean cloth.

2. Using a grease gun with a flexible hose, apply chassis lubricant to each grease fitting until the rubber caps begin to puff.

NOTE: *Do not over-lubricate, as the caps will separate from the suspension components.*

3. Apply a small amount of lubricant to the metal steering stops on the front suspension.

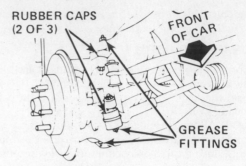

Front passenger side grease fittings

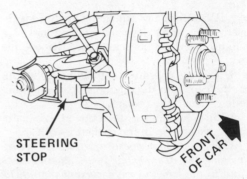

Front suspension steering stops (passenger side)

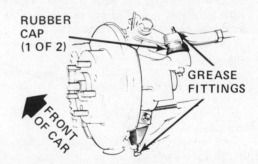

Rear suspension grease fittings (driver's side)

Body Lubrication

All mechanical parts of the body with contacting surfaces should be lubricated periodically.

Use a light penetrating oil in a spray can to lubricate hard to reach areas and a grease type lubricant such as Lubriplate or equivalent, for easily accessible surfaces, such as latches and strikers. Parts to be lubricated include: all hinges and latches at the doors and front and rear compartment lids, fuel filler door, headlight mechanism, manual transmission shift linkage, brake and clutch pedal pivot points.

Wheel Bearings

To maintain proper functioning of the front suspension, the front wheel bearings should be lubricated and correctly adjusted every 30,000 miles.

Please refer to Wheel Bearings in Chapter 9 for this procedure.

PUSHING AND TOWING

Your Fiero may be towed on all four wheels only if the steering and driveline are in normal operating condition. Keep in mind the following precautions when towing your vehicle:

1. If equipped with an automatic transaxle, do not exceed a speed of 35 mph or a distance of 50 miles.

2. Make sure the steering is unlocked, the transaxle is in neutral and the parking brake is released.

3. Connect to main structural parts of the car. Do not attach to bumpers or brackets.

4. Remember, with the engine off, the power assist for the brakes will not be operating.

If your Fiero is to towed by a wrecker, use the following precautions:

1. Follow the instructions of the wrecker manufacturer.

2. Since the Fiero is rear wheel drive, towing on the front wheels is preferred, however if necessary, it may be towed forwards on the rear drive wheels at speed up to 35 mph and for distances up to 50 miles on cars equipped with automatic transaxles. There is no restrictions on cars equipped with manual transaxles.

3. A safety chain system must be used for all towing.

JUMP STARTING

NOTE: *The battery is located directly under the right side engine compartment cover. Remove the cover by turning the two thumb screws counterclockwise until they come out. Grasp the cover at the front and rear and while raising the rear of the cover about one inch, pull back on the cover to disengage it from the locating pins.*

JACKING

The standard jack used with the Fiero is a scissors type which fits into a notch forward of the rear wheels. It is designed to lift both front and rear wheels of the side being jacked. The jack supplied with the car should never be used for any service operation other than changing a tire. Never get under the car while it is supported by only a jack. Always block the front and rear of the wheel opposite of the wheel being changed.

The service operations in this book often require that one end or the other, or both, of the car be raised and safely supported. The ideal method of course, would be a hydraulic hoist. Since this is beyond both the resource and re-

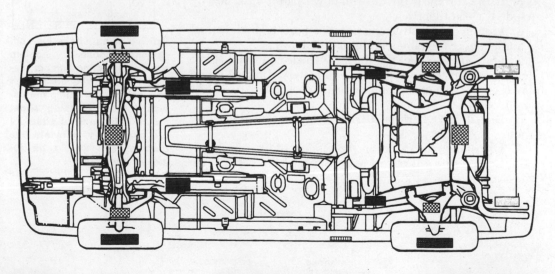

FRAME/BODY CONTACT HOIST

SERVICE STATION JACK

WHEEL LIFT HOIST

VEHICLE JACK

SAFETY STANDS

Body lifting points

JUMP STARTING A DEAD BATTERY

The chemical reaction in a battery produces explosive hydrogen gas. This is the safe way to jump start a dead battery, reducing the chances of an accidental spark that could cause an explosion.

Jump Starting Precautions

1. Be sure both batteries are of the same voltage.
2. Be sure both batteries are of the same polarity (have the same grounded terminal).
3. Be sure the vehicles are not touching.
4. Be sure the vent cap holes are not obstructed.
5. Do not smoke or allow sparks around the battery.
6. In cold weather, check for frozen electrolyte in the battery. Do not jump start a frozen battery.
7. Do not allow electrolyte on your skin or clothing.
8. Be sure the electrolyte is not frozen.
CAUTION: *Make certain that the ignition key, in the vehicle with the dead battery, is in the OFF position. Connecting cables to vehicles with on-board computers will result in computer destruction if the key is not in the OFF position.*

Jump Starting Procedure

1. Determine voltages of the two batteries; they must be the same.
2. Bring the starting vehicle close (they must not touch) so that the batteries can be reached easily.
3. Turn off all accessories and both engines. Put both cars in Neutral or Park and set the handbrake.
4. Cover the cell caps with a rag—do not cover terminals.
5. If the terminals on the run-down battery are heavily corroded, clean them.
6. Identify the positive and negative posts on both batteries and connect the cables in the order shown.
7. Start the engine of the starting vehicle and run it at fast idle. Try to start the car with the dead battery. Crank it for no more than 10 seconds at a time and let it cool off for 20 seconds in between tries.
8. If it doesn't start in 3 tries, there is something else wrong.
9. Disconnect the cables in the reverse order.
10. Replace the cell covers and dispose of the rags.

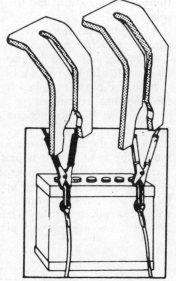

Side terminal batteries occasionally pose a problem when connecting jumper cables. There frequently isn't enough room to clamp the cables without touching sheet metal. Side terminal adaptors are available to alleviate this problem and should be removed after use.

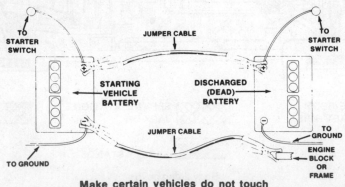

Make certain vehicles do not touch

This hook-up for negative ground cars only

quirement of the do-it-yourselfer, a small hydraulic floor jack accompanied by a set of sturdy jackstands will suffice for the procedures in this guide.

When using a floor jack, lift on the center of the front and rear control arms, on the center rear portion of the rear crossmember and the center of the front crossmember. Always set the parking brake and block the wheels. Jackstands should be positioned according to the illustration.

An alternate method of raising the car would be drive-on ramps, which are commercially available. However, driving up on ramps can be tricky and usually requires a helper to guide you on. Be sure to block the wheels when using ramps.

CAUTION: *Concrete blocks are not recommended for supporting the car. They are likely to crumble if the load is not evenly distributed. Boxes and milk crates of any description must not be used to support the car!*

Tune-Up and Performance Maintenance

TUNE-UP PROCEDURES

The procedures listed here are intended as specific procedure. More general procedures are given in Chapter 9, Troubleshooting.

Neither tune-up nor troubleshooting can be considered independently, since each has a direct bearing on the other.

An engine tune-up is a service designed to restore the maximum capability of power, performance, economy and reliability in an engine, and, at the same time, assure the owner of a complete check and more lasting results in efficiency and trouble-free performance. Engine tune-up becomes increasingly important each year, to ensure that pollutant levels are in compliance with federal emissions standards.

It is advisable to follow a definite and thorough tune-up procedure. Tune-up consists of three separate steps: analysis, the process of determining whether normal wear is responsible for performance loss, and whether parts require replacement or service; parts replacement or service; adjustment, where engine adjustments are returned to the original factory specifications.

The extent of an engine tune-up is usually determined by the length of time since the previous service, although the type of driving and general mechanical conditioning of the engine must be considered. Specific maintenance should also be performed at regular intervals, depending on operating conditions.

Troubleshooting is a logical sequence of procedures designed to lead the owner or service man to the particular cause of trouble. The troubleshooting chapter of this manual is general in nature, yet specific enough to locate the problem. Service usually comprises two areas: diagnosis, and repair. While the apparent cause of trouble, in many cases, is worn or damaged parts, performance problems are less obvious. The first job is to locate the problem and cause. Once the problem has been isolated, refer to the appropriate section for repair, removal or adjustment procedures.

It is advisable to read the entire chapter before beginning a tune-up, although those who are more familiar with tune-up procedures may wish to go directly to the instructions.

Spark Plugs

A typical spark plug consists of a metal shell surrounding a ceramic insulator. A metal electrode extends downward through the center of

Tune-Up Specifications

(When analyzing compression test results, look for uniformity among cylinders rather than specific pressures.)

Year	V.I.N. Code	Eng. No. Cyl. Displ. Cu. In.	Eng. Mfg.	hp	Spark Plugs Orig Type	Spark Plugs Gap (in.)	Ignition Timing (deg) Man Trans	Ignition Timing (deg) Auto Trans	Intake Valve Opens (deg)	Fuel Pump Pressure (psi)	Idle Speed (rpm) Man Trans	Idle Speed (rpm) Auto Trans
'84–'85	R	151	Pont.	90	R43TSX	.060	①	①	33	6–8	①	①
'85	9	173	Chev.	130	R42CTS	.060	①	①	25	6–8	①	①

NOTE: The underhood specifications sticker often reflects tune-up specification changes made in production. Sticker figures must be used if they disagree with those in this chart.
① See underhood sticker

the insulator and protrudes a small distance. Located at the end of the plug and attached to the side of the outer metal shell is the side electrode. The side electrode bends in at a 90° angle so that its tip is even with, and parallel to, the tip of the center electrode. The distance between these two electrodes (measured in thousandths of an inch) is called the spark plug gap. The spark plug in no way produces a spark but merely provides a gap across which the current can arc. The coil produces anywhere from 20,000-40,000 volts which travels to the distributor where it is distributed through the spark plug wires to the spark plugs. The current passes along the center electrode and jumps the gap to the side electrode, and, in so doing, ignites the air/fuel mixture in the combustion chamber.

SPARK PLUG HEAT RANGE

Spark plug heat range is the ability of the plug to dissipate heat. The longer the insulator (or the farther it extends into the engine), the hotter the plug will operate; the shorter the insulator, the cooler it will operate. A plug that absorbs little heat and remains too cool will quickly accumulate deposits of oil and carbon since it is not hot enough to burn them off. This leads to plug fouling and consequently to misfiring. A plug that absorbs too much heat will have no deposits, but, due to the excessive heat, the electrodes will burn away quickly and in some instances, pre-ignition may result. Pre-ignition takes place when plug tips get so hot that they glow sufficiently to ignite the fuel/air mixture before the actual spark occurs. This early ignition will usually cause a pinging during low speeds and heavy loads.

The general rule of thumb for choosing the correct heat range when picking a spark plug is: if most of your driving is long distance, high speed travel, use a colder plug; if most of your driving is stop and to, use a hotter plug. Original equipment plugs are compromise plugs, but most people never have occasion to change their plugs from the factory-recommended heat range.

```
  1 2 3   4   5
  ‾ ‾ ‾   ‾   ‾
  R 4 5   T S  X
```

1 — R--INDICATES RESISTOR-TYPE PLUG.
2 — "4" INDICATES 14 mm THREADS.
3 — HEAT RANGE
4 — TS--TAPERED SEAT
     S--EXTENDED TIP
5 — SPECIAL GAP

Spark plug coding using a AC-45TSX as an example

REPLACING SPARK PLUGS

A set of spark plugs usually requires replacement after about 10,000 miles on cars with conventional ignition systems and after about 20,000-30,000 miles on cars with electronic ignition, depending on your style of driving. In normal operation, plug gap increased about 0.001 in. for every 1,000–2,500 miles. As the gap increased, the plug's voltage requirement also increases. It requires a greater voltage to jump the wider gap and about two or three times as much voltage to fire a plug at high speeds than at idle.

When you're removing spark plugs, you should work on one at a time. Don't start by removing the plug wires all at once, because unless you number them, they may become mixed up. Take a minute before you begin and number the wires with tape. The best location for numbering is near where the wires come out of the cap.

NOTE: *On Fieros equipped with the 4 cyl. engine, the spark plugs are located on the front of the engine just below the valve cover. It may be necessary to remove the air cleaner, and set it to one side, without disconnecting any tubing or wiring.*

1. Twist the spark plug boot and remove the boot and wire from the plug. Do not pull on the wire itself as this will ruin the wire.

2. If possible, use a brush or rag to clean the area around the spark plug. Make sure that all

Check the spark plug gap using a filler gauge

Adjust the electrode gap by bending the side electrode

the dirt is removed so that none will enter the cylinder after the plug is removed.

3. Remove the spark plug using the proper size socket. Turn the socket counterclockwise to remove the plug. Be sure to hold the socket straight on the plug to avoid breaking the plug, or rounding off the hex on the plug.

4. Once the plug is out, check it against the plugs shown in the color section to determine engine condition. This is crucial since plug readings are vital signs of engine condition.

5. Use a round wire feeler gauge to check the plug gap. The correct size gauge should pass through the electrode gap with a slight drag. If you're in doubt, try one size smaller and one larger. The smaller gauge should go through easily while the larger one shouldn't go through at all. If the gap is incorrect, use the electrode bending tool on the end of the gauge to adjust the gap. When adjusting the gap, always bend the side electrode. The center electrode is non-adjustable.

6. Squirt a drop of penetrating oil on the threads of the new plug and install it. Don't oil the threads too heavily. Turn the plug in clockwise by hand until it is snug.

7. When the plug is finger tight, tighten it with a wrench. If you have a torque wrench, use it to tighten the plugs to 11 ft.lb. If you don't have a torque wrench, tighten the plug carefully.

8. Install the plug boot firmly over the plug. Proceed to the next plug.

CHECKING AND REPLACING SPARK PLUG CABLES

Visually inspect the spark plug cables for burns, cuts, or breaks in the insulation. Check the spark plug boots and the nipples on the distributor cap and coil. Replace any damaged wiring. If no physical damage is obvious, the wires can be checked with an ohmmeter for excessive resistance. (See the tune-up and troubleshooting section).

When installing a new set of spark plug cables, replace the cables one at a time so there will be no mix-up. Start by replacing the longest cable first. Install the boot firmly over the spark plug. Route the wire exactly the same as the original. Insert the nipple firmly into the tower on the distributor cap. Repeat the process for each cable.

FIRING ORDERS

To avoid confusion, replace spark plugs and wires one at a time. Or tag them with masking tape.

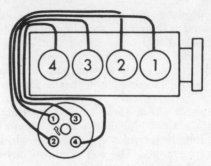

GM (Pontiac) 151-4 engine firing order: 1-3-4-2 Distributor rotation: clockwise

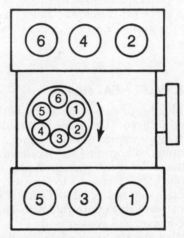

GM (Chevrolet) 173 V6 engine (2.8 L) engine firing order: 1-2-3-4-5-6 Distributor rotation: clockwise

Electronic Ignition

The High Energy Ignition distributor (H.E.I.) with Electronic Spark Timing (EST) combines all ignition components in one unit except the coil, which is mounted separately.

All spark timing changes in the H.E.I. (EST) distributor are done electronically by and Electronic Control Module (ECM) which monitors information from various engine sensors, computes the desired spark timing and signals the distributor to change the timing accordingly. A back-up spark advance system is incorporated to signal the ignition module in case of (ECM) failure. No vacuum or mechanical advance are used.

NOTE: *When using an auxiliary starter switch on HEI systems, the distributor BATT lead must be disconnected. Failure to do this may cause damage to the grounding circuit in the ignition switch.*

TACHOMETER HOOK-UP

The tachometer (Tach) terminal is next to the ignition switch (BAT) connector on the distributor cap.

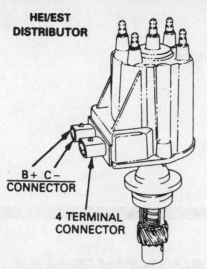

HEI/EST DISTRIBUTOR

B+ C−
CONNECTOR

4 TERMINAL CONNECTOR

Typical distributor using a separately mounted coil

CAUTION: *Never ground the TACH; serious module and ignition coil damage will result. If there is any doubt as to the correct tachometer hook-up, check with the tachometer manufacturer.*

IGNITION TIMING

1. Connect a timing light to the No. 1 spark plug wire according to the light manufacturer's instructions.
NOTE: *Do not pierce the spark plug wire to connect the timing light.*
2. Follow the instructions on the underhood engine decal for checking the ignition timing. These reflect the latest production changes for your vehicle.
3. Disconnect the 4 terminal connector at the distributor.
4. Start the engine and run it at idle speed.
5. Aim the timing light at the degree scale just over the harmonic balancer.
6. Adjust the timing by loosening the securing clamp and rotating the distributor until the desired ignition advance is achieved, then tighten the clamp.
7. Loosen the distributor retaining bolt. On some engines its necessary to slide the clamp back slightly. Do not remove the retaining bolt.
8. To advance the timing, rotate the distributor opposite the normal direction of rotor rotation. Retard the timing by rotating the distributor in the normal direction of rotor rotation.

Valve Lash

Hydraulic valve lifters are used to keep all parts of the valve train in constant contact. Each lifter is an automatic adjuster maintaining proper lash adjustment under all conditions. No routine adjustment is necessary.

Idle Speed And Mixture Adjustment

These adjustments are controlled by the Electronic Control Module (ECM). No adjustments are possible.

Engine and Engine Rebuilding

3

ENGINE ELECTRICAL

Distributor

REMOVAL AND INSTALLATION

1. Disconnect the negative battery cable.
2. Tag and disconnect all wires and harnesses leading from the distributor. Do not disconnect the plug wires.
3. Remove the distributor cap by turning the four latches counterclockwise. Set the distributor to one side with the plug wires intact.
4. Remove the hold down and clamp at the base of the V6 distributor. The four cylinder engine has two bolts and a clamp. Remove the outer bolt first, then loosen, but do not remove, the inner bolt. Slide the clamp back and remove it.
5. Before removing the distributor, note the position of the rotor. Scribe a mark on the distributor body indicating the initial position of the rotor.
6. Remove the distributor from the engine. The drive gear on the distributor shaft is helical, and the shaft will rotate slightly as the distributor is removed. Note and mark the position of the rotor at this second position. Do not crank the engine with the distributor removed.
7. To install the distributor, rotate the distributor shaft until the rotor aligns with the second mark you made (when the shaft stopped moving). Lubricate the drive gear with clean engine oil, install the distributor in the engine.
8. Install the clamp and hold down bolt. Tighten them until the distributor can just be moved with a little effort.
9. Connect all wires and harnesses and install the distributor cap.
10. Set the timing and tighten the hold bolt.

INSTALLATION IF THE ENGINE WAS DISTURBED

If the engine was cranked while the distributor was removed, you will have to place the engine on TDC of the compression stroke to obtain proper ignition timing.

1. Remove the No. 1 spark plug.
2. Place your thumb over the spark plug hole. Crank the engine slowly until compression is felt. It will be easier if you have someone rotate the engine by hand using a wrench on the crankshaft pulley.
3. Align the timing mark on the crankshaft pulley with the 0° mark on the timing scale attached to the front of the engine. This places the engine at TDC of the compression stroke.
4. Turn the distributor shaft until the rotor points between the No. 1 and No. 3 spark towers on the cap for the four cylinder engine, or between the No. 1 and No. 6 spark plug towers for the V6.
5. Install the distributor into the engine.
6. Perform Steps 9-12 of the preceding removal and installation procedure.

Alternator

ALTERNATOR PRECAUTIONS

To prevent damage to the alternator and regulator, the following precautions should be taken when working with the electrical system.

1. Never reverse the battery connections.
2. Booster batteries for starting must be connected properly: positive-to-positive and negative-to-negative.
3. Disconnect the battery cables before using a fast charger; the charger has a tendency to force current through the diodes in the opposite direction for which they were designed. This burns out the diodes.
4. Never use a fast charger as a booster for starting the vehicle.

5. Never disconnect the voltage regulator while the engine is running.

6. Avoid long soldering times when replacing diodes or transistors. Prolonged heat is damaging to AC generators.

7. Do not use test lamps of more than 12 volts (V) for checking diode continuity.

8. Do not short across or ground any of the terminals on the AC generator.

9. The polarity of the battery, generator, and regulator must be matched and considered before making any electrical connections within the system.

10. Never operate the alternator on an open circuit. Make sure that all connections within the circuit are clean and tight.

11. Disconnect the battery terminals when performing any service on the electrical system. This will eliminate the possibility of accidental reversal of polarity.

12. Disconnect the battery ground cable if arc welding is to be done on any part of the car.

REMOVAL AND INSTALLATION

1. Disconnect the negative battery cable.
2. Remove the air cleaner.

3. Disconnect the upper strut mount.

4. Disconnect the alternator adjusting bolt, upper adjusting bracket and drive belt.

5. Disconnect the wiring from the back of the alternator.

6. Lower the alternator mounting bracket and remove the alternator from the bottom of the vehicle.

7. Installation is the reverse of removal.

Regulator

The voltage regulator is a solid-state, non-adjustable unit integral with the alternator. The alternator must be disassembled to remove the regulator.

Starter

REMOVAL AND INSTALLATION

1. Disconnect the negative battery cable.
2. Raise and support the vehicle safely.
3. Disconnect all wires at the solenoid terminals. Note the color coding of the wires for installation.
4. Remove the starter support bracket mount bolts.

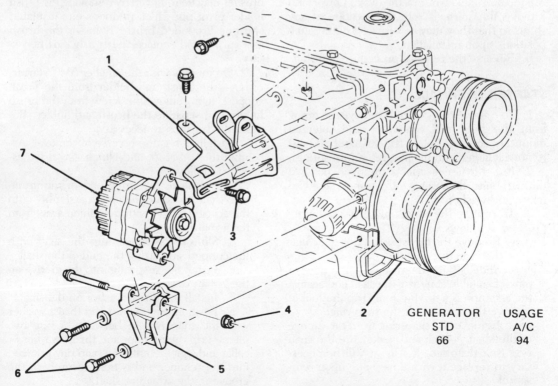

GENERATOR   USAGE
STD   A/C
66   94

1. Adjustment bracket	5. Generator support
2. Engine mount assy.	6. Bolt/screw 60 Nm (45 ft. lb.)
3. Bolt/screw (25Nm (19 ft. lb.)	7. Generator assy.
4. Nut 50 Nm (37 ft. lb.)	

Alternator removal and installation - four cyl. engine

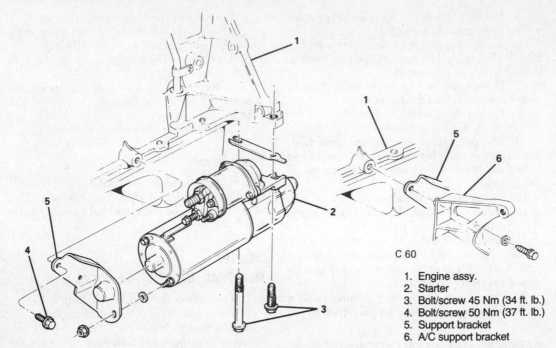

C 60

1. Engine assy.
2. Starter
3. Bolt/screw 45 Nm (34 ft. lb.)
4. Bolt/screw 50 Nm (37 ft. lb.)
5. Support bracket
6. A/C support bracket

Starter motor mounting - four cyl. shown

5. Loosen the front bracket bolt or nut and rotate the bracket out of the way. Lower and remove the starter. Note the location of any shims so that they may be replaced in the same positions upon installation.

6. Reverse the removal procedure to install.

STARTER OVERHAUL

1. To remove the solenoid, remove the screw from the field coil connector and solenoid mounting screws. Rotate the solenoid 90° and remove it along with the plunger return spring.

2. For further service, remove the two through-bolts, then remove the commutator end frame and washer.

3. To replace the clutch and drive assembly proceed as follows:

a. Remove the thrust washer or the collar from the armature shaft.

b. Slide a ⅝ in. deep socket or a piece of pipe of suitable size over the shaft and against the retainer as a driving tool. Tap the tool to remove the retainer off the snap ring.

c. Remove the snap ring from the groove in the shaft. Check and make sure the snap ring isn't distorted. If it is, it will be necessary to replace it with a new one upon reassembly.

d. Remove the retainer and clutch assembly from the armature shaft.

4. The shift lever may be disconnected from the plunger at this time by removing the roll pin.

5. On models with the standard starter, the brushes may be removed by removing the brush holder pivot pin which positions one insulated and one grounded brush. Remove the brush and spring and replace the brushes as necessary.

6. On models with the smaller 5MT starter, remove the brush and holder from the brush support, then remove the screw from the brush holder and separate the brush and holder. Replace the brushes as necessary.

7. Installation is the reverse of removal. Assemble the armature and clutch and drive assembly as follows:

a. Lubricate the drive end of the armature shaft and slide the clutch assembly onto the armature shaft with the pinion away from the armature.

b. Slide the retainer onto the shaft with the cupped side facing the end of the shaft.

c. Install the snap ring into the groove on the armature shaft.

d. Install the thrust washer on the shaft.

e. Position the retainer and thrust washer with the snap ring in between. Using two pliers, grip the retainer and thrust washer or collar and squeeze until the snap ring is forced into the retainer and is held securely in the groove in the armature shaft.

f. Lubricate the drive gear housing bushing.

g. Engage the shift lever yoke with the clutch and slide the complete assembly into the drive gear housing.

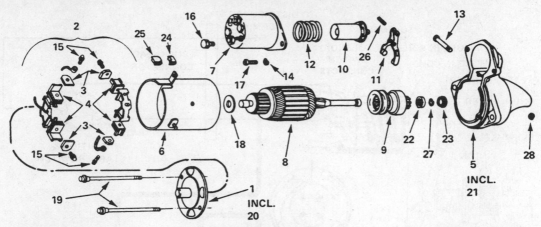

1. Frame—commutator end
2. Brush and holder pkg.
3. Brush
4. Brush holder
5. Housing—drive end
6. Frame and field asm.
7. Solenoid switch
8. Armature
9. Drive asm.
10. Plunger
11. Shift lever
12. Plunger return springer
13. Shift lever shaft
14. Lock washer
15. Screw—brush attaching
16. Screw—field lead to switch
17. Screw—switch attaching
18. Washer—brake
19. Thru bolt
20. Bushing—commutator end
21. Bushing—drive end
22. Pinion stop collar
23. Thrust collar
24. Grommet
25. Grommet
26. Plunger pin
27. Pinion stop retainer ring
28. Lever shaft retaining ring

Starter disassembled view

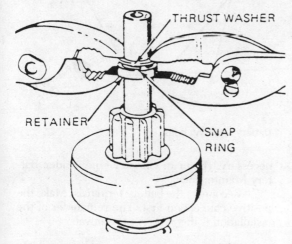

Installing the starter retainer washer and ring

NOTE: *When the starter motor has been disassembled or the solenoid has been replaced, it is necessary to check the pinion clearance. Pinion clearance must be correct to prevent the buttons on the shift lever yoke from rubbing on the clutch collar during cranking.*

CHECKING PINION CLEARANCE

1. Disconnect the motor field coil connector from the solenoid motor terminal and insulate it carefully.

2. Connect one 12 volt battery lead to the solenoid switch terminal and the other to the starter frame.

3. Flash a jumper lead momentarily from the solenoid motor terminal to the starter frame. This will shift the pinion into cranking position and it will remain there until the battery is disconnected.

4. Push the pinion back as far as possible to take up any movement, and check the clearance with a feeler gauge. The clearance should be 0.010–0.140 in.

5. There is no means for adjusting pinion clearance on the starter motor. If clearance does not fall within the limits, check for improper installation and replace all worn parts.

Checking the starter pinion clearance

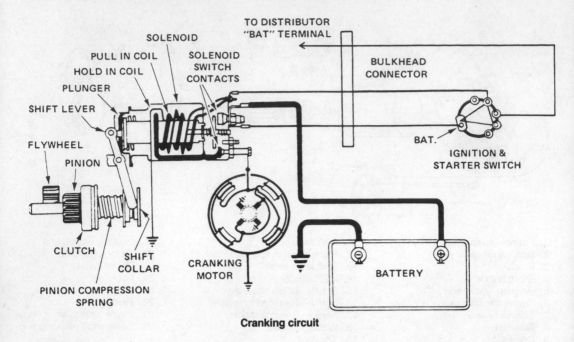

Cranking circuit

Battery

The battery is located in the rear compartment on the passenger's side of the vehicle, under a cover panel.

REMOVAL AND INSTALLATION

1. In the rear compartment remove the two thumb screws holding the battery cover panel to the body, and lift the panel out.

2. Remove the black negative cable, then the red positive cable from the battery.

3. Remove the battery retainer bolt, located on the bottom front side of the battery (terminal side).

4. Loosen the bolts which retain the heat shield and move the shield out of the way.

5. Carefully remove the battery.

6. Before installing a new battery, check the cables and terminals for corrosion and clean as

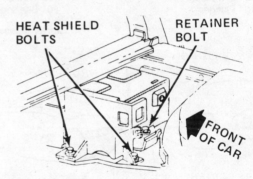

Battery retaining bolts

necessary. (Refer to Chapter One, under Battery Maintenance).

7. Reconnect the battery terminals. Make the positive connection first. The remainder of the installation is the reverse of removal.

ENGINE MECHANICAL

Engine Removal and Installation

All Engines

NOTE: *The engine assembly is removed from underneath the vehicle.*

1. Disconnect the battery cables.

2. Drain the engine coolant.

3. Remove the rear compartment lid and also the side panels on the V6 engine.

NOTE: *Do not remove the torsion rod retaining bolts.*

4. Remove the air cleaner assembly.

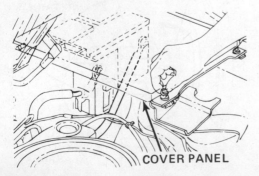

Removing the battery cover panel

General Engine Specifications

Year	Eng. V.I.N. Code	Engine Displacement Cu. In.	Eng. Mfg.	Fuel Delivery	Horsepower @ rpm■	Torque @ rpm (ft. lbs.)■	Bore x Stroke (in.)	Compression Ratio	Oil Pressure @ 2000 rpm
'84–'85	R	151	Pont.	TBI	90 @ 4000	132 @ 2800	4.000 x 3.000	9.0:1	36–41
'85	9	173	Chev.	PFI①	130 @ 5400	160 @ 3600	3.500 x 3.000	8.5:1/8.9:1	30–45

① Port Fuel Injection
■ SAE net

Valve Specifications

Year	V.I.N. Code	Engine No. Cyl. Displacement (cu. in.)	Eng. Mfg.	Seat Angle (deg)	Face Angle (deg)	Spring Test Pressure (lbs. @ in.)	Spring Installed Height (in.)	Stem to Guide Clearance (in.) Intake	Stem to Guide Clearance (in.) Exhaust	Stem Diameter (in.) Intake	Stem Diameter (in.) Exhaust
'84–'85	R	4-151	Pont.	45	45	176 @ 1.254	1.69	0.0010–0.0027	0.0010–0.0027	0.3418–0.3425	0.3418–0.3425
'85	9	6-173	Chev.	45	45	195 @ 1.181	1.57	0.0010–0.0027	0.0010–0.0027	0.3410–0.3416	0.3410–0.3416

Crankshaft and Connecting Rod Specifications
(All measurements are given in inches)

Year	V.I.N. Code	Engine No. Cyl. Displacement (cu. in.)	Eng. Mfg.	Crankshaft Main Brg. Journal Dia.	Crankshaft Main Brg. Oil Clearance	Crankshaft Shaft End-Play	Crankshaft Thrust on No.	Connecting Rod Journal Diameter	Connecting Rod Oil Clearance	Connecting Rod Side Clearance
'84–'85	R	4-151	Pont.	2.2995–2.3005	0.0005–0.0022	0.0035–0.0085	5	1.9995–2.0005	0.0005–0.0026	0.006–0.022
'85	9	6-173	Chev.	2.4937–2.4946	0.0016–0.0031	0.0023–0.0082	3	1.9984–1.9994	0.0014–0.0037	0.006–0.017

Camshaft Specifications
(All measurements in inches)

Year	V.I.N. Code	Engine	Eng. Mfg.	Journal Diameter 1	Journal Diameter 2	Journal Diameter 3	Journal Diameter 4	Journal Diameter 5	Bearing Clearance	Lobe Lift Intake	Lobe Lift Exhaust	Camshaft End Play
'84–'85	R	4-151	Pont.	1.869	1.869	1.869	—	—	0.0007–0.0027	0.398	0.398	0.0015–0.0050
'85	9	6-173	Chev.	1.869	1.869	1.869	—	—	0.0010–0.0040	0.231	0.263	—

Piston and Ring Specifications
(All measurements are given in inches. To convert inches to metric units, refer to the Metric Information section.)

Year	V.I.N. Code	Engine Type/ Disp. cu. in.	Eng. Mfg.	Piston-to-Bore Clearance	Ring Gap Top Compression	Ring Gap Bottom Compression	Ring Gap Oil Control	Ring Side Clearance Top Compression	Ring Side Clearance Bottom Compression	Ring Side Clearance Oil Control
'84–'85	R	4-151	Pont.	0.0025–0.0033	0.010–0.022	0.010–0.027	0.015–0.055	0.002–0.003	0.002–0.003	snug
'85	9	6-173	Chev.	0.0007–0.0017	0.0098–0.0197	0.0098–0.0197	0.020–0.055	0.0012–0.0028	0.0016–0.0037	.008 max

Torque Specifications

(All readings in ft. lbs.)

Year	V.I.N. Code	Engine No. Cyl. Displacement (cu. in.)	Eng. Mfg.	Cylinder Head Bolts	Rod Bearing Bolts	Main Bearing Bolts	Crankshaft Bolt	Flywheel to Crankshaft Bolts	Manifold	
									Intake	Exhaust
'84–'85	R	4-151	Pont.	92	32	70	200	44	29	44
'85	9	6-173	Chev.	65–90	34–40	63–74	66–84	45–55	20–25	22–28

5. Disconnect the throttle and shift cables.

6. Disconnect the heater hose at the intake manifold.

7. Disconnect the vacuum hoses from all non-engine components.

8. Disconnect the fuel lines and filter.

9. Disconnect the fuel pump relay and oxygen sensor.

10. On models with automatic transaxle, disconnect the transaxle cooler lines.

11. Disconnect the slave cylinder from manual transaxle equipped vehicles.

12. Disconnect the engine-to-chassis ground strap.

13. Discharge the A/C system, if so equipped, then disconnect the A/C lines at the compressor and seal the ends.

CAUTION: *Do not disconnect any refrigerant lines unless you have experience with air conditioning systems. Escaping refrigerant will freeze any surface it contacts, including your skin and eyes.*

14. Remove the rear console.

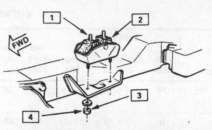

1. Insulator to support bracket studs
2. Engine insulator
3. Insulator to chassis attaching nut
4. 56 N·m (41 lb. ft.)

Engine mount to crossmember - four cyl. engine

15. Remove the ECM harness through the bulkhead panel.

16. Install an engine support fixture.

17. Remove the engine strut bracket and mark the bolt and bracket for reassembly.

18. Raise the vehicle. (Refer to the illustration).

19. Remove the rear wheels.

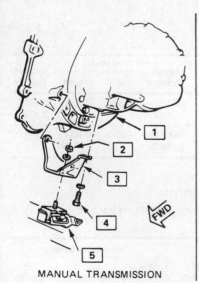

MANUAL TRANSMISSION

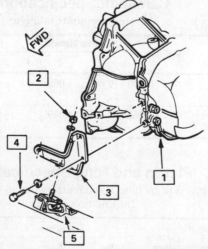

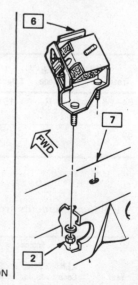

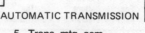

AUTOMATIC TRANSMISSION

1. Trans. asm.
2. 56 N·m (41 lb. ft.)
3. Forward transmission support bracket
4. 65 N·m (48 lb. ft.)

5. Trans. mtg. asm.
6. Forward transmission insulator
7. Crossmember asm.

Forward transaxle mount and mounting brackets - four cyl engine

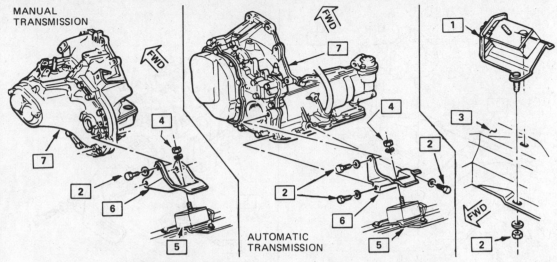

MANUAL
TRANSMISSION

AUTOMATIC
TRANSMISSION

1. Rear transmission insulator
2. 64 N·m (47 lb. ft.)
3. Crossmember asm.
4. 56 N·m (41 lb. ft.)
5. Mtg. asm.
6. Rear transmission support bracket
7. Trans. asm.

Rear transaxle mount and mounting brackets - four cyl. engine

20. On models equipped with an automatic transaxle, remove the torque converter bolts.

21. Remove the parking brake cable and calipers.

NOTE: *Do not disconnect the brake hoses. Support the caliper out of the way.*

22. Remove the strut bolts and mark the struts for realignment. (Refer to the Strut removal and installation procedure in Chapter 8).

23. Disconnect the A/C wiring, if so equipped.

24. Loosen the four engine cradle bolts.

25. On the 4 cylinder engine, release the parking brake cables at the cradle. A special tool No. J-34065 is available for this procedure.

CAUTION: *Support the engine/transaxle and cradle assembly on a jack. Be sure to support the outboard ends of the lower control arms. Disconnect the engine support fixture.*

26. Lower the car and attach the engine/transaxle assembly to a dolly. Remove the cradle bolts. Raise the car and roll the dolly from under the car.

27. Separate the engine and transaxle.

28. Installation is the reverse of removal.

Rocker Arm, Cover and Push Rod
REMOVAL AND INSTAllATION
Four Cylinder Engine

1. Remove the air cleaner assembly. (Refer to Chapter 1).

2. Remove the PCV valve and hose.

3. Remove the valve cover bolts.

4. Disconnect the wires from the spark plugs and clips.

5. Remove the valve cover by tapping lightly with a rubber hammer.

NOTE: *Prying on the cover could cause damage to the sealing surfaces.*

6. Remove the rocker arm bolt and ball.

7. If replacing the push rod only, loosen the rocker arm bolt and swing the arm clear of the push rod.

8. Remove the rocker arm and pushrod.

9. Installation is the reverse of removal. Torque the rocker arm bolt to 20 ft. lbs. Apply a continuous 3/16 in. diameter bead of RTV sealant or equivalent around the cylinder head sealaning surfaces inboard at the bolt holes.

NOTE: *Keep the sealant out of the bolt holes.*

V6 Engine

1. Disconnect the negative battery cable.

2. Remove the engine compartment lid and both side covers.

NOTE: *Do not remove the torsion rod retaining bolts.*

3. Disconnect the vacuum boost line and tube.

4. Disconnect the throttle and downshift cables and bracket.

5. Disconnect the cruise control cable, if applicable.

6. Disconnect the ground cable.

7. Remove the PCV valve from the cover.

8. Remove the oil dip stick tube.

9. Disconnect the plug wires and bracket.

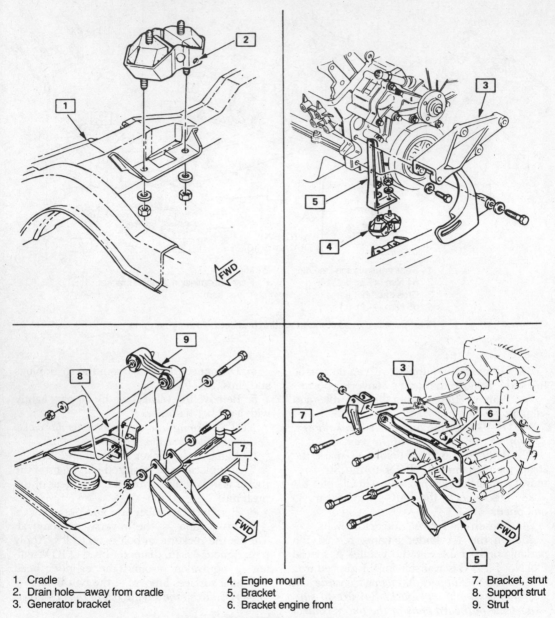

1. Cradle
2. Drain hole—away from cradle
3. Generator bracket
4. Engine mount
5. Bracket
6. Bracket engine front
7. Bracket, strut
8. Support strut
9. Strut

Engine mounts and torque strut - V6 engine

10. Remove the engine lift hook.

11. Remove the rocker arm cover bolts and carefully remove the cover by bumping with your hand or a rubber mallet. If prying is necessary do not distort the sealing flange.

12. Remove the rocker arm nuts.

NOTE: *Keep all components in order so that they may be installed in the same location.*

13. Remove the rocker arm pivot balls, arms and pushrods.

14. Before installation, coat the bearing surfaces of the rocker arms and pivot balls with "Molykote" or equivalent.

15. Install the push rods rocker arms and pivot balls. Make sure the push rods are seated in the valve lifters.

16. Adjust the rocker arm nuts until lash is eliminated.

a. Rotate the engine until the mark on the torsional damper lines up with the "0" mark on the timing tab, with the engine in the No. 1 firing position. This may be determined by placing fingers on the No. 1 rocker arms as the mark on the damper comes near the "0" mark. If the valves are not moving, the engine is in the No. 1 firing position.

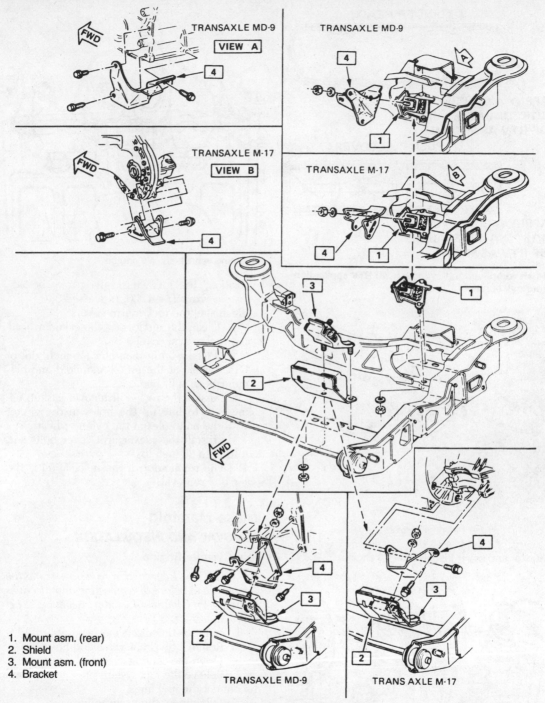

TRANSAXLE MD-9 VIEW A

TRANSAXLE MD-9

TRANSAXLE M-17 VIEW B

TRANSAXLE M-17

1. Mount asm. (rear)
2. Shield
3. Mount asm. (front)
4. Bracket

TRANSAXLE MD-9

TRANS AXLE M-17

Cradle and transaxle nuts - V6 engine

With the engine in the No. 1 firing position, the following valves may be adjusted: Exhaust—1,2,3; Intake—1,5,6.

b. Back out the adjusting nut until lash is felt at the pushrod, then turn the adjusting nut until all lash is removed. This can be determined by rotating the pushrod while turning the adjusting nut. When lash has been removed, turn the adjusting nut in 1½ additional turns to center the lifter plunger.

c. Crank the engine one revolution until the timing tab "0" mark and torsional damper mark are again in alignment. This is the No. 4 firing position. With the engine in this

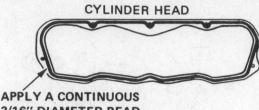

CYLINDER HEAD

**APPLY A CONTINUOUS
3/16" DIAMETER BEAD
OF RTV AS SHOWN**

PUSH ROD COVER

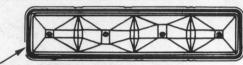

**APPLY A CONTINUOUS
3/16" DIAMETER BEAD
OF RTV AS SHOWN**

Push rod cover and cylinder head RTV application - four cyl. engine

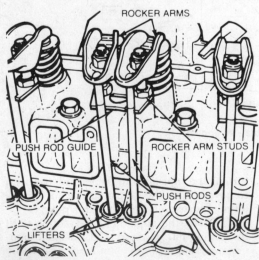

Rocker arm cover installation - V6 engine

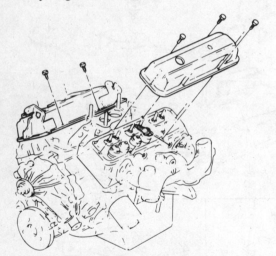

Valve mechanism - V6 engine

ROCKER ARMS

PUSH ROD GUIDE

ROCKER ARM STUDS

PUSH RODS

LIFTERS

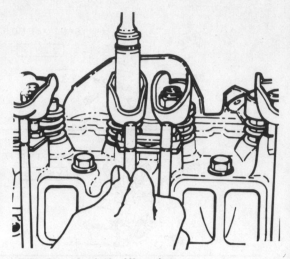

Adjusting valve lash - V6 engine

position, the following valves may be adjusted: Exhaust—4,5,6; Intake—2,3,4.

17. Install the rocker arm covers.

a. Clean the surfaces on the cylinder head and rocker arm cover.

b. Place a 3mm diameter (⅛ inch) dot of RTV sealer, at the intake manifold and cylinder head split line.

c. Install the rocker arm cover gasket, using care to line up the holes in the gasket with the bolt holes in the cylinder head.

d. Install the rocker arm cover bolts and torque to 90 inch lbs.

18. The remainder of the installation is the reverse of removal.

Intake Manifold

REMOVAL AND INSTALLATION

Four Cylinder Engine

CAUTION: *Relieve the pressure from the fuel system before disconnecting any fuel lines (Refer to Chapter 4 under Relieving Fuel Pressure).*

1. Remove the air cleaner assembly.
2. Remove the PCV valve and hose.
3. Drain the cooling system.
4. Relieve the fuel system pressure and and disconnect the fuel lines.
5. Disconnect the vacuum hoses.
6. Disconnect the wiring and the throttle linkage from the throttle body assembly.
7. Disconnect the cruise control linkage, if so equipped.
8. Disconnect the throttle linkage and bell crank and place to one side.
9. Disconnect the heater hose.
10. Remove the alternator upper bracket.
11. Remove the ignition coil, on vehicles with the separately mounted coil.

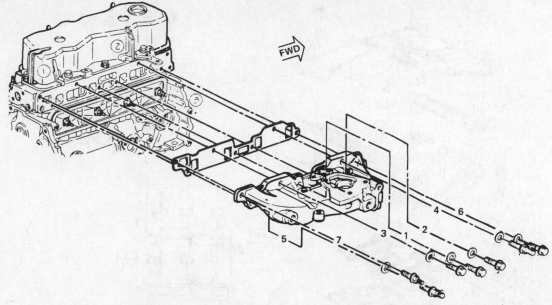

Intake manifold torque sequence - four cyl. engine

12. Remove the retaining bolts and remove the manifolds.

13. Installation is the reverse of removal. Torque all bolts in the sequence shown in the illustration. Torque the No. 7 bolt 37 ft. lbs. and all others to 25 ft. lbs.

V6 Engine

NOTE: *Refer to Chapter Four for the removal of the fuel injection unit.*

1. Disconnect the negative battery cable.
2. Remove both rocker arm covers.
3. Drain the engine coolant.
4. Disconnect the throttle body-to-elbow intake hose.
5. Remove the distributor and mark the position of the rotor.
6. Disconnect the shift and throttle linkage.
7. Remove the throttle body-to-upper plenum connector.
8. Disconnect the heater and radiator hoses.
9. Disconnect all wiring harness and vacuum hoses while noting their locations for reassembly.
10. Disconnect the vacuum booster pipe and bracket.
11. Disconnect the EGR pipe.
12. Remove the upper manifold plenum and gaskets.
13. Remove the intermediate intake manifold and gasket.
14. Remove the lower intake manifold and gaskets.

15. Clean all gasket surfaces on the intake manifolds and cylinder head.
16. Install the lower intake manifold and gasket and torque in sequence to 19 ft. lbs.
17. Install the intermediate intake manifold and gaskets and torque in sequence to 15 ft. lbs.
18. Install the upper manifold plenum and gaskets and torque in sequence.
19. The remainder of the installation is the reverse of removal. Check engine timing, coolant level and for leaks.

Exhaust Manifold

REMOVAL AND INSTALLATION

Four Cylinder Engine

1. Remove the air cleaner and the EFI bracket tube.
2. Raise the vehicle and support it with jack stands.
3. Remove the exhaust pipe and lower the vehicle.
4. Remove the retaining bolts and washers and remove the exhaust manifold and gasket.
5. Installation is the reverse of removal. Clean the sealing surfaces and use a new gasket. Torque the retaining bolts to the sequence shown in the illustration. Torque bolts No. 1,2,6, and 7 to 16 ft. lbs. Torque bolts No. 3,4, and 5 to 37 ft. lbs.

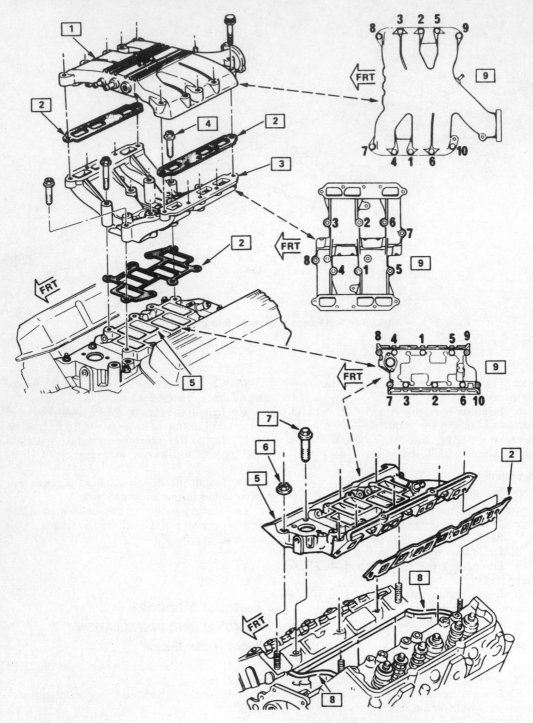

1. Manifold, upper plenum
2. Gasket
3. Intake manifold, intermediate
4. Bolt 21 N·m (15 lb. ft.)
5. Intake manifold, lower
6. Nut 26 N·m (19 lb. ft.)

7. Bolt 26 N·m (19 lb. ft.)
8. Apply a smooth—continuous bead approx. 2.0–3.0 mm wide and 3.0–3.5 mm thick on both surfaces. Bead configuration must insure complete sealing of water and oil. Surface must be free of oil and dirt to insure adequate seal.

Intake manifold assembly - V6 engine

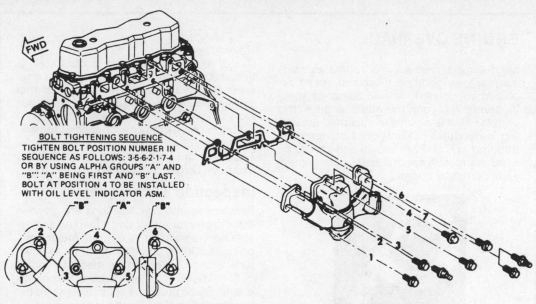

BOLT TIGHTENING SEQUENCE
TIGHTEN BOLT POSITION NUMBER IN
SEQUENCE AS FOLLOWS: 3-5-6-2-1-7-4
OR BY USING ALPHA GROUPS "A" AND
"B". "A" BEING FIRST AND "B" LAST.
BOLT AT POSITION 4 TO BE INSTALLED
WITH OIL LEVEL INDICATOR ASM.

Exhaust manifold torque sequence - four cyl. engine

Exhaust Manifold and Crossover

REMOVAL AND INSTALLATION

V6 Engine

FRONT

1. Disconnect the negative battery cable.
2. Remove the rear compartment lid.
NOTE: *Do not remove the torsion rod retaining bolts.*

3. Remove the brake vacuum hose.
4. Remove the manifold heat shield.
5. Remove the front crossover bolts.
6. Raise the car and remove the front converter heat shield and the lower manifold bolts.
7. Lower the car and remove the upper manifold bolts then remove the manifold.

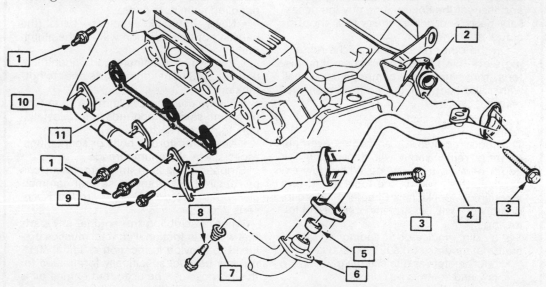

1. Bolt/stud lockwasher asm. (l.h. only) 24 N·m (18 lb. ft.)
2. Exhaust manifold asm. r.h.
3. Bolt—30 N·m (22 lb. ft.)
4. Crossover pipe
5. Seal
6. Muffler
7. Spring
8. Bolt—20 N·m (15 lb. ft.)
9. Bolt & lockwasher asm. 24 N·m (18 lb. ft.)
10. Exhaust manifold asm. l.h.
11. Gasket

Exhaust manifold - V6 engine

ENGINE OVERHAUL

Most engine overhaul procedures are fairly standard. In addition to specific parts replacement procedures and complete specifications for your individual engine, this chapter also is a guide to accepted rebuilding procedures. Examples of standard rebuilding practice are shown and should be used along with specific details concerning your particular engine.

Competent and accurate machine shop services will ensure maximum performance, reliability and engine life. Procedures marked with the symbol shown above should be performed by a competent machine shop, and are provided so that you will be familiar with the procedures necessary to a successful overhaul.

In most instances it is more profitable for the do-it-yourself mechanic to remove, clean and inspect the component, buy the necessary parts and deliver these to a shop for actual machine work.

On the other hand, much of the rebuilding work (crankshaft, block, bearings, pistons, rods, and other components) is well within the scope of the do-it-yourself mechanic.

Tools

The tools required for an engine overhaul or parts replacement will depend on the depth of your involvement. With a few exceptions, they will be the tools found in a mechanic's tool kit (see Chapter 1). More in-depth work will require any or all of the following:
- a dial indicator (reading in thousandths) mounted on a universal base
- micrometers and telescope gauges
- jaw and screw-type pullers
- scraper
- valve spring compressor
- ring groove cleaner
- piston ring expander and compressor
- ridge reamer
- cylinder hone or glaze breaker

- Plastigage®
- engine stand

Use of most of these tools is illustrated in this chapter. Many can be rented for a one-time use from a local parts jobber or tool supply house specializing in automotive work.

Occasionally, the use of special tools is called for. See the information on Special Tools and the Safety Notice in the front of this book before substituting another tool.

Inspection Techniques

Procedures and specifications are given in this chapter for inspecting, cleaning and assessing the wear limits of most major components. Other procedures such as Magnaflux and Zyglo can be used to locate material flaws and stress cracks. Magnaflux is a magnetic process applicable only to ferrous materials. The Zyglo process coats the material with a flourescent dye penetrant and can be used on any material. Check for suspected surface cracks can be more readily made using spot check dye. The dye is sprayed onto the suspected area, wiped off and the area sprayed with a developer. Cracks will show up brightly.

Overhaul Tips

Aluminum has become extremely popular for use in engines, due to its low weight. Observe the following precautions when handling aluminum parts:
- Never hot tank aluminum parts (the caustic hot-tank solution will eat the aluminum)
- Remove all aluminum parts (identification tag, etc.) from engine parts prior to hot-tanking.
- Always coat threads lightly with engine oil or anti-seize compounds before installation, to prevent seizure.
- Never over-torque bolts or spark plugs, especially in aluminum threads.

Stripped threads in any component can be repaired using any of several commercial repair kits (Heli-Coil, Microdot, Keenserts, etc.)

When assembling the engine, any parts that will be in frictional contact must be pre-lubed to provide lubrication at initial start-up. Any product specifically formulated for this purpose can be used, but engine oil is not recommended as a pre-lube.

When semi-permanent (locked, but removable) installation of bolts or nuts is desired, threads should be cleaned and coated with Loctite® or other similar, commercial non-hardening sealant.

Repairing Damaged Threads

Several methods of repairing damaged threads are available. Heli-Coil® (shown here), Keenserts® and Microdot® are among the most widely used. All involve basically the same principle—drilling out stripped threads, tapping the hole and installing a pre-wound insert—making welding, plugging and oversize fasteners unnecessary.

Two types of thread repair inserts are usually supplied—a standard type for most Inch Coarse, Inch Fine, Metric Coarse and Metric Fine thread sizes and a spark plug type to fit most spark plug port sizes. Consult the individual manufacturer's catalog to determine exact applications. Typical thread repair kits will contain a selection of pre-wound threaded inserts, a tap (corresponding to the outside diameter threads of the insert) and an installation tool. Spark plug inserts usually differ because they require a tap equipped with pilot threads and a combined reamer/tap section. Most manufacturers also supply blister-packed thread repair inserts separately in addition to a master kit containing a variety of taps and inserts plus installation tools.

Before effecting a repair to a threaded hole, remove any snapped, broken or damaged bolts or studs. Penetrating oil can be used to free frozen threads; the offending item can be removed with locking pliers or with a screw or stud extractor. After the hole is clear, the thread can be repaired, as follows:

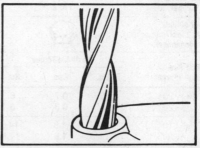

Drill out the damaged threads with specified drill. Drill completely through the hole or to the bottom of a blind hole

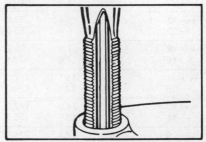

With the tap supplied, tap the hole to receive the thread insert. Keep the tap well oiled and back it out frequently to avoid clogging the threads

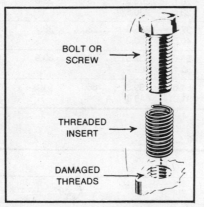

Damaged bolt holes can be repaired with thread repair inserts

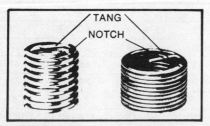

Standard thread repair insert (left) and spark plug thread insert (right)

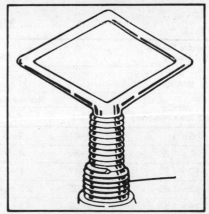

Screw the threaded insert onto the installation tool until the tang engages the slot. Screw the insert into the tapped hole until it is ¼–½ turn below the top surface. After installation break off the tang with a hammer and punch

Standard Torque Specifications and Fastener Markings

In the absence of specific torques, the following chart can be used as a guide to the maximum safe torque of a particular size/grade of fastener.
- There is no torque difference for fine or coarse threads.
- Torque values are based on clean, dry threads. Reduce the value by 10% if threads are oiled prior to assembly.
- The torque required for aluminum components or fasteners is considerably less.

U.S. Bolts

SAE Grade Number	1 or 2			5			6 or 7		
Number of lines always 2 less than the grade number.									
Bolt Size (Inches)—(Thread)	Maximum Torque			Maximum Torque			Maximum Torque		
	Ft./Lbs.	Kgm	Nm	Ft./Lbs.	Kgm	Nm	Ft./Lbs.	Kgm	Nm
¼—20	5	0.7	6.8	8	1.1	10.8	10	1.4	13.5
—28	6	0.8	8.1	10	1.4	13.6			
⁵⁄₁₆—18	11	1.5	14.9	17	2.3	23.0	19	2.6	25.8
—24	13	1.8	17.6	19	2.6	25.7			
³⁄₈—16	18	2.5	24.4	31	4.3	42.0	34	4.7	46.0
—24	20	2.75	27.1	35	4.8	47.5			
⁷⁄₁₆—14	28	3.8	37.0	49	6.8	66.4	55	7.6	74.5
—20	30	4.2	40.7	55	7.6	74.5			
½—13	39	5.4	52.8	75	10.4	101.7	85	11.75	115.2
—20	41	5.7	55.6	85	11.7	115.2			
⁹⁄₁₆—12	51	7.0	69.2	110	15.2	149.1	120	16.6	162.7
—18	55	7.6	74.5	120	16.6	162.7			
⁵⁄₈—11	83	11.5	112.5	150	20.7	203.3	167	23.0	226.5
—18	95	13.1	128.8	170	23.5	230.5			
¾—10	105	14.5	142.3	270	37.3	366.0	280	38.7	379.6
—16	115	15.9	155.9	295	40.8	400.0			
⅞— 9	160	22.1	216.9	395	54.6	535.5	440	60.9	596.5
—14	175	24.2	237.2	435	60.1	589.7			
1— 8	236	32.5	318.6	590	81.6	799.9	660	91.3	894.8
—14	250	34.6	338.9	660	91.3	849.8			

Metric Bolts

Relative Strength Marking	4.6, 4.8			8.8		
Bolt Markings						
Bolt Size Thread Size x Pitch (mm)	Maximum Torque			Maximum Torque		
	Ft./Lbs.	Kgm	Nm	Ft./Lbs.	Kgm	Nm
6 x 1.0	2–3	.2–.4	3–4	3–6	.4–.8	5–8
8 x 1.25	6–8	.8–1	8–12	9–14	1.2–1.9	13–19
10 x 1.25	12–17	1.5–2.3	16–23	20–29	2.7–4.0	27–39
12 x 1.25	21–32	2.9–4.4	29–43	35–53	4.8–7.3	47–72
14 x 1.5	35–52	4.8–7.1	48–70	57–85	7.8–11.7	77–110
16 x 1.5	51–77	7.0–10.6	67–100	90–120	12.4–16.5	130–160
18 x 1.5	74–110	10.2–15.1	100–150	130–170	17.9–23.4	180–230
20 x 1.5	110–140	15.1–19.3	150–190	190–240	26.2–46.9	160–320
22 x 1.5	150–190	22.0–26.2	200–260	250–320	34.5–44.1	340–430
24 x 1.5	190–240	26.2–46.9	260–320	310–410	42.7–56.5	420–550

CHECKING ENGINE COMPRESSION

A noticeable lack of engine power, excessive oil consumption and/or poor fuel mileage measured over an extended period are all indicators of internal engine wear. Worn piston rings, scored or worn cylinder bores, blown head gaskets, sticking or burnt valves and worn valve seats are all possible culprits here. A check of each cylinder's compression will help you locate the problems.

As mentioned in the "Tools and Equipment" section of Chapter 1, a screw-in type compression gauge is more accurate than the type you simply hold against the spark plug hole, although it takes slightly longer to use. It's worth it to obtain a more accurate reading. Follow the procedures below for gasoline and diesel-engined cars.

Gasoline Engines

1. Warm up the engine to normal operating temperature.
2. Remove all spark plugs.

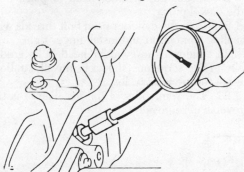

The screw-in type compression gauge is more accurate

3. Disconnect the high-tension lead from the ignition coil.
4. On carbureted cars, fully open the throttle either by operating the carburetor throttle linkage by hand or by having an assistant "floor" the accelerator pedal. On fuel-injected cars, disconnect the cold start valve and all injector connections.
5. Screw the compression gauge into the No. 1 spark plug hole until the fitting is snug.
NOTE: *Be careful not to crossthread the plug hole. On aluminum cylinder heads use extra care, as the threads in these heads are easily ruined.*
6. Ask an assistant to depress the accelerator pedal fully on both carbureted and fuel-injected cars. Then, while you read the compression gauge, ask the assistant to crank the engine two or three times in short bursts using the ignition switch.

7. Read the compression gauge at the end of each series of cranks, and record the highest of these readings. Repeat this procedure for each of the engine's cylinders. Compare the highest reading of each cylinder to the compression pressure specifications in the "Tune-Up Specifications" chart in Chapter 2. The specs in this chart are maximum values. A cylinder's compression pressure is usually acceptable if it is not less than 80% of maximum. The difference between each cylinder should be no more than 12–14 pounds.
8. If a cylinder is unusually low, pour a tablespoon of clean engine oil into the cylinder through the spark plug hole and repeat the compression test. If the compression comes up after adding the oil, it appears that that cylinder's piston rings or bore are damaged or worn. If the pressure remains low, the valves may not be seating properly (a valve job is needed), or the head gasket may be blown near that cylinder. If compression in any two adjacent cylinders is low, and if the addition of oil doesn't help the compression, there is leakage past the head gasket. Oil and coolant water in the combustion chamber can result from this problem. There may be evidence of water droplets on the engine dipstick when a head gasket has blown.

Diesel Engines

Checking cylinder compression on diesel engines is basically the same procedure as on gasoline engines except for the following:
1. A special compression gauge adaptor suitable for diesel engines (because these engines have much greater compression pressures) must be used.
2. Remove the injector tubes and remove the injectors from each cylinder.
NOTE: *Don't forget to remove the washer underneath each injector; otherwise, it may get lost when the engine is cranked.*

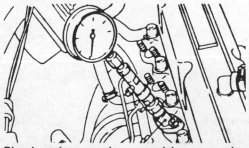

Diesel engines require a special compression gauge adaptor

3. When fitting the compression gauge adaptor to the cylinder head, make sure the bleeder of the gauge (if equipped) is closed.
4. When reinstalling the injector assemblies, install new washers underneath each injector.

8. Install the manifold and torque the upper bolts to 18 ft. lbs.

9. Raise the car and torque the lower bolts to 18 ft. lbs.

10. Install the front converter heat shield.

11. Lower the car and torque the crossover bolts to 22 ft. lbs.

12. The remainder of the installation is the reverse of removal. Check for exhaust or vacuum leaks.

REAR

1. Disconnect the manifold-to-crossover bolts.

2. Remove the manifold bolts then remove the manifold.

3. Installation is the reverse of removal. Torque the manifold bolts to 18 ft. lbs. and the manifold to crossover bolts to 22 ft. lbs.

Cylinder Head
REMOVAL AND INSTALLATION
Four Cylinder Engine

1. Drain the cooling system.

2. Raise the vehicle and support it safely with jack stands.

3. Remove the exhaust pipe.

4. Lower the vehicle.

5. Remove the oil level indicator tube.

6. Remove the air cleaner assembly.

7. Disconnect the EFI electrical connections and vacuum hoses.

8. Remove the EGR base plate.

9. Remove the heater hose from the intake manifold.

10. Remove the ignition coil from the lower mounting bolt and wiring connection.

11. Remove all wiring connections from the intake manifold and cylinder head.

12. Remove the engine strut bolt from the upper support.

13. Remove the alternator belt.

14. Remove the throttle cables from the intake manifold.

15. Remove the valve cover, rocker arms and pushrods.

16. Remove the cylinder head bolts and remove the cylinder head.

17. Before installing, clean the gasket surfaces of the head and block.

18. Make sure the retaining bolt threads and the cylinder block threads are clean since dirt could affect bolt torque.

19. Install a new gasket over the dowel pins in the cylinder block.

20. Install the cylinder head in place over the dowel pins.

21. Coat the cylinder head bolt threads with sealing compound and install finger tight.

22. Tighten the cylinder head bolts gradually in the sequence shown in the illustration. Final torque is 92 ft. lbs.

23. The remainder of the installation is the reverse of removal.

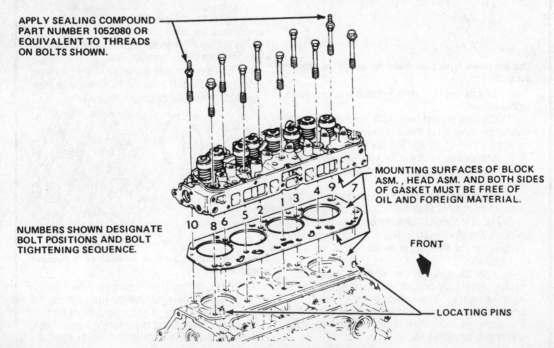

APPLY SEALING COMPOUND PART NUMBER 1052080 OR EQUIVALENT TO THREADS ON BOLTS SHOWN.

MOUNTING SURFACES OF BLOCK ASM., HEAD ASM. AND BOTH SIDES OF GASKET MUST BE FREE OF OIL AND FOREIGN MATERIAL.

NUMBERS SHOWN DESIGNATE BOLT POSITIONS AND BOLT TIGHTENING SEQUENCE.

FRONT

LOCATING PINS

Cylinder head torque sequence - four cyl. engine

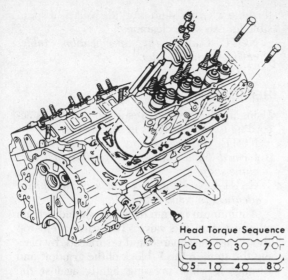

Head Torque Sequence

Cylinder head torque sequence - V6 engine

V6 Engine

Left Side

1. Raise the vehicle and drain the coolant from the block.
2. Lower the vehicle.
3. Remove the intake manifold.
4. Disconnect the exhaust crossover pipe.
5. Disconnect the generator bracket.
6. Remove the oil level indicator tube.
7. Loosen the rocker arms until you're able to remove the push rods.
8. Remove the cylinder head bolts then remove the cylinder head.
9. Before installing, clean the gasket surfaces on the head, cylinder block and intake manifold.
10. Place the gasket in position over the dowel pins with the note "This Side UP" showing.
11. Place the cylinder head into position.
12. Coat the cylinder head bolt threads with a sealer and install the bolts. Tighten the bolts in sequence to 66 ft. lbs.
13. Install the pushrods and loosely retain with the rocker arms. Make sure the lower ends of the pushrods are in the lifter seats then adjust the valve lash. Refer to the procedure under Rocker Arm , Cover and Push Rod.
14. The remainder of the installation is the reverse of removal.

V6 Engine

Right Side

1. Raise the vehicle, support it safely, then drain the cooling system.
2. Disconnect the exhaust pipe.
3. Lower the vehicle.

4. Disconnect the cruise control servo bracket.
5. Remove the intake manifold.
6. Disconnect the exhaust crossover pipe.
7. Follow steps 7 thru 14 of the left side cylinder head procedure above.

CLEANING AND INSPECTION

1. Remove all traces of carbon from the head, using a decarbon-type wire brush mounted in an electric drill. Do not use a motorized brush on any gasket mating surface.
2. Lay a straight edge across the cylinder head face and check between the straight edge and the head with feeler gauges. Make the check at six points minimum. Cylinder head flatness should be within .003-.006 inch. These surfaces may be reconditioned by parallel grinding. If more than 10% must be removed, the head should be replaced.

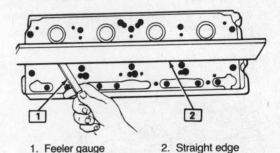

| 1. Feeler gauge | 2. Straight edge |

Checking cylinder head flatness

Valves

REMOVAL AND INSPECTION

1. Remove the cylinder head(s) from the vehicle as previously outlined.
2. Using a suitable valve spring compressor, compress the valve spring and remove the valve keys using a magnetic retrieval tool.
3. Slowly release the compressor and remove the valve spring caps (or rotors) and the valve springs.
4. Fabricate a valve arrangement board to use when you remove the valves, which will indicate the port in which each valve was originally installed (and which cylinder head on V6 models). Also note that the valve keys, rotators, caps, etc. should be arranged in a manner which will allow you to install them on the valve on which they were originally used.
5. Remove and discard the valve seals. On models using the umbrella type seals, note the location of the large and small seals for assembly purposes.
6. Thoroughly clean the valves on the wire wheel of a bench grinder, then clean the cyl-

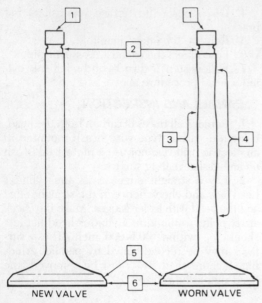

NEW VALVE   WORN VALVE

1. Valve tip
2. Keeper groove
3. Stem-least worn section
4. Stem-most worn section
5. Face
6. Margin

Valve wear

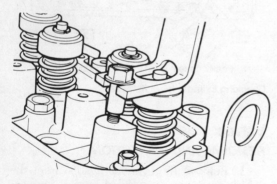

Compressing valve springs

inder head mating surface with a soft wire wheel, a soft wire brush, or a wooden scraper. Avoid using a metallic scraper, since this can cause damage to the cylinder head mating surface, especially on models with aluminum heads.

7. Using a valve guide cleaner chucked into a drill, clean all of the valve guides.

8. Install each valve into its respective port (guide) of the cylinder head.

9. Mount a dial indicator so that the stem is at 90° to the valve stem, as close to the valve guide as possible.

10. Move the valve off its seat, and measure the valve guide-to-stem clearance by rocking the stem back and forth to actuate the dial indicator.

11. Measure the valve stems using a micrometer, and compare to specifications, to de-

termine whether stem or guide wear is responsible for excessive clearance.

NOTE: *Consult the Specifications tables earlier in this chapter.*

REFACING

Using a valve grinder, resurface the valves according to specifications in this chapter.

NOTE: *All machine work should be performed by a competent, professional machine shop.*

CAUTION: *Valve face angle is not always identical to valve seat angle.*

A minimum margin of $\frac{1}{32}$ in. should remain after grinding the valve. The valve stem top should also be squared and resurfaced, by placing the stem in the V-block of the grinder, and turning it while pressing lightly against the grinding wheel. Be sure to chamfer the edge of the tip so that the squared edges don't dig into the rocker arm.

LAPPING

This procedure should be performed after the valves and seats have been machined, to insure that each valve mates to each seat precisely.

1. Invert the cylinder head, lightly lubricate the valve stems, and install the valves in the head as numbered.

2. Coat valve seats with fine grinding compound, and attach the lapping tool suction cup to a valve head.

NOTE: *Moisten the suction cup.*

3. Rotate the tool between your palms, changing position and lifting the tool often to prevent grooving.

4. Lap the valve until a smooth, polished seat is evident.

5. Remove the valve and tool, and rinse away all traces of grinding compound.

Valve Guide Service

The valve guides used in these engines are integral with the cylinder head, that is, they cannot be replaced.

NOTE: *Refer to the previous "Valves—Removal and Installation" to check the valve guides for wear.*

Valve guides are most accuratley repaired using the bronze wall rebuilding method. In this operation, "threads" are cut into the bore of the valve guide and bronze wire is turned into the threads. The bronze "wall" is then reamed to the proper diameter. This method is well received for a number of reasons: it is relatively

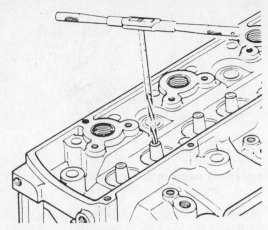

Reaming valve guides

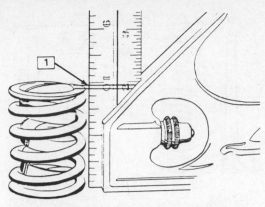

1. Not more than 1/16" variance while rotating spring

Checking valve springs

inexpensive, it offers better valve lubrication (the wire forms channels which retain oil), it offers less valve friction, and it preserves the original valve guide-to-seat relationship.

Another popular method of repairing valve guides is to have the guides "knurled." The knurling entails cutting into the bore of the valve guide with a special tool. The cutting action "raises" metal off of the guide bore which actually narrows the inner diameter of the bore, thereby reducing the clearance between the valve guide bore and the valve stem. This method offers the same advantages as the bronze wall method, but will generally wear faster.

Either of the above services must be performed by a professional machine shop which has the specialized knowledge and tools necessary to perform the service.

Valve Seat Service

The valve seats are integral with the cylinder head on all engines. On all engines the seats are machined into the cylinder head casting itself.

Valve Spring Testing

Place the spring on a flat surface next to a square. Measure the height of the spring, and rotate it against the edge of the square to measure distortion. If spring height varies (by comparison) by more than 1/16 in. or if distortion exceeds 1/16 in., replace the spring.

In addition to evaluating the spring as above, test the spring pressure at the installed and compressed (installed height minus valve lift) height using a valve spring tester. Spring pressure should be ± 1 lb. of all other springs in either position.

VALVE AND SPRING INSTALLATION

NOTE: *Be sure that all traces of lapping compound have been cleaned off before the valves are installed.*

1. Lubricate all of the valve stems with a light coating of engine oil, then install the valves into the proper ports/guides.

2. If umbrella-type valve seals are used, install them at this time. Be sure to use a seal protector to prevent damage to the seals as they are pushed over the valve keeper grooves. If O-ring seals are used, don't install them yet.

3. Install the valve springs and the spring retainers (or rotators), and using the valve compressing tool, compress the springs.

4. If umbrella-type seals are used, just install the valve keepers (white grease may be used to hold them in place) and release the pressure on the compressing tool. If O-ring type seals are used, carefully work the seals into the second groove of the valve (closest to the head), install the valve keepers and release the pressure on the tool.

NOTE: *If the O-ring seals are installed BE-*

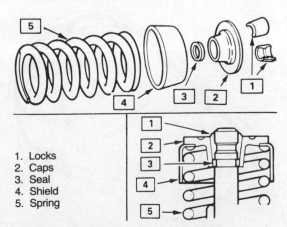

1. Locks
2. Caps
3. Seal
4. Shield
5. Spring

Upper valve train parts - four cyl. engine

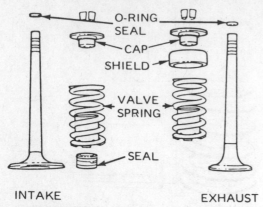

Valve train parts - V6 engine

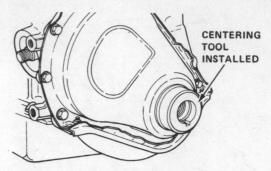

Front cover centering tool - four cyl. engine

FORE the springs and retainers are compressed, the seal will be destroyed.

5. After all of the valves are installed and retained, tap each valve spring retainer with a rubber mallet to seat the keepers in the retainer.

Timing Cover and Oil Seal

REMOVAL AND INSTALLATION

Four Cylinder Engine

1. Remove the crankshaft hub. It is may be necessary to remove the inner fender splash shield.

2. It may be necessary to remove the alternator lower bracket.

3. Remove the front engine mounts.

4. Using a floor jack, raise the engine.

5. Remove the engine mount mounting bracket-to-cylinder block bolts. Remove the bracket and mount as an assembly.

6. Remove the oil pan-to-front cover bolts.

7. Remove the front cover-to-block screws.

8. Pull the cover slightly forward, just

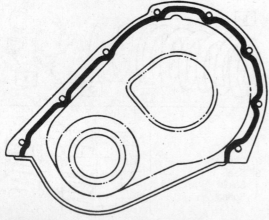

Timing cover sealer application - four cyl. engine

enough to allow cutting of the oil pan front seal flush with the block on both sides.

9. Remove the front cover and the attached portion of the pan seal.

10. Clean the gasket surfaces throughly.

11. Cut the tabs from the new oil pan front seal

12. Install the seal on the front cover, pressing the tips into the holes provided.

13. Coat the new gasket with sealer and position it on the front cover.

14. Apply a 1/8 in. bead of silicone sealer to the joint formed at the oil pan and block.

15. Align the front cover seal with a centering tool and install the front cover. Tighten the screws evenly.

16. Install the hub and torque the hub bolt to 160 ft. lbs.

NOTE: *Coat the pulley-to-hub bolts with a locking sealant.*

Front Cover

REMOVAL AND INSTALLATION

V6 Engine

1. Disconnect the negative battery cable.

2. Remove the A/C compressor and bracket, without disconnecting the refrigerant lines, and position out of the way.

3. Remove the water pump.

4. Raise the vehicle and support it safely.

5. Remove the torsional damper.

6. Remove the oil pan to cover bolts.

7. Lower the vehicle and remove the front cover.

8. Before installing, clean the sealing surfaces on the front cover and cylinder block. Install a new gasket and apply a 1/8 in. bead of RTV sealer to the oil pan sealing surface of the front cover.

9. Place the front cover on the engine and install the stud bolt and bolts.

10. The remainder of the installation is the reverse of removal.

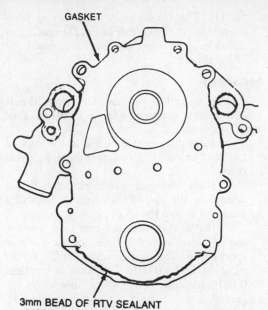

3mm BEAD OF RTV SEALANT
#1052366 OR EQUIVALENT
Front cover sealant replacement - V6 engine

Timing chain and sprocket - V6 engine

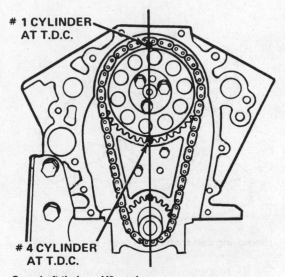

Camshaft timing - V6 engine

Front Cover Oil Seal
REMOVAL AND INSTALLATION
V6 Engine

1. Remove the torsional damper.
2. Pry out the seal using a suitable tool.
3. Before installing, lubricate the seal with clean engine oil.
4. Insert the seal in the front cover with the lip facing the engine.
5. Using Tool No. J23042 Seal Installer, drive the seal into place.
6. Install the torsional damper and check for leaks.

Timing Chain and Sprockets
REMOVAL AND INSTALLATION
V6 Engine

1. Remove the crankcase front cover.
2. Place the No. 1 piston at top dead center, with the marks on the camshaft and crankshaft sprockets aligned.
3. Remove the camshaft sprocket and chain. NOTE: *It may be necessary to use a plastic mallet on the lower edge of the sprocket to dislodge it.*
4. Remove the camshaft sprocket with Tool No. J5825.
5. Install the sprocket with Tool No. J5590.
6. Apply "Molykote" or equivalent to the sprocket thrust surface.
7. Hold the sprocket with the chain hanging down and align the marks on the camshaft and crankshaft sprockets.
8. Align the dowel in the camshaft with the dowel hole in the camshaft sprocket.
9. Draw the camshaft sprocket onto the camshaft, using the mounting bolts and torque to 15-20 ft. lbs.
10. Lubricate the timing chain with engine oil.
11. Install the crankcase front cover.

Camshaft and Timing Gear
FOUR CYLINDER ENGINE
Removal

1. Remove the engine as previously described.
2. Install the engine on a stand.
3. Remove the rocker arm cover, loosen the valve rocker arm bolts and swing the rocker arms clear of the push rods.

Removing camshaft thrust plate screws - four cyl. engine

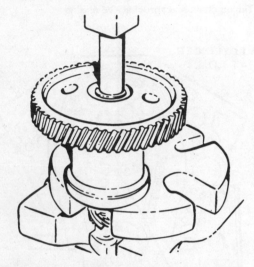

Removing camshaft timing gear - four cyl. engine

4. Remove the distributor and fuel pump.

5. Remove the pushrod cover, pushrods and valve lifters.

6. Remove the alternator, lower alternator bracket and front engine mount bracket assembly.

7. Remove the oil pump driveshaft and gear assembly.

8. Remove the front pulley hub and timing gear cover.

9. Remove the two camshaft thrust plate screws by working through the holes in the camshaft gear.

10. Remove the camshaft and gear assembly by pulling it out through the front of the block.

NOTE: *Support the shaft carefully when removing so as not to damage the camshaft bearings.*

11. If the gear must be removed from the shaft, use the press plate and adapter J-971 on the press.

12. Place the tools on the table of the press. Place the camshaft through the openings in the tools, then press the shaft out of the gear using a socket or other suitable tool.

NOTE: *The thrust plate must be so positioned that the woodruff key in the shaft does not damage it when the shaft is pressed out of the gear.*

Installation

1. To assemble the camshaft gear, thrust plate and gear spacer ring to the camshaft, proceed as follows:

a. Firmly support the shaft at the back of the front journal in an arbor press using press plate adapters.

b. Place the gear spacer ring and thrust plate over the end of the shaft, and install a woodruff key in the shaft keyway.

c. Install the camshaft gear and press it onto the shaft until it bottoms against the gear spacer ring. The end clearance of the thrust plate should be 0.0010–0.0050 in. If less than 0.0015 in., the thrust plate should be replaced.

2. Thoroughly coat the camshaft journals with a high quality engine oil supplement.

3. Install the camshaft assembly into the engine, being careful not to damage the bearings or cam.

4. Turn the crankshaft and camshaft so that the valve timing marks on the gear teeth will line up. The engine is now in the No. 4 firing position. Install the camshaft thrust plate-to-block screws and tighten to 75 in. lbs.

5. Install the timing gear cover and gasket.

6. Line up the keyway in the hub with the key on the crankshaft and slide the hub onto the shaft. Install the center bolt and torque to 160 ft. lbs.

7. Install the valve lifters, pushrods, pushrod cover, oil pump shaft and gear assembly and fuel pump as previously described.

8. Install the distributor as follows:

a. Turn the crankshaft 360° to the firing position of the No. 1 cylinder (number 1 exhaust and intake valve lifters both on base circle of camshaft and timing mark on the

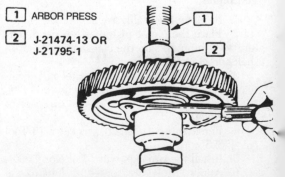

1 ARBOR PRESS

2 J-21474-13 OR J-21795-1

Camshaft timing gear/thrust plate end clearance - four cyl. engine

harmonic balancer indexed with the TDC mark on the timing pad).

  b. Install the distributor in its original position and align the shaft so the rotor arm points toward the No. 1 cylinder spark plug contact.

9. Swing the rocker arms over the pushrods. With the lifters on the base circle of the camshaft, tighten the rocker arm bolt to 20 ft. lbs. Do not over torque.

10. Install the front mount assembly, lower alternator bracket and alternator.

11. Complete engine installation as described earlier in this chapter.

Camshaft
REMOVAL AND INSTALLATION
V6 Engine

1. Remove the engine (on cradle).
2. Remove the valve lifters.
3. Remove the crankcase front cover.
4. Remove the timing chain and sprocket.
5. Remove the rear cover.
6. Carefully remove the camshaft to avoid damage to the bearings.
7. Before installation, lubricate the camshaft journals with engine oil.

NOTE: *If a new camshaft is to be installed, coat the lobes with an engine oil supplement such as GM E.O.S. or its equivalent.*

8. The remainder of installation is the reverse of removal.

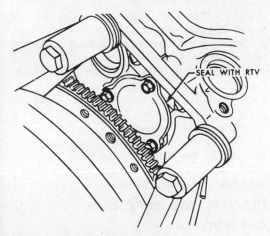

Camshaft rear cover - V6 engine

Camshaft Bearings
REMOVAL AND INSTALLATION
4-151 Engine

1. Remove the engine from the vehicle as previously outlined.

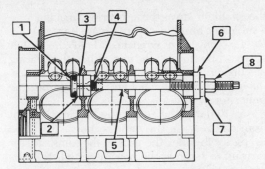

1. Back-up nut	5. 2 piece puller screw
2. Expanding collet	6. Pulling plate
3. Bearing	7. Thrust bearing
4. Expanding mandrel	8. Pulling nut

Removal and installation of camshaft bearings - typical

2. Remove the camshaft from the engine as previously outlined.

3. Unbolt and remove the engine flywheel.

4. Drive the rear camshaft expansion plug out of the engine block from the inside.

5. Using a camshaft bearing service tool, drive the front camshaft bearing towards the rear and the rear bearing towards the front.

6. Install the appropriate extension on the service tool and drive the center bearing out towards the rear.

7. Drive all of the new bearings into place in the opposite direction of which they were removed, making sure to align the oil holes in the engine block bores.

NOTE: *The front camshaft bearing must be driven approximately 1/8 in. behind the front of the cylinder block to uncover the oil hole to the timing gear oiling nozzle.*

8. Install the camshaft into the engine then install the engine as previously outlined.

6-173 Engine

Camshaft bearings can be replaced with engine completely or partially disassembled. To replace bearings without complete disassembly remove the camshaft and crankshaft leaving cylinder heads attached and pistons in place. Before removing crankshaft, tape threads of connecting rod bolts to prevent damage to crankshaft. Fasten connecting rods against sides of engine so they will not be in the way while replacing camshaft bearings.

1. Remove the camshaft rear cover.

2. Using Tool J-6098 or its equivalent, with the nut and thrust washer installed to the end of the threads, index the pilot in the camshaft front bearing and install the puller screw through the pilot.

3. Install the remover and installer tool with

the shoulder toward the bearing, making sure a sufficient number of threads are engaged.

4. Using two wrenches, hold the puller screw while turning the nut. When the bearing has been pulled from the bore, remove the remover and installer tool and bearing from the puller screw.

5. Remove the remaining bearings (except front and rear) in the same manner. It will be necessary to index the pilot in the camshaft rear bearing to remove the rear intermediate bearing.

6. Assemble the remover and installer tool on the driver handle and remove the camshaft front and rear bearings by driving towards the center of the cylinder block.

The camshaft front and rear bearings should be installed first. These bearings will act as guides for the pilot, and center the remaining bearings being pulled into place.

7. Assemble the remover and installer tool on the driver handle and install the camshaft front and rear bearings by driving them towards the center of the cylinder block.

8. Using Tool Set J-6098, or its equivalent with the nut and thrust washer installed to end of the threads, index the pilot into the camshaft front bearing and install the puller screw through the pilot.

9. Index the camshaft bearing into the bore (with oil hole aligned as outlined below), then install the remover and installer tool on the puller screw with the shoulder toward the bearing.

The rear and intermediate bearing oil holes must be aligned at 2:30 o'clock.

The front bearing oil holes must be aligned at 1:00 and 2:30 o'clock (two holes).

10. Using two wrenches, hold the puller screw while turning the nut. After the bearing has been pulled into the bore, remove the remover and installer tool from the puller screw and check the alignment of the oil holes in the camshaft bearings.

11. Install the remaining bearings in the same manner. It will be necessary to index the pilot in the camshaft rear bearing to install the rear intermediate bearing.

Clean the rear cover mating surfaces and bolt holes then apply a ⅛ in. bead of RTV sealer to the cover. Install the cover.

Pistons and Connecting Rod Assemblies

REMOVAL

1. Remove the engine assembly from the car, see "Engine Removal and Installation".

2. Remove the intake manifold, cylinder head or heads.

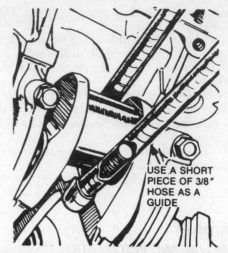

USE A SHORT PIECE OF 3/8" HOSE AS A GUIDE

Use lengths of vacuum hose or rubber tubing to protect the crankshaft journals and cylinder walls during piston installation

3. Remove the oil pan.

4. Remove the oil pump assembly.

5. Stamp the cylinder number on the machine surfaces of the bolt bosses of the connecting rod and cap for identification when reinstalling. If the pistons are to be removed from the connecting rod, mark the cylinder number on the piston with a silver pencil or quick drying paint for proper cylinder indentification and cap-to-rod location. The 4-151 engine is numbered 1-4 from front to back; the V6-173 is numbered 1-3-5 on the right bank, 2-4-6 on the left bank.

6. Examine the cylinder bore above the ring travel. If a ridge exists, remove the ridge with a ridge reamer before attempting to remove the piston and rod assembly.

7. Remove the rod bearing cap and bearing.

8. Install a guide hose over threads of rod bolts. This is to prevent damage to bearing journal and rod bolt threads.

9. Remove the rod and piston assembly through the top of the cylinder bore.

10. Remove any other rod and piston assemblies in the same manner.

CLEANING AND INSPECTION

Connecting Rods

Wash connecting rods in cleaning solvent and dry with compressed air. Check for twisted or bent rods and inspect for nicks or cracks. Replace connecting rods that are damaged.

Pistons

Clean varnish from piston skirts and pins with a cleaning solvent. DO NOT WIRE BRUSH ANY PART OF THE PISTON. Clean the ring grooves with a groove cleaner and make sure oil ring holes and slots are clean.

Inspect the piston for cracked ring lands, skirts or pin bosses, wavy or worn ring lands, scuffed or damaged skirts, eroded areas at the top of the piston. Replace pistons that are damaged or show signs of excessive wear. Inspect the grooves for nicks or burrs that might cause the rings to hang up.

Measure piston skirt (across center line of piston pin) and check piston clearance.

PISTON PIN REMOVAL AND INSTALLATION

Use care at all times when handling and servicing connecting rods and pistons. To prevent possible damage to these units, do not clamp the rod or piston in a vise since they may become distorted. Do not allow the pistons to strike against one another, against hard objects or bench surfaces, since distortion of the piston contour or nicks in the soft aluminum material may result.

1. Remove the piston rings using a suitable piston ring remover.

2. Install the guide bushing of the piston pin removing and installing tool.

3. Install the piston and connecting rod assembly on a support, and place the assembly in an arbor press. Press the pin out of the connecting rod, using the appropriate piston pin tool.

MEASURING THE OLD PISTONS

Check used piston-to-cylinder bore clearance as follows:

1. Measure the cylinder bore diameter with a telescope gauge.

2. Measure the piston diameter. When measuring the pistons for size or taper, measurements must be made with the piston pin removed.

3. Subtract the piston diameter from the cylinder bore diameter to determine piston-to-bore clearance.

4. Compare the piston-to-bore clearances obtained with those clearances recommended. Determine if the piston-to-bore clearance is in the acceptable range.

5. When measuring taper, the largest reading must be at the bottom of the skirt.

SELECTING NEW PISTONS

1. If the used piston is not acceptable, check the service piston size and determine if a new piston can be selected. (Service pistons are available in standard, high limit and standard 0.254mm (0.010 in.) oversize.).

2. If the cylinder bore must be reconditioned, measure the new piston diameter, then hone the cylinder bore to obtain the prefered clearance.

3. Select a new piston and mark the piston to identify the cylinder for which it was fitted. (On some cars, oversize pistons may be found. These pistons will be 0.254mm (0.010 in.) oversize).

CYLINDER HONING

1. When cylinders are being honed, follow the manufacturer's recommendations for the use of the hone.

2. Occasionally during the honing operation, the cylinder bore should be thoroughly cleaned and the selected piston checked for correct fit.

3. When finish-honing a cylinder bore, the hone should be moved up and down at a sufficient speed to obtain a very fine uniform surface finish in a cross-hatch pattern of approximately 45-65 degrees included angle. The finish marks should be clean but not sharp, free from imbedded particles and torn or folded metal.

4. Permanently mark the piston for the cylinder to which it has been fitted and proceed to hone the remaining cylinders.

NOTE: *Handle pistons with care. Do not attempt to force pistons through cylinders until the cylinders have been honed to correct size. Pistons can be distorted through careless handling.*

5. Thoroughly clean the bores with hot water and detergent. Scrub well with a stiff bristle brush and rinse thoroughly with hot water. It is extremely essential that a good cleaning operation be performed. If any of the abrasive material is allowed to remain in the cylinder bores, it will rapidly wear the new rings and cylinder bores. The bores should be swabbed several times with light engine oil and a clean cloth and then wiped with a clean dry cloth. CYLINDERS SHOULD NOT BE CLEANED WITH KEROSENE OR GASOLINE. Clean the remainder of the cylinder block to remove the excess material spread during the honing operation.

CHECKING CYLINDER BORE

Cylinder bore size can be measured with inside micrometers or a cylinder gauge. The most wear will occur at the top of the ring travel.

Reconditioned cylinder bores should be held to not more than 0.025mm (0.001 in.) taper.

If the cylinder bores are smooth, the cylinder walls should not be deglazed. If the cylinder walls are scored, the walls may have to be honed before installing new rings. It is important that reconditioned cylinder bores be thoroughly washed with a soap and water solution to remove all traces of abrasive material to eliminate premature wear.

Piston Rings

The pistons have three rings (two compression rings and one oil ring). The oil ring consists of two rails and an expander. Pistons do not have oil drain holes behind the rings.

RING TOLERANCES

When installing new rings, ring gap and side clearance should be checked as follows:

Piston Ring and Rail Gap

Each ring and rail gap must be measured with the ring or rail positioned squarely and at the bottom of the ring-travel area of the bore.

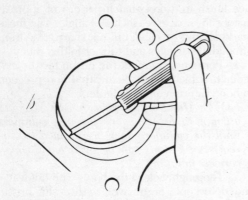

Measuring piston ring gap - typical

Side Clearance

Each ring must be checked for side clearance in its respective piston groove by inserting a feeler gauge between the ring and its upper land. The piston grooves must be cleaned before checking the ring for side clearance specifications. To check oil ring side clearance, the oil rings must be installed on the piston.

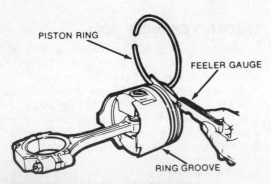

Measuring piston ring side clearance

RING INSTALLATION

For service ring specifications and detailed installation productions, refer to the instructions furnished with the parts package.

Connecting Rod Bearings

If you have already removed the connecting rod and piston assemblies from the engine, follow only Steps 3-7 of the following procedure.

REMOVAL, INSPECTION, INSTALLATION

The connecting rod bearings are designed to have a slight projection above the rod and cap

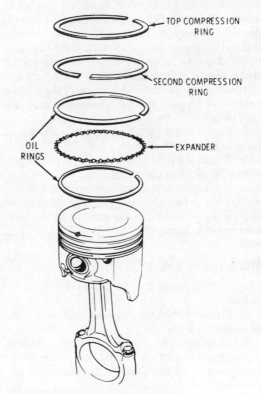

Piston and rod assembly - typical

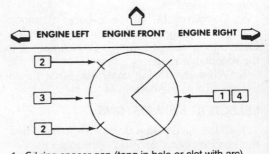

1. Oil ring spacer gap (tang in hole or slot with arc)
2. Oil ring rail gaps
3. 2nd compression ring gap
4. Top compression ring gap

Piston ring gap location - typical

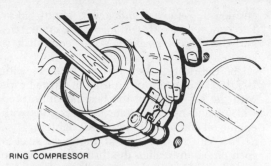

RING COMPRESSOR

Installing a piston using a piston ring compressor

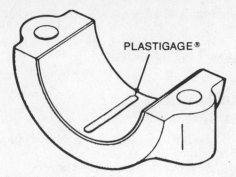

PLASTIGAGE®

Plastigage®

faces to insure a positive contact. The bearings can be replaced without removing the rod and piston assemblies from the engine.

1. Remove the oil pan. See the Oil Pan procedures, below. It may be necessary to remove the oil pump to provide access to rear connecting rod bearings.

2. With the the connecting rod journal at the bottom, stamp the cylinder number on the machined surfaces of the connecting rod and cap for identification when installing, then remove the caps.

3. Inspect journals for roughness and wear. Slight roughness may be removed with a fine grit polishing cloth saturated with engine oil. Burrs may be removed with a fine oil stone by moving the stone on the journal circumference. Do not move the stone back and forth across the journal. If the journals are scored or ridged, the crankshaft must be replaced.

4. The connecting rod journals should be checked for out-of-round and correct size with a micrometer.

NOTE: *Crankshaft rod journals will normally be standard size. If any undersized bearings are used, all will be 0.254mm undersize and 0.254mm will be stamped on the number 4 counterweight.*

If plastic gauging material is to be used:

5. Clean oil from the journal bearing cap, connecting rod and outer and inner surfaces of the bearing inserts. Position the insert so that the tang is properly aligned with the notch in the rod and cap.

6. Place a piece of plastic gauging material in the center of lower bearing shell.

7. Remove the bearing cap and determine the bearing clearances by comparing the width of the flattened plastic gauging material at its widest point with the graduation on the container. The number within the graduation on the envelope indicates the clearance in thousandths of an inch or millimeters. If this clearance is excessive, replace the bearing and recheck the clearance with the plastic gauging material. Lubricate the bearing with engine oil before installation. Repeat Steps 2-7 on the remaining connecting rod bearings. All rods must be connected to their journals when rotating the crankshaft, to prevent engine damage.

Piston and Connecting Rod Assembly

INSTALLATION

1. Install some lengths of rubber tubing over the connecting rod bolts to prevent damage to the journals.

2. Apply engine oil to the rings and piston, then install a piston ring compressing tool on the piston.

3. Install the assembly in its respective cylinder bore.

4. Lubricate the crankshaft journal with engine oil and install the connecting rod bearing and cap, with the bearing index tang in rod and cap on same side.

NOTE: *When more than one rod and piston assembly is being installed, the connecting rod cap attaching nuts should be tightened only enough to keep each rod in position until all have been installed. This will aid installation of the remaining piston assemblies.*

5. Torque the rod bolt nuts to specification.

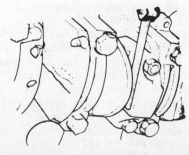

Check the connecting rod side clearance with a feeler gauge

6. Install all other parts in reverse order of removal.

7. Install the engine in the car. See Engine Removal and Installation.

Crankshaft

REMOVAL

1. Remove the engine assembly as previously outlined.

2. Remove the engine front cover.

3. Remove the timing chain and sprockets.

4. Remove the oil pan.

5. Remove the oil pump.

6. Stamp the cylinder number on the machined surfaces of the bolt boses of the connecting rods and caps for identification when installing. If the pistons are to be removed from the connecting rod, mark the cylinder number on each piston with an indelible marker, silver pencil or quick drying paint for proper cylinder identification and cap to rod location.

7. Remove the connecting rod caps and store them so that they can be installed in their original positions.

9. Remove all the main bearing caps.

10. Note the position of the keyway in the crankshaft so it can be installed in the same position.

11. Lift the crankshaft out of the block. The rods will pivot to the center of the engine when the crankshaft is removed.

12. Remove both halves of the rear main oil seal.

INSTALLATION

1. Measure the crankshaft journals with a micrometer to determine the correct size rod and main bearings to be used. Whenever a new or reconditioned crankshaft is installed, new connecting rod bearings and main bearings should be installed. See Main Bearings and Rod Bearings.

2. Clean all oil passages in the block (and crankshaft if it is being reused).

NOTE: *A new rear main seal should be installed anytime the crankshaft is removed or replaced.*

3. Install sufficient oil pan bolts in the block to align with the connecting rod bolts. Use rubber bands between the bolts to position the connecting rods as required. Connecting rod position can be adjusted by increasing the tension on the rubber bands with additional turns around the pan bolts or thread protectors.

4. Position the upper half of main bearings in the block and lubricate them with engine oil.

5. Position crankshaft keyway in the same position as removed and lower it into block. The connecting rods will follow the crank pins into the correct position as the crankshaft is lowered.

6. Lubricate the thrust flanges with 10501609 Lubricant or equivalent. Install caps with the lower half of the bearings lubricated with engine oil. Lubricate the cap bolts with engine oil and install, but do not tighten.

7. With a block of wood, bump the shaft in each direction to align the thrust flanges of the main bearing. After bumping the shaft in each direction, wedge the shaft to the front and hold it while torquing the thrust bearing cap bolts.

NOTE: *In order to prevent the possibility of cylinder block and/or main bearing cap damage, the main bearing caps are to be tapped into their cylinder block cavity using a wood or rubber mallet before the bolts are installed. Do not use attaching bolts to pull the main bearing caps into their seats. Failure to observe this information may damage the cylinder block or a bearing cap.*

8. Torque all main bearing caps to specification.

9. Remove the connecting rod bolt thread protectors and lubricate the connecting rod bearings with engine oil.

10. Install the connecting rod bearing caps in their original position. Torque the nuts to specification.

11. Complete the installation by reversing the removal steps.

Main Bearings

CHECKING BEARING CLEARANCE

1. Remove the bearing cap and wipe the oil from the crankshaft journal and the outer and inner surfaces of the bearing shell.

2. Place a piece of plastic gauging material in the center of the bearing.

3. Use a floor jack or other means to hold the crankshaft against the upper bearing shell. This is necessary to obtain accurate clearance readings when using plastic gauging material.

4. Install the bearing cap and bearing. Place engine oil on the cap bolts and install. Torque the bolts to specification.

5. Remove the bearing cap and determine the bearing clearance by comparing the width of the flattened plastic gauging material at its widest point with the graduations on the gauging material container. The number within the graduation on the envelope indicates the clearance in millimeters or thousandths of an inch. If the clearance is greater than allowed, RE-PLACE BOTH BEARING SHELLS AS A SET. Recheck the clearance after replacing the shells. (Refer to Main Bearing Replacement).

REPLACEMENT

Main bearing clearances must be corrected by the use of selective upper and lower shells. UNDER NO CIRCUMSTANCES should the use of shims behind the shells to compensate for wear be attempted. To install the main bearing shells, proceed as follows:

1. Remove the oil pan as outlined below. On some models, the oil pump may also have to be removed.

2. Loosen all main bearing caps.

3. Remove the bearing cap and remove the lower shell.

4. Insert a flattened cotter pin or roll pin in the oil passage hole in the crankshaft, then rotate the crankshaft in the direction opposite to cranking rotation. The pin will contact the upper shell and roll it out.

5. The main bearing journals should be checked for roughness and wear. Slight roughness may be removed with a fine grit polishing cloth saturated with engine oil. Burrs may be removed with a fine oil stone. If the journals are scored or ridged, the crankshaft must be replaced.

The journals can be measured for out-of-round with the crankshaft installed by using a crankshaft caliper and inside micrometer or a main bearing micrometer. The upper bearing shell must be removed when measuring the crankshaft journals. Maximum out-of-round of the crankshaft journals must not exceed 0.037mm (0.0015 in.).

6. Clean the crankshaft journals and bearing caps thoroughly for installing new main bearings.

7. Apply special lubricant, No. 1050169 or equivalent, to the thrust flanges of bearing shells.

8. Place a new upper shell on the crankshaft journal with locating tang in the correct position and rotate the shaft to turn it into place using a cotter pin or roll pin as during removal.

9. Place a new bearing shell in the bearing cap.

10. Install a new oil seal in the rear main bearing cap and block.

11. Lubricate the main bearings with engine oil. Lubricate the thrust surface with lubricant 1050169 or equivalent.

12. Lubricate the main bearing cap bolts with engine oil.

NOTE: *In order to prevent the possibility of cylinder block and/or main bearing cap damage, the main bearing caps are to be tapped into their cylinder block cavity using a wood or rubber mallet before the attaching bolts are installed. Do not use attaching bolts to pull the main bearing caps into their*

seats. Failure to observe this information may damage the cylinder block or a bearing cap.

13. Torque the main bearing cap bolts to 145 Nm (107 ft. lbs.).

Oil Pan

REMOVAL AND INSTALLATION

Four Cylinder Engine

1. On some models it may be necessary to remove the engine cradle from the car as follows:

NOTE: *The cradle can be removed from the car without removing the engine or transaxle.*

a. Using engine support fixture J-28467 or equivalent, raise the engine enough to take tension off the engine mounts.

b. Raise the vehicle and support it safely with jackstands.

c. Remove the exhaust pipe bolts at the manifold.

d. Remove the rear wheel and tire assemblies.

e. Remove both lower control arms at the knuckles.

f. Remove both toe-link rods at the knuckle.

g. Remove the emergency brake cable at the cradle.

h. Remove the engine and transmission mounting bolts.

i. Remove the cradle bolts and remove the cradle assembly.

2. Drain the engine oil.

3. Remove the nuts from the engine mount to the support bracket.

4. Disconnect the exhaust pipe at the manifold and the rear transaxle mount.

5. Remove the starter and flywheel cover.

6. Remove the upper alternator bracket.

7. Support the engine with Tool J28467 or equivalent.

8. Remove the lower alternator bracket and engine support bracket.

9. Remove the oil pan retaining bolts and remove the oil pan.

10. Installation is the reverse of removal. Apply RTV sealant or equivalent as shown in the illustration. The two bolts in the timing gear cover should be installed last after the pan bolts are tight.

When installing the engine cradle, torque the following as indicated:

- Rear cradle bolts: 76 ft. lbs.
- Front cradle nut: 67 ft. lbs.
- Engine mount assembly: 42 ft. lbs.
- Rear mount assembly: 18 ft. lbs.
- Front mount assembly: 36 ft. lbs.

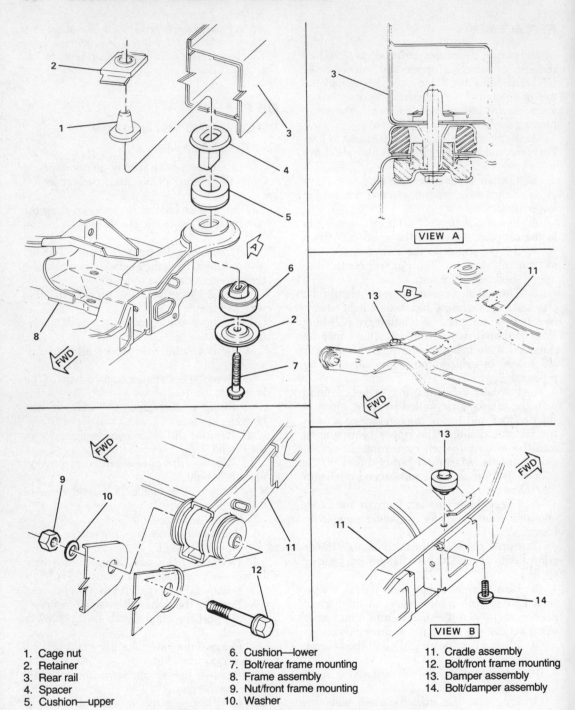

1. Cage nut
2. Retainer
3. Rear rail
4. Spacer
5. Cushion—upper
6. Cushion—lower
7. Bolt/rear frame mounting
8. Frame assembly
9. Nut/front frame mounting
10. Washer
11. Cradle assembly
12. Bolt/front frame mounting
13. Damper assembly
14. Bolt/damper assembly

Cradle mountings and damper - four cyl. engine

- Lower control arm at knuckle: 33 ft. lbs.
- Lower control arm at cradle: 69 ft. lbs.

V6 Engine

1. Disconnect the negative battery cable.
2. Raise the vehicle and support it safely.
3. Drain the crankcase.
4. Remove the flywheel shield or clutch housing cover.
5. Remove the starter.
6. Remove the oil pan.
7. Before installation, clean all mating surfaces.
8. Place a ⅛ in. bead of RTV sealant on the oil pan sealing flange.
9. Install the oil pan and torque the 1 in. bolts to 6–9 ft. lbs. and the 1.5 inch bolts to 14–22 ft. lbs.

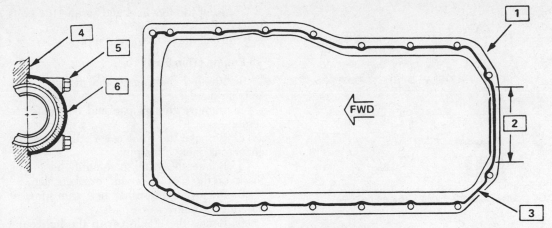

1. Oil pan
2. Apply a ⅜" wide by ³⁄₁₆" thick bead of RTV sealer in area indicated
3. Apply a ³⁄₁₆" wide by ⅛" thick bead of RTV sealer in area indicated
4. Engine block assembly
5. Rear bearing
6. Groove in main bearing cap must be filled flush to ⅛" above surface with RTV

Oil pan sealer application - 4 cyl. engine

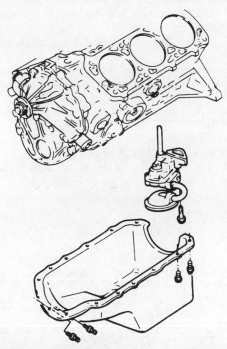

Oil pan and pump - V6 engine

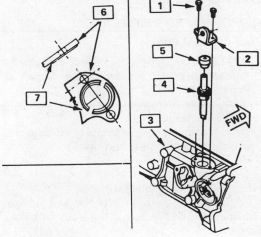

1. 14 N·m (10 lb. ft.)
2. Plate assembly
3. Cylinder block
4. Shaft and gear assembly
5. Bearing
6. Plate
7. Apply a continuous ¹⁄₁₆" diam. bead of RTV as shown

Oil pump and driveshaft - four cyl. engine

10. The remainder of the installation is the reverse of removal.

Oil Pump

REMOVAL AND INSTALLATION

Four Cylinder Engine

1. Remove the oil pan as described earlier.
2. Remove the two flange mounting bolts and the nut from the main bearing cap bolt.

3. Remove the pump and screen as an assembly.
4. Installation is the reverse of removal. Align the pump shaft with the driveshaft tang. Torque the pump retaining bolts 20 ft. lbs.

V6 Engine

1. Remove the oil pan.
2. Remove the pump and driveshaft extension.

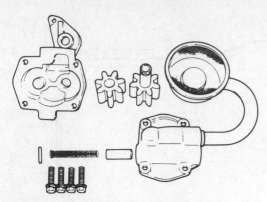

Oil pump - exploded view - V6 engine

3. To install, engage the driveshaft extension in the cover end of the distributor drive gear.

4. Install the pump-to-rear bearing cap bolt and torque to 26-35 ft. lbs.

5. Install the oil pan and refill with oil.

Rear Main Oil Seal

REMOVAL AND INSTALLATION

Four Cylinder Engine

NOTE: *This is a one piece seal and can be replaced without removal of the oil pan or crankshaft.*

1. Remove the transaxle assembly.
2. Remove the flywheel.
3. If equipped with a manual transaxle, remove the pressure plate and disc.
4. Pry out the rear main seal.
5. Before installing, clean the block and crankshaft-to-seal mating surfaces.
6. Lubricate the outside of the seal for ease of installation and press into the block with your fingers.

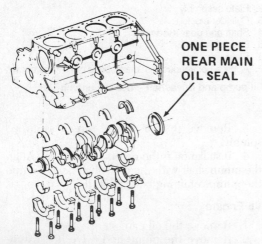

ONE PIECE REAR MAIN OIL SEAL

Rear main oil seal - four cyl. engine

7. Install the flywheel and torque the bolts to 44 ft. lbs.
8. Install the transaxle assembly.

V6 Engine (Thin Seal)

1. Remove the engine and mount it on a suitable stand.
2. Remove the oil pan and oil pump assembly.
3. Remove the front cover, then lock the chain tensioner with a pin.
4. Rotate the crankshaft until the timing marks on the cam and crank sprockets align.
5. Remove the camshaft bolt, cam sprocket and timing chain.
6. Rotate the crankshaft to the horizontal position.
7. Remove the rod bearing nuts, caps and bearings.
8. Remove the crankshaft and the old oil seal.
9. Apply a light coat of G.M. 1052726 or equivalent to the outside of the seal.
10. Install the new seal and tool in the rear area of the crankshaft.
11. Install the crankshaft and tool in the engine.
12. Position the seal tool so that the arrow points toward the cylinder block and remove the tool.
13. Put a light coat of oil on the crankshaft journals.
14. Seal the rear main bearing split line surface with G.M. 1052726 or equivalent.
15. The remainder of the installation is the reverse of removal. Torque to specifications.

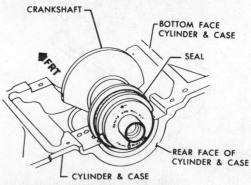

CRANKSHAFT —

BOTTOM FACE CYLINDER & CASE

SEAL

FRT

REAR FACE OF CYLINDER & CASE

CYLINDER & CASE

CAUTION RETAINER SPRING SIDE OF SEAL MUST FACE TOWARD FRONT OF CYLINDER & CASE.

Installing the thin seal - V6 engine

V6 Engine (Thick Seal)

1. Refer to the "Transaxle, Removal and Installation" procedures in this section and remove the transaxle.

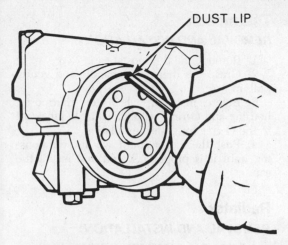

Removing thick seal - V6 engine

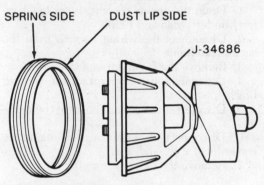

SEAL BORE TO SEAL SURFACE
TO BE LUBRICATED
WITH ENGINE OIL BEFORE
ASSEMBLY

Installing the thick seal - V6 engine

NOTE: *If equipped with an manual transaxle, remove the pressure plate and the clutch.*

2. Remove the flywheel from the crankshaft.

3. Using a small pry bar, pry the rear oil seal from the housing.

NOTE: *When prying the oil seal from the housing, be careful not to damage the machined surfaces.*

4. Using the seal installation tool J-34686, lubricate the new oil seal lip and slide it onto the installation (dust lip side against the tool) until it seats against the tool.

5. Align the installation tool's dowel pin with the dowel pin hole in the crankshaft. Torque the mounting screws to 2-5 ft. lbs.

6. Turn the "T" handle and push the seal into the housing, until it bottoms out against the housing.

7. Loosen the "T" handle until it comes to a stop. Remove the mounting screws of the installation tool.

8. Check the seal and make sure that it is squarely seated in the bore.

9. To complete the installation, reverse the removal procedures. Torque the flywheel bolts to 50 ft. lbs.

Flywheel

For removal and installation of the flywheel, please refer to the transaxle removal and installation procedure in Chapter 6.

Water Pump

CAUTION: *Keep hands, tools, and clothing away from the engine cooling fan to help prevent personal injury. This fan is electric and can come on whether or not the engine is running. The fan can start automatically in response to a heat sensor with the ignition in the 'ON' position.*

REMOVAL AND INSTALLATION

1. Disconnect the negative battery cable.

2. Remove the accessory drive belts.

3. Remove the water pump attaching bolts and remove the water pump.

4. If installing a new water pump, transfer the pulley from the old unit. With sealing surfaces cleaned, place a ⅛ in. bead of sealant, GM # 1052289 or equivalent, on the water pump sealing surface. While the sealant is still wet, install the pump and torque the bolts to 6 ft. lbs. on the 4 cyl. engine. On the V6 engine, torque all bolts to 22 ft. lbs. except the two directly below the water pump center shaft. Torque these two bolts to 7 ft. lbs.

5. Install the accessory drive belts.

6. Reconnect the negative battery cable.

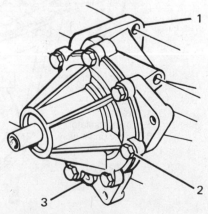

1. Body   2. Bolt   3. Housing

Water pump mounting - four cyl. engine

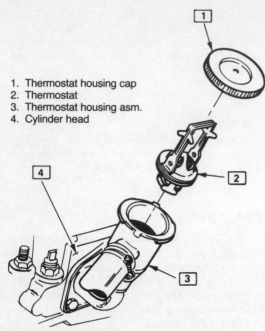

1. Thermostat housing cap
2. Thermostat
3. Thermostat housing asm.
4. Cylinder head

Thermostat and housing - typical

Thermostat

REMOVAL AND INSTALLATION

1. Remove the thermostat cap.
2. Grasp the thermostat handle and gently pull up.
3. Before installing, clean the thermostat housing and O-ring. Apply a suitable lubricant to the O-ring for easier installation.
4. Push the thermostat down into the housing until it is properly seated and install the cap.

Radiator

REMOVAL AND INSTALLATION

NOTE: *See CAUTION under Water Pump removal and installation.*

1. Drain the engine coolant. Refer to Chapter 1 under Drain and Refill.
2. Disconnect the wiring harness from the fan and fan frame.
3. Remove the fan and frame assembly.
4. Disconnect the upper radiator support bracket.
5. Disconnect the coolant hoses at the radiator.
6. Disconnect the transmission/engine oil cooler lines at the radiator.
7. Remove the radiator from the car.

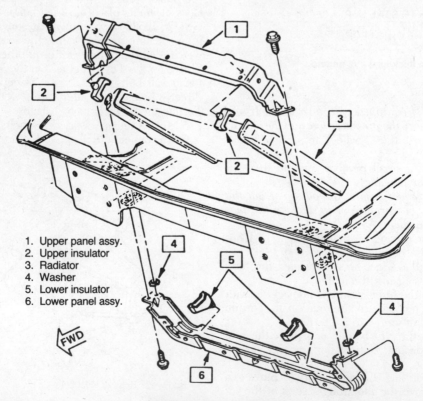

1. Upper panel assy.
2. Upper insulator
3. Radiator
4. Washer
5. Lower insulator
6. Lower panel assy.

Radiator support - typical

8. Installation is the reverse of removal. After installation run the engine and check for leaks.

Exhaust System

The muffler is a tri-flow design, located at the rear of the vehicle, mounted transversely. The complete exhaust system is a one piece design constructed of stainless steel. When servicing a welded connection it should be cut and the new connection clamped when installing replacement parts. Also, coat the slip joints with exhaust system sealer before assembling.

Spring type hangers are used to support the complete exhaust system. It is very important that they be installed properly to avoid annoying vibrations which are difficult to diagnose.

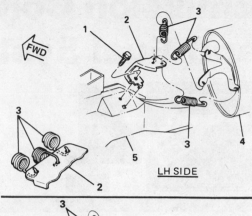

LH SIDE

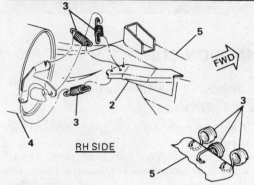

RH SIDE

1. Bolt/screw
2. Bracket
3. Springs (must be installed as shown)
4. Muffler assembly
5. Frame assembly

Muffler spring installation - typical

Emission Controls and Fuel System

EMISSION CONTROLS

Crankcase Ventilation

DESCRIPTION

A Positive Crankcase Ventilation system (PCV) is used to provide more complete burning of the crankcase vapors. Fresh air from the air cleaner or intake duct (V6), is supplied to the crankcase, mixed with blow-by gases and then passed through a Positive Crankcase Ventilation valve (PCV) into the intake manifold (four cyl.) or the Air Plenum (V6).

INSPECTION

A clogged PCV valve or plugged hose could cause rough idling. Check the valve as follows:

1. Remove the valve from the rocker arm cover.

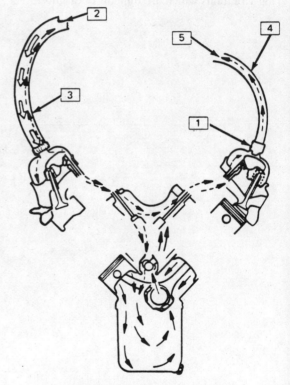

⇨ CLEAN AIR

⟶ VOLATILE OIL FUMES

--⟶ MIXTURE OF AIR AND FUMES

1. PCV valve
2. To throttle body
3. Crankcase vent hose
4. PCV valve hose
5. To intake manifold

PCV flow - typical - V6 engine

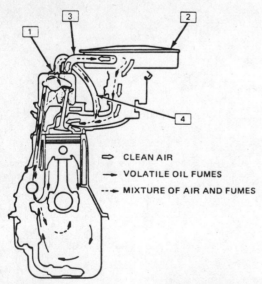

⇨ CLEAN AIR

⟶ VOLATILE OIL FUMES

--⟶ MIXTURE OF AIR AND FUMES

1. PCV valve
2. Air cleaner
3. Crankcase vent hose
4. PCV valve hose

PCV flow - typical - 4 cyl. engine

2. Run the engine at idle.

3. Place your thumb over the end of the valve to check for vacuum. If there is no vacuum at the valve, check for plugged hoses at manifold port or PCV valve. Replace plugged or deteriorated hoses .

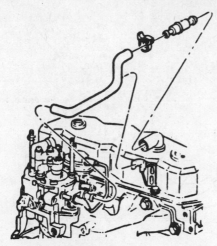

PCV system - 4 cyl. engine

4. Turn off the engine and remove the PCV valve . Shake the valve and listen for the rattle of the check needle inside the valve. If the valve does not rattle replace the valve.

Evaporative Emission Control System

DESCRIPTION

This method transfers fuel vapor from the fuel tank to an activated carbon (charcoal) storage canister to hold the vapors when the vehicle is not operating. When the engine is running, the fuel vapor is purged from the carbon element by intake air flow and consumed in the normal combustion process.

FUEL VAPOR CANISTER

Removal and installation

1. Remove the hoses on the canister and mark them for installation.
2. Remove the canister.
3. Installation is the reverse of removal.

Exhaust Emission Controls

EXHAUST GAS RECIRCULATION VALVE (EGR)

Description

The EGR System is used to lower the NOx (oxides of nitrogen) emission levels caused by high combustion temperature. It does that by decreasing combustion temperature. The main element of the system is the EGR valve mounted on the intake manifold (4 cyl.) and on the exhaust manifold (V6). The EGR valve feeds small amounts of exhaust gas back into the combustion chamber.

Removal and Installation

1. Remove the air cleaner on the 4 cylinder engine.
2. Disconnect the vacuum line.
3. Remove the bolts and remove the valve from the manifold.
4. Installation is the reverse of removal.

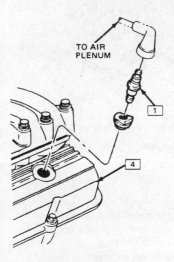

TO AIR PLENUM

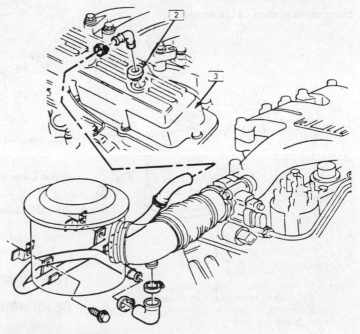

1. PCV
2. Fresh air inlet
3. Front valve cover
4. Rear valve cover

PCV system - V6 engine

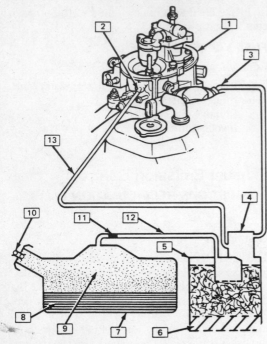

1. TBI
2. Canister purge port
3. Vacuum signal
4. Purge valve
5. Vapor storage canister
6. Purge air
7. Fuel tank
8. Fuel
9. Vapor
10. Pressure–vacuum relief gas cap
11. Vent restricter
12. Fuel tank vent
13. Purge line

Evaporative system - 4 cyl. engine

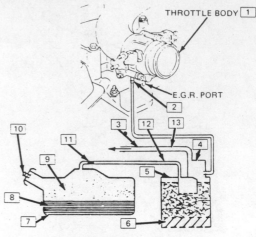

1. Throttle body
2. Canister purge
3. Vacuum
4. Purge valve
5. Vapor storage canister
6. Purge air
7. Fuel tank
8. Fuel
9. Vapor
10. Pressure–vacuum relief gas cap
11. Vent restricter
12. Fuel tank vent
13. Purge line

Evaporative system - V6 engine

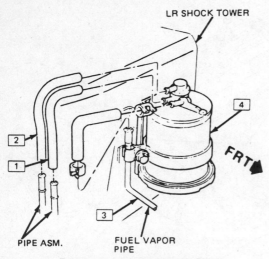

1. Purge vacuum hose (ported signal)
2. Vacuum hose (manifold vacuum)
3. Fuel tank vent pipe
4. Vapor canister

Evaporator canister - V6 engine

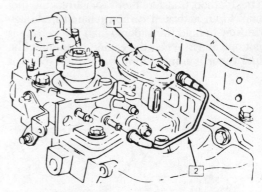

1. EGR valve   2. EGR valve tube

EGR valve - 4 cyl. engine

Valve Cleaning

1. Using a wire wheel, clean the deposits from the mounting surface and around the valve.

2. Scrape any exhaust deposits around the valve outlet with a suitable tool.

3. Clean all mounting surfaces.

Thermostatic Air Cleaner

DESCRIPTION

This system used on the four cylinder engines uses heated air and manifold vacuum to give

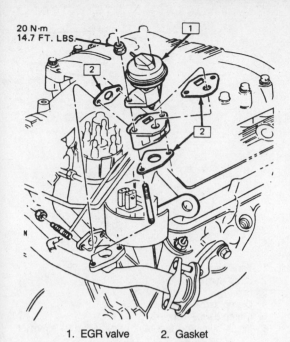

1. EGR valve   2. Gasket

EGR valve - V6 engine

good drivability under varying climatic conditions.

Air can enter the air cleaner from outside the engine compartment or from the heat stove built around the exhaust manifold. A vacuum diaphragm motor, built into the air cleaner snorkel, moves the damper door, to admit hot air from the exhaust manifold, outside air, or a combination of both. Inside the air cleaner is a temperature sensor that reacts to air intake

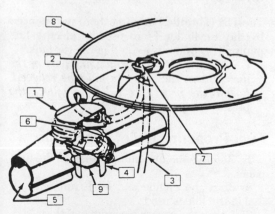

1. Vacuum diaphragm motor
2. Temperature sensor
3. Vacuum hose (to manifold vacuum)
4. Heat stove duct
5. Snorkel
6. Linkage
7. Air bleed valve
8. Air cleaner asm.
9. Damper door

Thermostatic air cleaner system - typical

temperature and controls the amount of vacuum going to the motor.

INSPECTION

1. Checked for kinked, plugged or deteriorated hoses.
2. Check the condition of the gasket or seal between the air cleaner and TBI unit.
3. With the air cleaner assembly installed, the damper door should be open to the outside air.
4. Start the engine. Watch the damper door in the air cleaner snorkel. When the engine is first started, the damper door should move and close off outside air.
5. As the air cleaner warms up, the damper door should open slowly to the outside air.
6. If the air cleaner fails to operate as described above, the vacuum motor or the temperature sensor may be defective.

GENERAL FUEL SYSTEM SERVICE

Electric Fuel Pump

REMOVAL AND INSTALLATION

1. Relieve the fuel system pressure. (Refer to the procedure below)
2. Drain the fuel tank.
3. Disconnect the wiring from the tank.
4. Remove the ground wire retaining screw from under the body.
5. Disconnect all hoses from the tank.
6. Support the tank on a jack and remove the retaining strap nuts.
7. Lower the tank and remove it.
8. Remove the fuel gauge/pump retaining

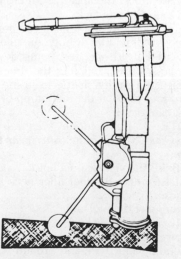

Electric fuel pump and sending unit - typical

ring using a spanner wrench such as tool J-24187.

9. Remove the gauge unit and the pump.

10. Installation is the reverse of removal. Always replace the O-ring under the gauge/pump retaining ring.

Oxygen Sensor
REMOVAL AND INSTALLATION

NOTE: *The oxygen sensor uses a permanently attached pigtail and connector. This pigtail should not be removed from the oxygen sensor. Damage or removal of the pigtail or connector could affect proper operation of the oxygen sensor.*

The oxygen sensor is installed in the exhaust manifold and is removed in the same manner as a spark plug. The sensor may be difficult to remove when the engine temperature is below 120 deg. F (48 deg. C) and excessive force may damage threads in the exhaust manifold or exhaust pipe. Exercise care when handling the oxygen sensor; the electrical connector and louvered end must be kept free of grease, dirt, or other contaminants. Avoid using cleaning solvents of any kind and don't drop or roughly handle the sensor. A special anti-seize compound is used on the oxygen sensor threads when installing and care should be used NOT to get compound on the sensor itself. Disconnect the negative battery cable when servicing the oxygen sensor and torque to 30 ft. lbs. (41 Nm) when installing.

Fuel Tank
REMOVAL AND INSTALLATION

1. Relieve the fuel system pressure.
2. Disconnect the negative battery cable.
3. Drain the fuel tank.

   a. If possible, use a hand operated pump device to drain fuel through the filler tube.

   b. If a hand operated pump device cannot be used to complete the draining process, use a siphon at the main (not the return) fuel pipe, at the fuel pump or the fuel tank gauge unit.

NOTE: *As a precaution, keep a dry chemical (Class B) fire extinguisher near the work area.*

4. Raise the vehicle on a hoist.
5. Disconnect the fuel filler neck hose and vent hose.
6. Support the fuel tank.
7. Remove the fuel tank strap support bolts and lower the tank enough to disconnect the fuel sending unit wire and ground wire, if so equipped.

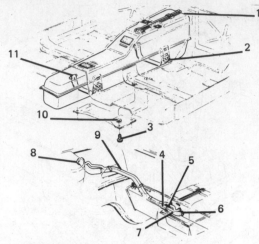

1. Tank asm.
2. Strap asm.—rr
3. Bolt (4)
4. Clamp asm.—filler—2
5. Clamp asm.—vent—2
6. Install hoses on fuel tank pipes within 0–3 mm of fuel tank surface
7. Hose asm.
8. Cap asm.
9. Pipe asm.
10. Washer (4)
11. Strap asm.—frt

Fuel tank - typical

8. Remove the tank.
9. Installation is the reverse of removal.

4-CYLINDER ENGINE FUEL SYSTEM

The TBI (Throttle Body Injection) system used by the 4-cylinder Fiero uses an electric fuel pump. This pump is located in the gas tank.

CAUTION: *Before opening any part of the fuel system, the pressure must be relieved. Follow the procedure below to relieve the pressure:*

Fuel Pressure Relief Procedure

1. Remove the fuel pump fuse from the fuse panel.
2. Start the engine and let it run until all fuel in the line is used.
3. Crank the starter an additional three seconds to relieve any residual pressure.
4. With the ignition OFF, replace the fuse.

Throttle Body (TBI) Fuel Injection

The Model 300 Throttle Body Injection is used on the 2.5 liter 4 cyl. engine. The Throttle Body Injection unit or TBI is centrally located on the intake manifold. Its function compares to that of a carburetor in supplying an air/fuel mixture into the intake.

The TBI unit is simple in construction and very precise in controlling the air fuel mixture as it is completely controlled by the ECM (Electronic Control Module).

The unit is made primarily of aluminum and consist of two major casting assemblies, a throttle body and fuel metering assembly.

With the TBI system, air is drawn into a single bore. The fuel is then injected into the air stream under pressure. The unit contains a pressure regulator, idle air control valve, and an electrically operated solenoid that activates the fuel injector. Also attached to the TBI is a throttle position sensor, a fuel inlet and a fuel return fitting.

NOTE: *The assembly identification number is stamped on the low mounting flange located on the TPS side of the throttle body, and should be noted before servicing the unit.*

FUEL INJECTOR

Removal

1. Remove the air cleaner.
2. Remove the injector connector by squeezing the two tabs together and pulling straight up.
3. Remove the fuel meter cover as follows:
    a. Remove the five meter cover screws and lockwashers while holding the cover on the fuel meter body.
    b. Lift off the fuel meter cover including the fuel pressure regulator assembly.
    c. Discard the fuel outlet passage gasket but leave the fuel meter cover gasket on the fuel meter body.
CAUTION: *Do not remove the four screws securing the pressure regulator assembly to the fuel meter cover. The fuel pressure regulator cover contains a large spring under heavy tension, which could cause injury if released.*
NOTE: *Do not immerse the fuel meter cover including the pressure regualtor in any type*

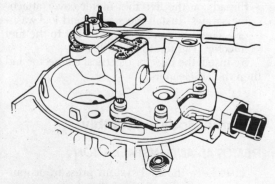

Removing the fuel injector

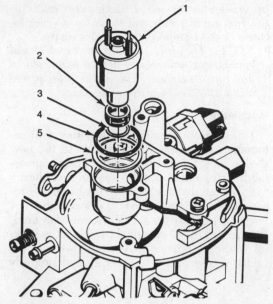

1. Fuel injector
2. Filter
3. Large "O" ring
4. Steel back-up washer
5. Small "O" ring

Fuel injector components

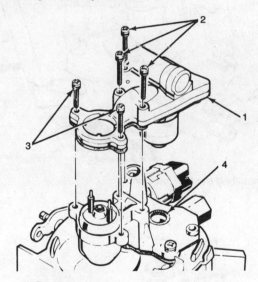

1. Fuel meter cover with regulator/compensator
2. Screws—long
3. Screws—short
4. Dust seal

Fuel meter cover removal

of cleaner as it will damage the internal diaphragms and gaskets.

    d. Remove the sealing ring (dust seal) for the base of the fuel pressure regulator, from the fuel meter body.
4. Remove the injector being carefull not to damage the electrical connector pins on the top of the injector.
5. Remove the large O ring and steel back-

up washer at the top of the injector cavity in the fuel meter body and the small O-ring located in the bottom of the injector cavity.

NOTE: *The fuel injector is an electrical component and should not be immersed in any type of cleaner. The fuel injector is serviced as a complete assembly only.*

Installation

1. Lubricate the new, small O-ring with automatic transmission fluid; then push the new O-ring on the nozzle end of the injector pressing the ring up against the injector fuel filter.

2. Install the steel back-up washer in the recess of the fuel meter body. Lubricate the new large O-ring with automatic transmission fluid, then install the O-ring directly above the back-up washer, pressing the O-ring down into the cavity recess. The O-ring is located properly

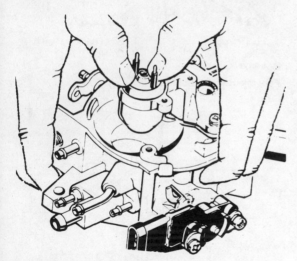

Installing the fuel injector

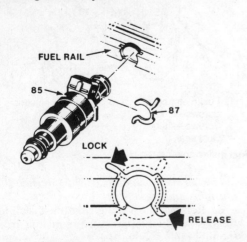

85 INJECTOR - PORT
87 CLIP-INJECTOR RETAINER

Rotate the injector retaining clips to release the injectors

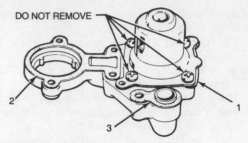

1. Fuel meter cover
2. Fuel meter cover gasket (install on fuel meter body)
3. Fuel return passage gasket (install on fuel meter cover)

Fuel meter cover installation

when it is flush with the fuel meter body casting surface.

NOTE: *Do not attempt to reverse this procedure and install the back-up washer and O-ring after the injector is located in the cavity as this would prevent seating of the O-ring in the cavity recess.*

3. Install the injector by using a pushing/twisting motion to the center the nozzle O-ring in the bottom of the injector cavity and aligning the raised lug on the injector base with the notch cast into the fuel meter body. Push down on the injector making sure it is fully seated in the cavity.

NOTE: *Injector installation is correct with the lug seated in the notch and the electrical terminals parallel to the throttle shaft in the throttle body.*

4. Install the fuel meter cover as follows:

a. Install a new dust seal, for the fuel pressure regulator, into the recess on the fuel meter body.

b. Install a new fuel return passage gasket on the fuel meter cover.

c. Install a new fuel meter gasket on the fuel meter body.

d. Install the fuel meter cover, making sure the pressure regulator dust seal and cover gaskets are in place. Apply a thread locking compound, supplied in service kits, to the threads on the five fuel meter cover attaching screws. Install the screws and lockwashers. The two short screws go next to the fuel injector. Tighten to 28 in. lbs.

5. Install the injector electrical connector and then the air cleaner.

Throttle Body Assembly

REMOVAL AND INSTALLATION

1. Relieve the fuel system pressure as outlined earlier.

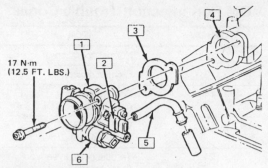

1. Throttle body
2. T.P.S.
3. Gasket
4. Air plenum
5. Cold start valve air tube
6. I.A.C. valve

Throttle body service

2. Remove the THERMAC hose from the engine fitting and air cleaner.

3. Disconnect all electrical harness connectors.

4. Disconnect the throttle linkage and return spring, also the cruise control, if so equipped.

5. Disconnect the vacuum hoses from the throttle body. Identify for reconnection.

6. Using a back-up wrench to hold the fuel line nuts on the throttle body, disconnect the fuel supply and return lines.

7. Remove the three bolts securing the throttle body to the engine and remove the throttle body assembly.

8. Installation is the reverse of removal. Torque the retaining nuts to 17 ft. lbs. Check the O-rings at the end of the fuel lines and replace if necessary.

6-CYLINDER ENGINE FUEL SYSTEM

On 1985 and later models, equipped with the V6 engine, a new multi-port fuel injection (MFI) system is available. The MFI system is controlled by an electronic control module (ECM) which monitors engine operations and generates output signals to provide the correct air/fuel mixture, ignition timing and engine idle speed control. Input to the control unit is provided by an oxygen sensor, coolant temperature sensor, detonation sensor, hot film air mass sensor and throttle position sensor. The ECM also receives information concerning engine rpm, road speed, transmission gear position, power steering and air conditioning.

The system uses Bosch injectors, one at each intake port, rather than the single injector found on the earlier throttle body system. The injectors are mounted on a fuel rail and are activated by a signal from the electronic control module. The injector is a solenoid-operated valve which remains open depending on the width of the electronic pulses (length of the signal) from the ECM; the longer the open time, the more fuel is injected. In this manner, the air/fuel mixture can be precisely controlled for maximum performance with minimum emissions.

Fuel is pumped from the tank by a high pressure fuel pump, located inside the fuel tank. It is a positive displacement roller vane pump. The impeller serves as a vapor separator and pre-charges the high pressure assembly. A pressure regulator maintains 28-36 psi (28-50 psi on turbocharged engines) in the fuel line to the injectors and the excess fuel is fed back to the tank. On MFI systems, a fuel accumulator is used to dampen the hydraulic line hammer in the system created when all injectors open simultaneously.

The Mass Air Flow Sensor is used to measure the mass of air that is drawn into the engine cylinders. It is located just ahead of the air throttle in the intake system and consists of a heated film which measures the mass of air, rather than just the volume. A resistor is used to measure the temperature of the incoming air and the air mass sensor maintains the temperatue of the film at 75 degrees above ambient temperature. As the ambient (outside) air temperature rises, more energy is required to maintain the heated film at the higher temperature and the control unit uses this difference in required energy to calculate the mass of the incoming air. The control unit uses this information to determine the duration of fuel injection pulse, timing and EGR.

The throttle body incorporates an idle air control (IAC) that provides for a bypass channel through which air can flow. It consists of an orifice and pintle which is controlled by the ECM through a stopper motor. The IAC provides air flow for idle and allows additional air during cold start until the engine reaches operating temperature. As the engine temperature rises, the opening through which air passes is slowly closed.

The throttle postion sensor (TPS) provides the control unit with information on throttle position, in order to determine injector pulse width and hence correct mixture. The TPS is connected to the throttle shaft on the throttle body and consists of a potentiometer with one end connected to a 5 volt source from the ECM and the other to ground. A third wire is connected to the ECM to measure the voltage output from the TPS which changes as the throttle valve angle is changed (accelerator pedal moves). At the closed throttle position, the output is low (approximately .4 volts); as the throttle valve opens, the output increases to a maximum 5 volts at wide open throttle (WOT). The TPS can be misadjusted open, shorted, or loose and, if it is out of adjustment, the idle quality or WOT performance may be poor. A loose TPS can cause intermittent bursts of fuel from the injectors and an unstable idle because the ECM thinks the throttle is moving. This should cause a trouble code to be set. Once a trouble code is set, the ECM will use a preset value for TPS and some vehicle performance may return. A small amount of engine coolant is routed through the throttle assembly to prevent freezing inside the throttle bore during cold operation.

CHECK ENGINE LIGHT

The "check engine" light on the instrument panel is used as a warning lamp to tell the driver that a problem has occured in the electronic engine control system. When the self-diagnosis mode is activated by grounding the test terminal of the diagnostic connector, the check engine light will flash stored trouble codes to help isolate system problems. The electronic control module (ECM) has a memory that knows what certain engine sensors should be, under certain conditions. If a sensor reading is not what the ECM thinks it should be, the control unit will illuminate the check engine light and store a trouble code in its memory. The trouble code indicates what circuit the problem is in, each circuit consisting of a sensor, the wiring harness and connectors to it and the ECM.

The Assembly Line Communications Link (ALCL) is a diagnostic connector located in the passenger compartment, usually under the left side of the instrument panel. It has terminals which are used in the assembly plant to check that the engine is operating properly before shipment. Terminal B is the diagnostic test terminal and Terminal A is the ground. By connecting the two terminals together with a jumper wire, the diagnostic mode is activated and the control unit will begin to flash trouble codes using the check engine light.

NOTE: *Some models have a "Service Engine Soon" light instead of a "Check Engine" display.*

When the test terminal is grounded with the key ON and the engine stopped, the ECM will display code 12 to show that the system is working. The ECM will usually display code 12 three times, then start to display any stored trouble codes. If no trouble codes are stored, the ECM will continue to display code 12 until the test terminal is disconnected. Each trouble code will be flashed three times, then code 12 will display again. The ECM will also energize all controlled relays and solenoids when in the diagnostic mode to check function.

GM Port Injection Trouble Codes

Trouble Code	Circuit
12	Normal operation
13	Oxygen sensor
14	Coolant sensor (low voltage)
15	Coolant sensor (high voltage)
21	Throttle position sensor (high voltage)
22	Throttle position sensor (low voltage)
24	Speed sensor
32	FGR vacuum control
33	Mass air flow sensor
34	Mass air flow sensor
42	Electronic spark timing
43	Electronic spark control
44	Lean exhaust
45	Rich exhaust
51	PROM failure
52	CALPAK
55	ECM failure

When the test terminal is grounded with the engine running, it will cause the ECM to enter the Field Service Mode. In this mode, the service engine soon light will indicate whether the system is in Open or Closed Loop operation. In open loop, the light will flash 2½ times per second; in closed loop, the light will flash once per second. In closed loop, the light will stay out most of the time if the system is too lean and will stay on most of the time if the system is too rich.

NOTE: *The vehicle may be driven in the Field Service mode and system evaluated at any steady road speed. This mode is useful in diagnosing driveability problems where the system is rich or lean too long.*

Trouble codes should be cleared after service is completed. To clear the trouble code memory, disconnect the battery for at least 10 seconds. This may be accomplished by disconnecting the ECM harness from the positive battery pigtail or by removing the ECM fuse.

CAUTION: *The ignition switch must be OFF when disconnecting or reconnecting power to the ECM. The vehicle should be driven after the ECM memory is cleared to allow the system to readjust itself. The vehicle should be driven at part throttle under mod-*

erate acceleration with the engine at normal operating temperature. A change in performance should be noted initially, but normal performance should return quickly.

FUEL SYSTEM PRESSURE TEST

When the ignition switch is turned ON, the in-tank fuel pump is energized for as long as the engine is cranking or running and the control unit is receiving signals from the HEI distributor. If there are no reference pulses, the control unit will shut off the fuel pump within two seconds. The pump will deliver fuel to the fuel rail and injectors, then the pressure regulator where the system pressure is controlled to maintain 26–46 psi.

1.   Connect pressure gauge J-34370-1, or equivalent, to fuel pressure test point on the fuel rail. Wrap a rag around the pressure tap to absorb any leakage that may occur when installing the gauge.

2. Turn the ignition ON and check that pump pressure is 34–40 psi. This pressure is controlled by spring pressure within the regulator assembly.

3.   Start the engine and allow it to idle. The fuel pressure should drop to 28–32 psi due to the lower manifold pressure.

NOTE: *The idle pressure will vary somewhat depending on barometric pressure. Check for a drop in pressure indicating regulator control, rather than specific values.*

4. If the fuel pressure drops, check the operation of the check valve, the pump coupling connection, fuel pressure regulator valve and the injectors. A restricted fuel line or filter may also cause a pressure drop. To check the fuel pump output, rstrict the fuel return line and run 12 volts to the pump. The fuel pressure should rise to approximately 75 psi with the return line restricted.

CAUTION: *Before attempting to remove or service any fuel system component, it is necessary to relieve the fuel system pressure as outlined below.*

RELIEVING FUEL SYSTEM PRESSURE

1. Connect fuel gauge J-34730-1, or equivalent, to the fuel pressure valve. Wrap a heavy rag around the fitting while connecting the gauge to avoid spillage.

2. Install a bleed hose into a container approved for gasoline, and open the valve to bleed off pressure.

Fuel Injectors
REMOVAL AND INSTALLATION

Use care in removing the fuel injectors to prevent damage to the electrical connector pins on the injector and the nozzle. The fuel injector is serviced as a acomplete assembly only and should not be immersed in any kind of cleaner.

1. Relieve fuel system pressure.

2. Remove the injector electrical connections.

3. Remove the fuel rail.

4. Separate the injector from the fuel rail.

5. Installation is the reverse of removal. Replace the O-rings when installing injectors into intake manifold.

Fuel Pressure Regulator
REMOVAL AND INSTALLATION

1. Relieve fuel system pressure.

2. Remove pressure regulator from fuel rail. Place a rag around the base of the regulator to catch any spilled fuel.

3. Installation is the reverse of removal.

Idle Air Control Valve
REMOVAL AND INSTALLATION

1. Remove electrical connector from idle air control valve.

2. Remove the idle air control valve using a suitable wrench.

3. Installation is the reverse of removal. Before installing the idle air control valve, measure the distance that the valve is extended. Measurement should be made from the motor housing to the end of the cone. The distance should not exceed 1½ inches, or damage to the valve may occur when installed. Use a new gasket and turn the ignition on then off again to allow the ECM to reset the idle air control valve.

NOTE: *Identify replacement IAC valve as being either Type 1 (with collar at electric terminal end) or Type 2 (without collar). If measuring distance is greater than specified above, proceed as follows:*

Type 1: Press on valve firmly to retract it.

Type 2: Compress retaining spring from valve while turning valve inwith a clockwise motion. Return spring to original positionwith straight portion of spring end aligned with flat surface of valve.

Throttle Position Sensor
REMOVAL AND INSTALLATION

1. Disconnect the electrical connector from the sensor.

2. Remove the attaching screws, lockwashers and retainers.

3. Remove the throttle position sensor. If necessary, remove the screw holding the actuator to the end of the throttle shaft.

4. With the throttle valve in the normal closed idle position, install the throttle position sensor on the throttle body assembly, making sure the sensor pickup lever is located above the tang on the throttle actuator lever.

5. Install the retainers, screws and lockwashers using a thread locking compound. DO NOT tighten the screws until the throttle position switch is adjusted.

6. Install three jumper wires between the throttle position switch and the harness connector.

7. With the ignition switch ON, use a digital voltmeter connected to terminals B and C and adjust the switch to obtain 0.35-0.45 volts.

8. Tighten the mounting screws, then recheck the reading to insure that the adjustment hasn't changed.

9. Turn ignition OFF, remove jumper wires, then reconnect harness to throttle position switch.

CHILTON'S
FUEL ECONOMY
& TUNE-UP TIPS

Tune-up • Spark Plug Diagnosis • Emission Controls

Fuel System • Cooling System • Tires and Wheels

General Maintenance

CHILTON'S FUEL ECONOMY & TUNE-UP TIPS

Fuel economy is important to everyone, no matter what kind of vehicle you drive. The maintenance-minded motorist can save both money and fuel using these tips and the periodic maintenance and tune-up procedures in this Repair and Tune-Up Guide.

There are more than 130,000,000 cars and trucks registered for private use in the United States. Each travels an average of 10-12,000 miles per year, and, and in total they consume close to 70 billion gallons of fuel each year. This represents nearly ⅔ of the oil imported by the United States each year. The Federal government's goal is to reduce consumption 10% by 1985. A variety of methods are either already in use or under serious consideration, and they all affect you driving and the cars you will drive. In addition to "down-sizing", the auto industry is using or investigating the use of electronic fuel delivery, electronic engine controls and alternative engines for use in smaller and lighter vehicles, among other alternatives to meet the federally mandated Corporate Average Fuel Economy (CAFE) of 27.5 mpg by 1985. The government, for its part, is considering rationing, mandatory driving curtailments and tax increases on motor vehicle fuel in an effort to reduce consumption. The government's goal of a 10% reduction could be realized — and further government regulation avoided — if every private vehicle could use just 1 less gallon of fuel per week.

How Much Can You Save?

Tests have proven that almost anyone can make at least a 10% reduction in fuel consumption through regular maintenance and tune-ups. When a major manufacturer of spark plugs sur-

TUNE-UP

1. Check the cylinder compression to be sure the engine will really benefit from a tune-up and that it is capable of producing good fuel economy. A tune-up will be wasted on an engine in poor mechanical condition.

2. Replace spark plugs regularly. New spark plugs alone can increase fuel economy 3%.

3. Be sure the spark plugs are the correct type (heat range) for your vehicle. See the Tune-Up Specifications.

Heat range refers to the spark plug's ability to conduct heat away from the firing end. It must conduct the heat away in an even pattern to avoid becoming a source of pre-ignition, yet it must also operate hot enough to burn off conductive deposits that could cause misfiring.

The heat range is usually indicated by a number on the spark plug, part of the manufacturer's designation for each individual spark plug. The numbers in bold-face indicate the heat range in each manufacturer's identification system.

Periodically, check the spark plugs to be sure they are firing efficiently. They are excellent indicators of the internal condition of your engine.

Manufacturer	Typical Designation
AC	R **45** TS
Bosch (old)	WA **145** T30
Bosch (new)	HR **8** Y
Champion	RBL **15** Y
Fram/Autolite	4**15**
Mopar	P-**62** PR
Motorcraft	BRF-**42**
NGK	BP **5** ES-15
Nippondenso	W **16** EP
Prestolite	14GR **5** 2A

On AC, Bosch (new), Champion, Fram/Autolite, Mopar, Motorcraft and Prestolite, a higher number indicates a hotter plug. On Bosch (old), NGK and Nippondenso, a higher number indicates a colder plug.

4. Make sure the spark plugs are properly gapped. See the Tune-Up Specifications in this book.

5. Be sure the spark plugs are firing efficiently. The illustrations on the next 2 pages show you how to "read" the firing end of the spark plug.

6. Check the ignition timing and set it to specifications. Tests show that almost all cars have incorrect ignition timing by more than 2°.

veyed over 6,000 cars nationwide, they found that a tune-up, on cars that needed one, increased fuel economy over 11%. Replacing worn plugs alone, accounted for a 3% increase. The same test also revealed that 8 out of every 10 vehicles will have some maintenance deficiency that will directly affect fuel economy, emissions or performance. Most of this mileage-robbing neglect could be prevented with regular maintenance.

Modern engines require that all of the functioning systems operate properly for maximum efficiency. A malfunction anywhere wastes fuel. You can keep your vehicle running as efficiently and economically as possible, by being aware of your vehicle's operating and performance characteristics. If your vehicle suddenly develops performance or fuel economy problems it could be due to one or more of the following:

PROBLEM	POSSIBLE CAUSE
Engine Idles Rough	Ignition timing, idle mixture, vacuum leak or something amiss in the emission control system.
Hesitates on Acceleration	Dirty carburetor or fuel filter, improper accelerator pump setting, ignition timing or fouled spark plugs.
Starts Hard or Fails to Start	Worn spark plugs, improperly set automatic choke, ice (or water) in fuel system.
Stalls Frequently	Automatic choke improperly adjusted and possible dirty air filter or fuel filter.
Performs Sluggishly	Worn spark plugs, dirty fuel or air filter, ignition timing or automatic choke out of adjustment.

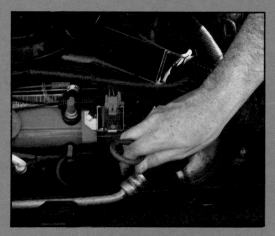

Check spark plug wires on conventional point type ignition for cracks by bending them in a loop around your finger.

Be sure that spark plug wires leading to adjacent cylinders do not run too close together. (Photo courtesy Champion Spark Plug Co.)

7. If your vehicle does not have electronic ignition, check the points, rotor and cap as specified.

8. Check the spark plug wires (used with conventional point-type ignitions) for cracks and burned or broken insulation by bending them in a loop around your finger. Cracked wires decrease fuel efficiency by failing to deliver full voltage to the spark plugs. One misfiring spark plug can cost you as much as 2 mpg.

9. Check the routing of the plug wires. Misfiring can be the result of spark plug leads to adjacent cylinders running parallel to each other and too close together. One wire tends to pick up voltage from the other causing it to fire "out of time".

10. Check all electrical and ignition circuits for voltage drop and resistance.

11. Check the distributor mechanical and/or vacuum advance mechanisms for proper functioning. The vacuum advance can be checked by twisting the distributor plate in the opposite direction of rotation. It should spring back when released.

12. Check and adjust the valve clearance on engines with mechanical lifters. The clearance should be slightly loose rather than too tight.

SPARK PLUG DIAGNOSIS

Normal

APPEARANCE: This plug is typical of one operating normally. The insulator nose varies from a light tan to grayish color with slight electrode wear. The presence of slight deposits is normal on used plugs and will have no adverse effect on engine performance. The spark plug heat range is correct for the engine and the engine is running normally.

CAUSE: Properly running engine.

RECOMMENDATION: Before reinstalling this plug, the electrodes should be cleaned and filed square. Set the gap to specifications. If the plug has been in service for more than 10-12,000 miles, the entire set should probably be replaced with a fresh set of the same heat range.

Oil Deposits

APPEARANCE: The firing end of the plug is covered with a wet, oily coating.

CAUSE: The problem is poor oil control. On high mileage engines, oil is leaking past the rings or valve guides into the combustion chamber. A common cause is also a plugged PCV valve, and a ruptured fuel pump diaphragm can also cause this condition. Oil fouled plugs such as these are often found in new or recently overhauled engines, before normal oil control is achieved, and can be cleaned and reinstalled.

RECOMMENDATION: A hotter spark plug may temporarily relieve the problem, but the engine is probably in need of work.

Incorrect Heat Range

APPEARANCE: The effects of high temperature on a spark plug are indicated by clean white, often blistered insulator. This can also be accompanied by excessive wear of the electrode, and the absence of deposits.

CAUSE: Check for the correct spark plug heat range. A plug which is too hot for the engine can result in overheating. A car operated mostly at high speeds can require a colder plug. Also check ignition timing, cooling system level, fuel mixture and leaking intake manifold.

RECOMMENDATION: If all ignition and engine adjustments are known to be correct, and no other malfunction exists, install spark plugs one heat range colder.

Carbon Deposits

APPEARANCE: Carbon fouling is easily identified by the presence of dry, soft, black, sooty deposits.

CAUSE: Changing the heat range can often lead to carbon fouling, as can prolonged slow, stop-and-start driving. If the heat range is correct, carbon fouling can be attributed to a rich fuel mixture, sticking choke, clogged air cleaner, worn breaker points, retarded timing or low compression. If only one or two plugs are carbon fouled, check for corroded or cracked wires on the affected plugs. Also look for cracks in the distributor cap between the towers of affected cylinders.

RECOMMENDATION: After the problem is corrected, these plugs can be cleaned and reinstalled if not worn severely.

MMT Fouled

APPEARANCE: Spark plugs fouled by MMT (Methycyclopentadienyl Maganese Tricarbonyl) have reddish, rusty appearance on the insulator and side electrode.

CAUSE: MMT is an anti-knock additive in gasoline used to replace lead. During the combustion process, the MMT leaves a reddish deposit on the insulator and side electrode.

RECOMMENDATION: No engine malfunction is indicated and the deposits will not affect plug performance any more than lead deposits (see Ash Deposits). MMT fouled plugs can be cleaned, regapped and reinstalled.

High Speed Glazing

APPEARANCE: Glazing appears as shiny coating on the plug, either yellow or tan in color.

CAUSE: During hard, fast acceleration, plug temperatures rise suddenly. Deposits from normal combustion have no chance to fluff-off; instead, they melt on the insulator forming an electrically conductive coating which causes misfiring.

RECOMMENDATION: Glazed plugs are not easily cleaned. They should be replaced with a fresh set of plugs of the correct heat range. If the condition recurs, using plugs with a heat range one step colder may cure the problem.

Ash (Lead) Deposits

APPEARANCE: Ash deposits are characterized by light brown or white colored deposits crusted on the side or center electrodes. In some cases it may give the plug a rusty appearance.

CAUSE: Ash deposits are normally derived from oil or fuel additives burned during normal combustion. Normally they are harmless, though excessive amounts can cause misfiring. If deposits are excessive in short mileage, the valve guides may be worn.

RECOMMENDATION: Ash-fouled plugs can be cleaned, gapped and reinstalled.

Detonation

APPEARANCE: Detonation is usually characterized by a broken plug insulator.

CAUSE: A portion of the fuel charge will begin to burn spontaneously, from the increased heat following ignition. The explosion that results applies extreme pressure to engine components, frequently damaging spark plugs and pistons.

Detonation can result by over-advanced ignition timing, inferior gasoline (low octane) lean air/fuel mixture, poor carburetion, engine lugging or an increase in compression ratio due to combustion chamber deposits or engine modification.

RECOMMENDATION: Replace the plugs after correcting the problem.

Photos Courtesy Champion Spark Plug Co.

EMISSION CONTROLS

13. Be aware of the general condition of the emission control system. It contributes to reduced pollution and should be serviced regularly to maintain efficient engine operation.

14. Check all vacuum lines for dried, cracked or brittle conditions. Something as simple as a leaking vacuum hose can cause poor performance and loss of economy.

15. Avoid tampering with the emission control system. Attempting to improve fuel econ-

FUEL SYSTEM

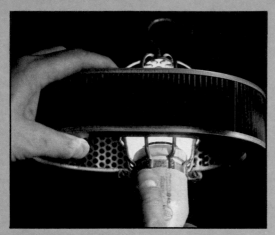

Check the air filter with a light behind it. If you can see light through the filter it can be reused.

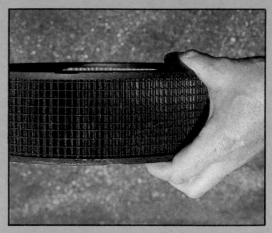

Extremely clogged filters should be discarded and replaced with a new one.

18. Replace the air filter regularly. A dirty air filter richens the air/fuel mixture and can increase fuel consumption as much as 10%. Tests show that ⅓ of all vehicles have air filters in need of replacement.

19. Replace the fuel filter at least as often as recommended.

20. Set the idle speed and carburetor mixture to specifications.

21. Check the automatic choke. A sticking or malfunctioning choke wastes gas.

22. During the summer months, adjust the automatic choke for a leaner mixture which will produce faster engine warm-ups.

COOLING SYSTEM

29. Be sure all accessory drive belts are in good condition. Check for cracks or wear.

30. Adjust all accessory drive belts to proper tension.

31. Check all hoses for swollen areas, worn spots, or loose clamps.

32. Check coolant level in the radiator or expansion tank.

33. Be sure the thermostat is operating properly. A stuck thermostat delays engine warm-up and a cold engine uses nearly twice as much fuel as a warm engine.

34. Drain and replace the engine coolant at least as often as recommended. Rust and scale

TIRES & WHEELS

38. Check the tire pressure often with a pencil type gauge. Tests by a major tire manufacturer show that 90% of all vehicles have at least 1 tire improperly inflated. Better mileage can be achieved by over-inflating tires, but never exceed the maximum inflation pressure on the side of the tire.

39. If possible, install radial tires. Radial tires deliver as much as ½ mpg more than bias belted tires.

40. Avoid installing super-wide tires. They only create extra rolling resistance and decrease fuel mileage. Stick to the manufacturer's recommendations.

41. Have the wheels properly balanced.

omy by tampering with emission controls is more likely to worsen fuel economy than improve it. Emission control changes on modern engines are not readily reversible.

16. Clean (or replace) the EGR valve and lines as recommended.

17. Be sure that all vacuum lines and hoses are reconnected properly after working under the hood. An unconnected or misrouted vacuum line can wreak havoc with engine performance.

23. Check for fuel leaks at the carburetor, fuel pump, fuel lines and fuel tank. Be sure all lines and connections are tight.

24. Periodically check the tightness of the carburetor and intake manifold attaching nuts and bolts. These are a common place for vacuum leaks to occur.

25. Clean the carburetor periodically and lubricate the linkage.

26. The condition of the tailpipe can be an excellent indicator of proper engine combustion. After a long drive at highway speeds, the inside of the tailpipe should be a light grey in color. Black or soot on the insides indicates an overly rich mixture.

27. Check the fuel pump pressure. The fuel pump may be supplying more fuel than the engine needs.

28. Use the proper grade of gasoline for your engine. Don't try to compensate for knocking or "pinging" by advancing the ignition timing. This practice will only increase plug temperature and the chances of detonation or pre-ignition with relatively little performance gain.

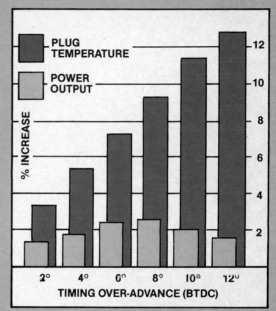

Increasing ignition timing past the specified setting results in a drastic increase in spark plug temperature with increased chance of detonation or preignition. Performance increase is considerably less. (Photo courtesy Champion Spark Plug Co.)

that form in the engine should be flushed out to allow the engine to operate at peak efficiency.

35. Clean the radiator of debris that can decrease cooling efficiency.

36. Install a flex-type or electric cooling fan, if you don't have a clutch type fan. Flex fans use curved plastic blades to push more air at low speeds when more cooling is needed; at high speeds the blades flatten out for less resistance. Electric fans only run when the engine temperature reaches a predetermined level.

37. Check the radiator cap for a worn or cracked gasket. If the cap does not seal properly, the cooling system will not function properly.

42. Be sure the front end is correctly aligned. A misaligned front end actually has wheels going in differed directions. The increased drag can reduce fuel economy by .3 mpg.

43. Correctly adjust the wheel bearings. Wheel bearings that are adjusted too tight increase rolling resistance.

Check tire pressures regularly with a reliable pocket type gauge. Be sure to check the pressure on a cold tire.

GENERAL MAINTENANCE

Check the fluid levels (particularly engine oil) on a regular basis. Be sure to check the oil for grit, water or other contamination.

A vacuum gauge is another excellent indicator of internal engine condition and can also be installed in the dash as a mileage indicator.

44. Periodically check the fluid levels in the engine, power steering pump, master cylinder, automatic transmission and drive axle.

45. Change the oil at the recommended interval and change the filter at every oil change. Dirty oil is thick and causes extra friction between moving parts, cutting efficiency and increasing wear. A worn engine requires more frequent tune-ups and gets progressively worse fuel economy. In general, use the lightest viscosity oil for the driving conditions you will encounter.

46. Use the recommended viscosity fluids in the transmission and axle.

47. Be sure the battery is fully charged for fast starts. A slow starting engine wastes fuel.

48. Be sure battery terminals are clean and tight.

49. Check the battery electrolyte level and add distilled water if necessary.

50. Check the exhaust system for crushed pipes, blockages and leaks.

51. Adjust the brakes. Dragging brakes or brakes that are not releasing create increased drag on the engine.

52. Install a vacuum gauge or miles-per-gallon gauge. These gauges visually indicate engine vacuum in the intake manifold. High vacuum = good mileage and low vacuum = poorer mileage. The gauge can also be an excellent indicator of internal engine conditions.

53. Be sure the clutch is properly adjusted. A slipping clutch wastes fuel.

54. Check and periodically lubricate the heat control valve in the exhaust manifold. A sticking or inoperative valve prevents engine warm-up and wastes gas.

55. Keep accurate records to check fuel economy over a period of time. A sudden drop in fuel economy may signal a need for tune-up or other maintenance.

Chassis Electrical

5

UNDERSTANDING AND TROUBLESHOOTING ELECTRICAL SYSTEMS

For any electrical system to operate, it must make a complete circuit. This simply means that the power flow from the battery must make a complete circle. When an electrical component is operating, power flows from the battery to the component, passes through the component causing it to perform its function (lighting a light bulb), and then returns to the battery through the ground of the circuit. This ground is usually (but not always) the metal part of the car or truck on which the electrical component is mounted.

Perhaps the easiest was to visualize this is to think of connecting a light bulb, with two wires attached to it, to the battery. If one of the two wires attached to the light built were attached to the negative post of the battery and the other were attached to the positive post of the battery, you would have a complete circuit. Current from the battery would flow to the light bulb, causing it to light, and return to the negative post of the battery.

The normal automotive circuit differs from this simple example in two ways. First, instead of having a return wire from the bulb to the battery, the light bulb returns the current to the battery through the chassis of the vehicle. Since the negative battery cable is attached to the chassis and the chassis is made of electrically conductive metal, the chassis of the vehicle can serve as ground wire to complete the circuit. Secondly, most automotive circuits contain switches to turn components on and off as required.

Every complete circuit from a power source must include a component which is using the power from the power source. If you were to disconnect the light bulb from the wires and touch the two wires together (don't do this) the power supply wire to the component would be grounded before the normal ground connection for the circuit.

Because grounding a wire from a power source makes a complete circuit, less the required component to use the power, this phenomenon is called a short circuit. Common causes are: broken insulation (exposing the metal wire to a metal part of the car), or a shorted switch.

Some electrical components which require a large amount of current to operate also have a relay in their circuit. Since these circuits carry a large amount of current, the thickness of the wire in the circuit (gauge size) is also greater. If this large wire were connected from the component to the control switch on the instrument panel, and then back to the component, a voltage drop would occur in the circuit. To prevent this potential drop in voltage, an electromagnetic switch (relay) is used. The large wires in the circuit are connected from the battery to one side of the relay, and from the opposite side of the relay to the component. The relay is normally open, preventing current from passing through the circuit. An additional, smaller, wire is connected from the relay to the control switch for the circuit. When the control switch is turned on, it grounds the smaller wire from the relay and completes the circuit. This closes the relay and allows current to flow from the battery to the component. The horn, headlight, and starter circuits are three which use relays.

It is possible for larger surges of current to pass through the electrical system of your car or truck. If this surge of current were to reach an electrical component, it could burn it out. To prevent this, fuses, circuit breakers or fusible links are connected into the current supply wires of most of the major electrical systems. When an electrical current of excessive power passes through the component's fuse, the fuse blows out and breaks the circuit, saving the component from destruction.

A circuit breaker is basically a self-repairing fuse. The circuit breaker opens the circuit the same way a fuse does. However, when either the short is removed from the circuit or the surge subsides, the circuit breaker resets itself and does not have to be replaced as a fuse does.

A fuse link is a wire that acts as a fuse. It is normally connected between the starter relay and the main wiring harness. This connection is usually under the hood. The fuse link (if installed) protects all the chassis electrical components, and is the probable cause of trouble when none of the electrical components function, unless the battery is disconnected or dead.

Electrical problems generally fall into one of three areas:

1. The component that is not functioning is not receiving current.
2. The component itself is not functioning.
3. The component is not properly grounded.

The electrical system can be checked with a test light and a jumper wire. A test light is a device that looks like a pointed screwdriver with a wire attached to it and has a light bulb in its handle. A jumper wire is a piece of insulated wire with an alligator clip attached to each end.

If a component is not working, you must follow a systematic plan to determine which of the three causes is the villain.

1. Turn on the switch that controls the inoperable component.
2. Disconnect the power supply wire from the component.
3. Attach the ground wire on the test light to a good metal ground.
4. Touch the probe end of the test light to the end of the power supply wire that was disconnected from the component. If the component is receiving current, the test light will go on.

NOTE: *Some components work only when the ignition switch is turned on.*

If the test light does not go on, then the problem is in the circuit between the battery and the component. This includes all the switches, fuses and relays in the system. Follow the wire that runs back to the battery. The problem is an open circuit between the battery and the component. If the fuse is blown and, when replaced, immediately blows again, there is a short circuit in the system which must be located and repaired. If there is a switch in the system, bypass it with a jumper wire. This is done by connecting one end of the jumper wire to the power supply wire into the switch and the other end of the jumper wire to the wire coming out of the switch. If the test light lights with the jumper wire installed, the switch or whatever was bypassed is defective.

NOTE: *Never substitute the jumper wire for the component, since it is required to use the power from the power source.*

5. If the bulb in the test light goes on, then the current is getting to the component that is not working. This eliminates the first of the three possible causes. Connect the power supply wire and connect a jumper wire from the component to a good metal ground. Do this with the switch which controls the component turned on, and also the ignition switch turned on if it is required for the component to work. If the component works with the jumper wire installed, then it has a bad ground. This is usually caused by the metal area on which the component mounts to the chassis being coated with some type of foreign matter.

6. If neither test located the source of the trouble, then the component itself is defective. Remember, that for any electrical system to work, all connections must be clean and tight.

HEATER

Blower Motor

REMOVAL AND INSTALLATION

1. Disconnect the negative battery cable.
2. Remove the cooling tube.
3. Disconnect all electrical connections.
4. Remove the heater retaining screws and remove the blower and cage assembly.
5. Installation is the reverse of removal.

Heater Core

REMOVAL AND INSTALLATION

With A/C

1. Under the hood, disconnect and plug the heater hoses at the heater.
2. Remove the speaker grille and the speaker.
3. Remove the heater core cover, retainers and the heater core.
4. Installation is the reverse of removal. Refill the cooling system as required.

Without A/C

1. Disconnect the negative battery cable.
2. Disconnect the following wire connections:
   a. Heater relay.
   b. Heater blower resistor.
   c. Heater blower switch.
   d. Heater ground connection.
   e. Forward courtesy lamp socket.

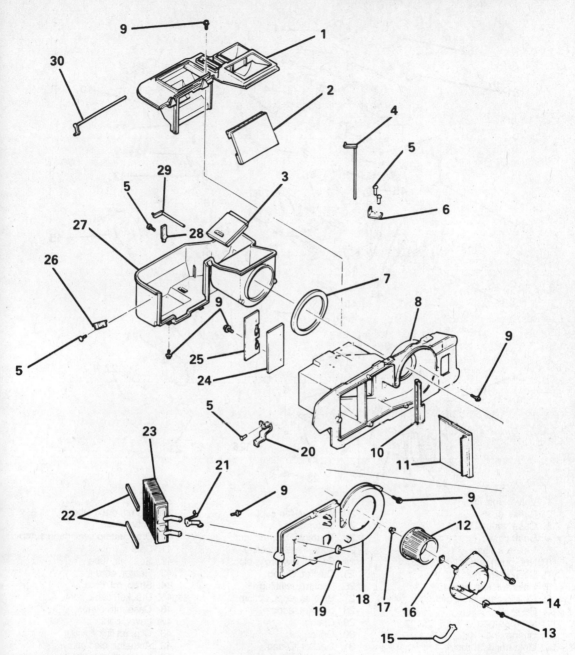

1. Cover, air inl. & dist.
2. Valve, vent
3. Valve, defr.
4. Shaft, w/lvr., temp. vlv.
5. Rivet, truss hd (⁹⁄₁₆″ x ¼″)
6. Bracket, cbl. mtg.
7. Seal, htr. & blo. case
8. Case, htr.
9. Screw, hwh tap (M4.2 x 1.41 x 13)
10. Baffle, air
11. Valve, temp.
12. Fan, blo.
13. Screw, hwh tap (M4.2 x 1.41 x 14)
14. Terminal, blo. mtr. grd. (2.530)
15. Tube, mtr. clg. (9.218)
16. Washer, fan supt. (9.216)
17. Nut, blo. fan
18. Cover, blo.
19. Seal, htr. core tube
20. Bracket, mt.
21. Clamp, core mt.
22. Seal, htr. core
23. Core, htr.
24. Seal, htr. core case
25. Clip, htr. core mt.
26. Bracket, cbl. mt.
27. Case, air inl. & distr.
28. Bracket, cbl. mt.
29. Shaft, w/lvr., defr. vlv.
30. Shaft, w/lvr., vent vlv.

Heater module - exploded view

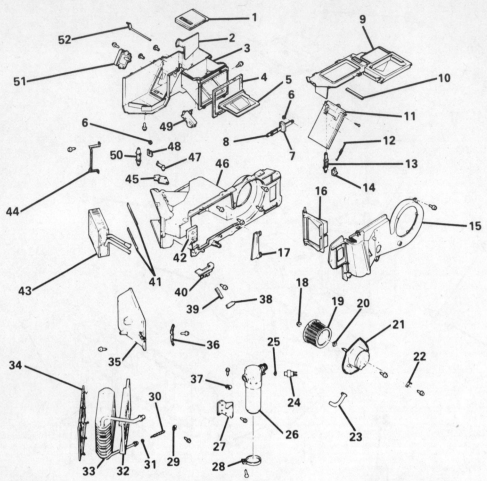

A/C module - exploded view

1. Valve, defr.
2. Baffle, air
3. Case, air int. & dist.
4. Seal, case
5. Valve, w/fitting
6. Nut, push on (M3.6 x 11.23)
7. Seal, opg. link
8. Link, adj. spr. defr.
9. Cover, case al. & defr.
10. Seal
11. Valve, mode
12. Spring, ext.
13. Link, adj. spr. mode
14. Retainer
15. Case, blower
16. Valve, temp.
17. Baffle, air
18. Nut
19. Fan
20. Washer, fan supt.
21. Motor, elec.
22. Terminal, blo. mtr. grd.
23. Tube, motor cooling
24. Switch, low press elec.
25. Gasket, O-ring
26. Accum., w/fitting
27. Bracket, supt. accum.
28. Bracket, accum.
29. Clamp
30. Orifice
31. Gasket, O-ring
32. Seal, core evap.
33. Core, w/tube asm. evap.
34. Filter, water core
35. Cover, heater
36. Clip, spl. mt. core
37. Clamp
38. Clamp, drain tube
39. Tube, drain
40. Drain, sump seal, drain sump
41. Seal
42. Seal, htr. tube
43. Heater, core
44. Strap, mt. core
45. Bracket, cable cont.
46. Case, htr. evap.
47. Lever, cont.
48. Clip, tet link
49. Actuator, elec. al.
50. Link, adj. spr. al.
51. Actuator, elec. mode
52. Shaft, w/lever defr.

3. Remove the windshield washer fluid container.

4. Disconnect the heater core inlet and outlet hoses.

5. Remove the heater core grommets.

6. Remove the heater case cover.

7. Remove the heater core retainer and remove the heater core.

8. Installation is the reverse of removal. Refill the cooling system as required.

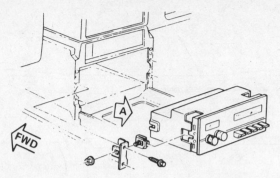

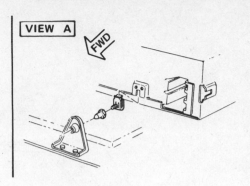

Radio mounting

RADIO

REMOVAL AND INSTALLATION

1. Remove the console trim plate assembly.
2. Disconnect the side retaining nuts and the rear retaining bolt.
3. Disconnect the electrical and antenna connections.
4. Remove the radio out through the front of the console.
5. Installation is the reverse of removal.

NOTE: *It is very important when doing any radio work to avoid pinching the speaker wires. A short circuit to ground from either wire will cause damage to the output circuit of the radio.*

WINDSHIELD WIPERS

Wiper Arm Replacement

The wiper arms are retained on the serrated transmission spindle shaft by an integral locking clip. Carefully lift up on the wiper arm using Tool J-8966 or equivalent.

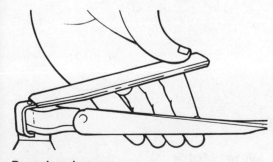

Removing wiper arm

Wiper Blade Replacement

To replace the wiper element (rubber insert) only, refer to Chapter One.

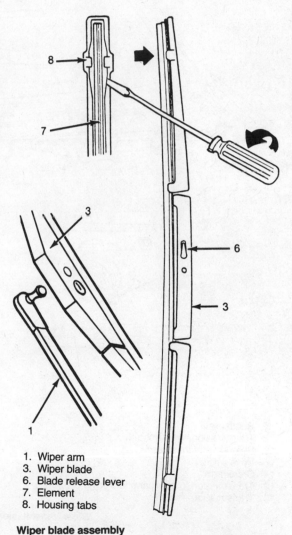

1. Wiper arm
3. Wiper blade
6. Blade release lever
7. Element
8. Housing tabs

Wiper blade assembly

1. Depress the release lever and remove the blade from the arm.
2. To install, position the blade over the pin on the arm and press until the release lever engages with the groove in the pin.

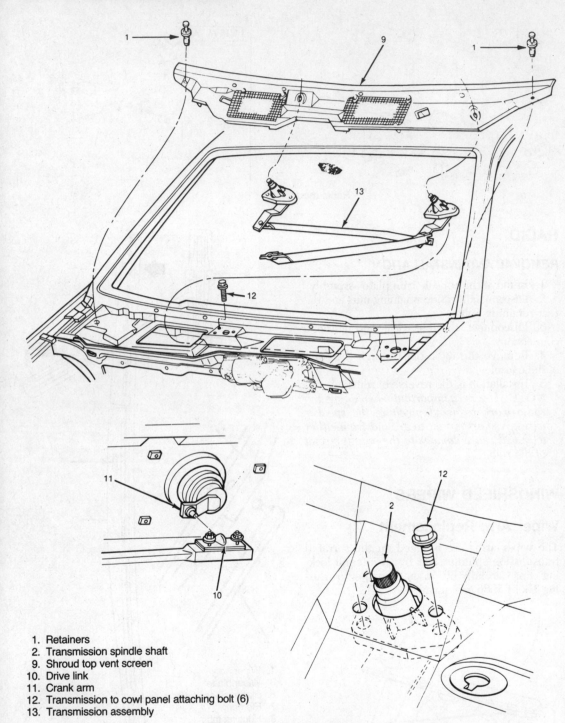

1. Retainers
2. Transmission spindle shaft
9. Shroud top vent screen
10. Drive link
11. Crank arm
12. Transmission to cowl panel attaching bolt (6)
13. Transmission assembly

Wiper transmission assembly

Wiper Switch

The windshield wiper switch is an integral part of the multi-function switch (windshield wiper/washer, headlight beam selector, directional signal) within the steering column. Please refer to Multi-Function Switch, Disassembly and Assembly in Chapter 8.

Wiper Motor

REMOVAL AND INSTALLATION

1. Remove the wiper arms.
2. Remove the shroud top vent screen.
3. Remove the drive link from the crank arm.
4. Disconnect the electrical leads.

5. Remove the three attaching screws and remove the wiper arm.

6. Installation is the reverse of removal. Make sure the wiper motor is in the park position before installing the wiper arms and the shroud top screen.

Wiper Transmission Assembly (Linkage)

REMOVAL AND INSTALLATION

1. Remove the wiper arms.
2. Remove the shroud top vent screen.
3. Remove the drive link from the crank arm.
4. Remove the six bolts attaching the transmission to the cowl panel and remove the transmission.
5. Installation is the reverse of removal.

INSTRUMENT CLUSTER

REMOVAL AND INSTALLATION

1. Disconnect the negative battery cable.
2. Remove the rear cluster cover.

3. Remove the front trim plate.
4. Remove the steering column cover.
5. Remove the cluster attaching screws, disconnect the wiring harness, and remove the cluster assembly.

NOTE: *The speedometer, tach, and gauges may be serviced by removing the front cluster lens.*

Quartz Electric Speedometer

The quartz speedometer utilizes an accurate clock signal supplied by a quartz crystal, along with intergrated electronic circuitry to process an electrical speed signal. This eliminates the need for the conventional speedometer cable. The speed signal is used by the circuitry to drive the core gage and odometer stepper motor. The electrical speed signal is generated by a permanent magnet (PM) generator mounted in the transmission. This speed signal is transmitted to the speedometer assembly buffering circuit contained in the instrument cluster circuitry.

NOTE: *You can gain access to the speedometer and tach by removing the front cluster lens, however, knowledge of instrument circuit checks will help in determining if op-*

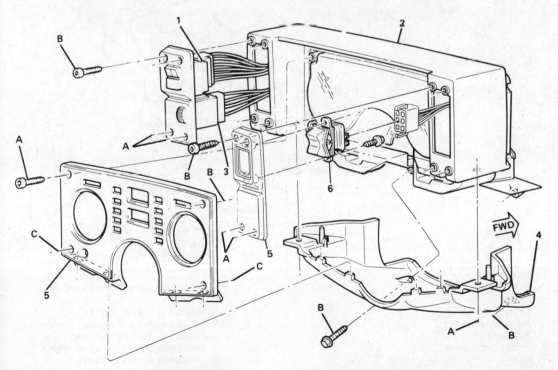

1. Headlamp switch
2. Cluster pad asm.
3. Dimmer switch
4. Cover asm.
5. Trim plate
6. Deck lid switch

A. Install these bolt/screws first
B. Install these bolt/screws second
C. Install these bolt/screws last

Cluster trim plates

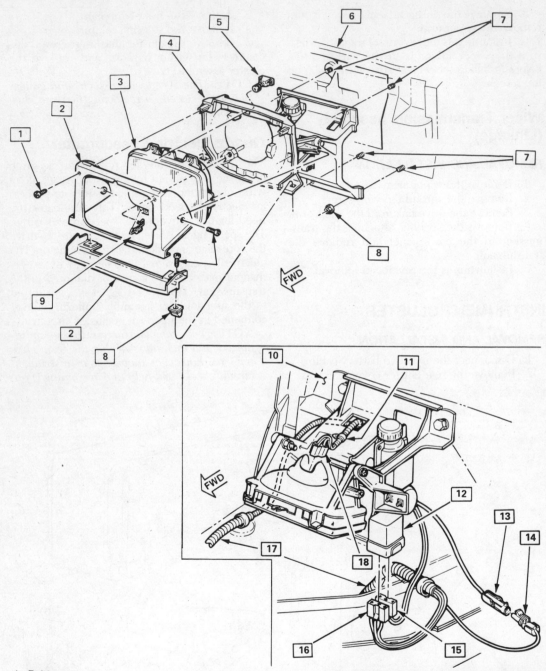

1. Bolt/screw
2. Bezel
3. Lamp asm.
4. Actuator asm.
5. Adjuster
6. Front compt. panel
7. Stud
8. Nut
9. Spring

10. Panel front compt. & headlamp mounting
11. Clip
12. Headlamp relay assembly
13. Headlamp motor to actuator connection
14. Headlamp actuator connection
15. Headlamp motor to relay connection
16. Headlamp relay connection
17. Wire assembly front end
18. Headlamp connection

Headlamp assembly

erating difficulties lie in the instrument itself or its related circuit. The speedometer and tach themselves should be serviced by a Specified Service Center. If a speedometer problem develops, it is suggested that you contact an authorized Pontiac dealer.

LIGHTING

Headlamp

REMOVAL AND INSTALLATION

1. Open the hood and disconnect the electrical connections at the lamps.
2. Raise the headlamps, then close the hood.
3. Remove the Torx screw at the top right and left side of the bezel.
4. Remove the black plastic bezel.
5. Raise the hood.
6. Using a hooked tool, pull the retaining spring to one side to release the lamp assembly.
7. Remove the lamp assembly from the retaining pins.
8. Remove the four screws from the chrome retaining ring and remove the headlight.
10. Installation is the reverse of removal.

Headlight Switch

REMOVAL AND INSTALLATION

1. Disconnect the negative battery cable.
2. Remove the headlight/dimmer switch trim plate screws.
3. Disconnect the electrical connector and remove the switch assembly.
4. Installation is the reverse of removal.

CIRCUIT PROTECTION

Fuse Block

The fuse block is a swing-down unit located in the underside of the instrument panel left of the steering column. The fuse block uses miniaturized fuses, designed for increased circuit protection and greater reliability. Various convenience connectors, which snap-lock into the fuse block, add to the serviceability of this unit.

Convenience Center

The convenience center is a stationary unit. It is located on the right side of the heater or A/C module in the vehicle, under the instrument

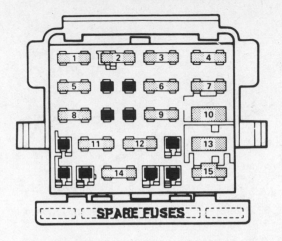

1. FUSE 10 AMP. IGN. RED (E. F. I. E. C. M. & INJ.) (C. C. C., E. C. M.)

2. FUSE 10 AMP. IGN. RED (FUEL PUMP RELAY & OIL PRESSURE SW. FEED)

3. FUSE 20 AMP. BATT. YEL. (STOP LAMP SW., HAZARD FLASHER, CHIME)

4. FUSE 20 AMP. IGN. YEL. (COOLANT FAN RELAY COIL)

5. FUSE 20 AMP. IGN. YEL. (TURN SIGNAL FLASHER, BACK-UP LAMPS)

6. FUSE 20 AMP BATT. YEL (TAIL LAMPS, PARKING, SIDE MARKER & LICENSE LAMPS)

7. FUSE 20 AMP. IGN. YEL. (HEATER, A/C)

8. FUSE 20 AMP. IGN. RED (C49 RELAY, C49 OFF-ON SW, CHIME, VOLTMETER, CRUISE, V. S. S., A/C RELAY T. C. C. BRAKE SW. & R.R. DECK LID)

9. FUSE 20 AMP BATT YEL (DOME LAMPS, HORN RELAY, CLOCK, LIGHTER, POWER LOCKS RELAY, POWER MIRROR)

10. CIRCUIT BREAKER 30 AMP. (POWER WINDOWS)

11. FUSE 5 AMP. IGN. TAN (INST. PANEL LAMPS, HEADLAMP WARNING)

12. FUSE 10 AMP. IGN. RED (RADIO FEED & CRUISE)

13. CIRCUIT BREAKER 30 AMP. (AU3/C49) (POWER LOCKS, REAR DEFOG)

14. FUSE 20 AMP. IGN. YEL. (WINDSHIELD WIPER MOTOR)

15. FUSE 3 AMP. IGN. TAN (CRANK SIGNAL TO E. C. M.)

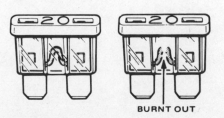

BURNT OUT

Fuse location

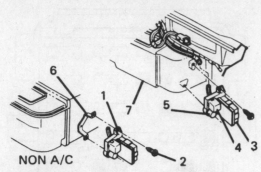

NON A/C

1. Convenience center
2. Screw
3. Alarm
4. Relay (horn)
5. Flasher (4-way)
6. Bracket
7. Heater and A/C module

Convenience center and components

panel. This location provides easy access to the audio alarm, hazard warnings, the horn relay and the seatbelt key and headlamp warning alarm. All units are serviced by plug-in replacements.

Fusible Link

Added protection is provided to all battery feed circuits and other selected circuits by a fusible link. This link is a short piece of copper wire approximately 4 inches long, inserted in series with the circuit and acts as a fuse. The link is two (2) or more gauges smaller in size than the circuit wire it is protecting and will burn out without damage to the circuit in case of current overload.

FUSIBLE LINK REPLACEMENT

1. Disconnect the battery.
2. Locate the burned out link.
3. Strip away all melted harness insulation.
4. Cut the burned link ends from the circuit wire.
5. Strip the circuit wire back approximately ½ inch to allow soldering of new link.
6. Using a fusible link four (4) gauges smaller than the protected circuit (approximately 10 inches long), solder a new link into the circuit.

NOTE: *Use only resin core solder. Under no circumstances should an acid solder be used nor should a link be connected in any other manner except by soldering. Use of acid core solder may result in corrosion.*

7. Tape the soldered ends securely, using suitable electrical tape.
8. After taping the wire, tape the harness leaving an exposed loop of wire approximately 5 inches in length.
9. Reconnect the battery.

WIRING DIAGRAMS

Wiring diagrams have been left out of this book. As cars have become more complex, and available with longer and longer option lists, wiring diagrams have grown in size and complexity also. It has become virtually impossible to provide a readable reproduction in a reasonable number of pages. Information on ordering wiring diagrams from the vehicle manufacturer can be found in the owner's manual.

TRANSAXLES

NOTE: *The following procedure is for both automatic and manual transaxles.*

REMOVAL

1. Remove the air cleaner assembly.
2. Disconnect the negative battery cable.
3. Disconnect the ground cable at the transaxle.
4. Disconnect the shift cable at the transaxle.
5. Remove the upper transaxle-to-engine bolts.
6. Install engine support fixture J-28467 or equivalent.
7. Raise the car and support it safely with jackstands.
8. Remove the rear wheels and tires.
9. Remove the axleshafts.
10. Remove the heat shield from the catalytic converter.
11. Disconnect the exhaust pipe from the exhaust manifold.
12. Remove the engine mount-to-cradle nuts.

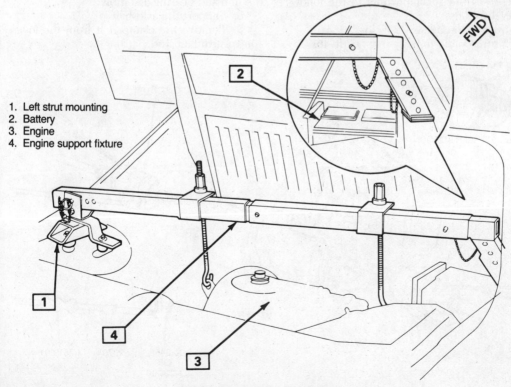

1. Left strut mounting
2. Battery
3. Engine
4. Engine support fixture

Engine support fixture installed

13. Support the cradle with an adjustable stand.

14. Remove the rear cradle-to-body bolts.

15. Remove the forward cradle-to-body mounting bolts.

16. Lower the cradle and move it out of the way.

17. Remove the starter and inspection cover shields and remove the starter.

18. Remove the flywheel-to-converter bolts.

19. Disconnect and plug the cooler lines, if equipped with automatic transmission.

20. Position a transmission stand under the transaxle.

21. On manual transaxles, remove the lower transaxle-to-engine bolts, and remove the transaxle.

22. On automatic transaxles, remove the transaxle-to-support mounting bolts on the right side.

INSTALLATION

1. Install the starter and inspection cover shields.

2. Hoist the cradle into position.

NOTE: *Lower the cradle at the front and raise the car. Work the cradle at the rear into position on the mounts, then raise the front into position.*

3. The remainder of the installation is the reverse of removal.

4. Torque the retaining nuts to the following specifications:
   - Starter-to-engine: 32 ft. lbs.
   - Front cradle-to-body nuts: 67 ft. lbs.

- Rear cradle-to-body bolts: 76 ft. lbs.
- Exhaust pipe-to-exhaust manifold: 25 ft.lb.
- Transaxle mounts-to-cradle nuts, rear: 18 ft. lbs.
- Engine mounts-to-cradle nuts: 40 ft. lbs.
- Upper transaxle-to-engine bolts: 55 ft. lbs.
- Cooler lines: 20 ft. lbs.
- Support bracket-to-transaxle (automatic): 37 ft. lbs.

Drive Axle

REMOVAL AND INSTALLATION

CAUTION: *Use care when removing the drive axle. Tri-pot joints can be damaged if the drive axle is over-extended.*

1. Remove and discard the hub nut.

2. Raise the car and remove the wheel and tire.

3. Install a drive boot seal protector No. J-28712, or its equivalent, on the outer seal.

4. Disconnect the toe link rod at the knuckle assembly.

5. Disconnect the parking brake cables at the cradle.

6. Disconnect the brake line bracket at the underbody in the inner wheelhouse opening.

7. Using tool No. J-28733, or its equivalent hub spindle remover, remove the axleshaft from the hub and bearing assembly.

8. Support the axleshaft.

9. Remove the clamp bolt from the lower control arm ball stud.

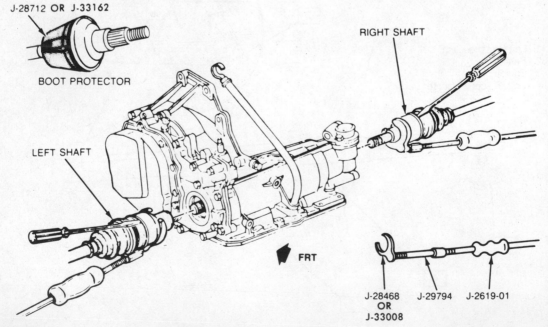

Removing the driveaxle from the transaxle

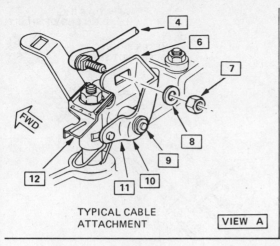

TYPICAL CABLE
ATTACHMENT

VIEW A

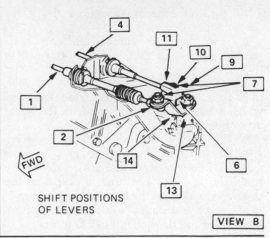

SHIFT POSITIONS
OF LEVERS

VIEW B

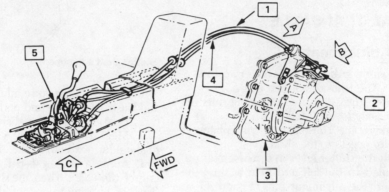

VIEW C

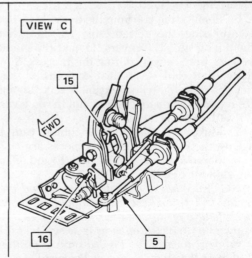

1. Cable A	7. Nut E	13. R 3rd 1st
2. Lever F	8. P washer	14. 2nd 4th
3. Transaxle asm.	9. R	15. Alignment pin F
4. Cable B	10. 1st 2nd	16. Alignment pin G
5. Trans control asm. C	11. 4th 3rd	
6. Lever D	12. Retainer clip J	

Manual transaxle cable adjustment

10. Separate the knuckle from the lower control arm.

11. Pull the strut, knuckle and caliper assembly away from the body and secure it in this position.

12. Using tool no. J-33008 and No. J-2619-01 or their equivalents, disengage the snap rings which are retaining the drive axle at the transaxle, then remove the drive axle.

NOTE: *If the drive axle is being replaced, replace the knuckle seal.*

13. When attaching the drive axle to the transaxle, seat the axle using a prybar in the groove provided on the inner retainer. The remainder of installation is the reverse of removal. Torque the hub nut to 225 ft. lbs.

MANUAL TRANSAXLE

Cable Adjustment

1. Disconnect the negative battery cable.
2. Place the transaxle in first gear.
3. Loosen the shift cable attaching nuts (E) at the transaxle levers (D) and (F).
4. Remove the console and trim plates as required for access to the shifter.
5. With the shifter lever in the first gear position (pulled to the left and held against the stop), insert the alignment pins (F) and (G) as shown in view (D).
6. Remove the lash from the transaxle by first compressing the select cable (B) and then tightening nut (E). Levers (D) and (F) should be kept from moving during this process. Similarly, shift cable (A) is first compressed, and nut (E) then tightened. Again, levers (D) and (F) remain stationary. Tighten nut (E) on levers (D) and (F) to 20 ft. lbs.
7. Make sure the reverse inhibit cam is against the roller, and align it if necessary.
8. Remove the alignment pins (F) and (G) at the shifter assembly.

NOTE: *While cycling from 1st to 2nd and 2nd to 1st, the select cable should not move. Difficulty in shifting the transaxle to reverse may be corrected by moving select lever (D) inboard toward the 1st-3rd-reverse position during the shift cable (A) adjustment.*

Shifter Shaft Adjustment

If the shift cables are properly adjusted , and a " hang-up" occurs when shifting in the 1-2 gear range, it may be necessary to check the washer on the shaft. This washer helps position the shifter shaft for proper shifting characteristics. Perform the following procedure to obtain the correct washer:

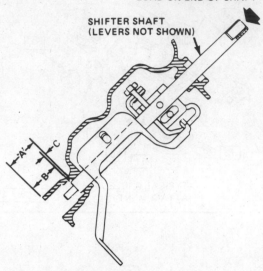

APPLY A 4-6 Kg
LOAD ON END OF SHAFT

SHIFTER SHAFT
(LEVERS NOT SHOWN)

Shifter shaft adjustment

1. Remove the reverse inhibitor fitting spring and washer from the end of the housing.
2. Position the shifter shaft in 2nd gear.
3. Measure Dimension A (End of housing-to-shoulder just behind the end of the shaft).
4. Apply a load of 4–6 Kg on the opposite end of the shaft. Then measure Dimension B (End of housing-to-end of shifter shaft major diameter).
5. Subtract: Dimension A minus Dimension B equals distance C.
6. Compare the result of step 5 with the chart, and choose the proper shim for use in installation.

Shim Part No.	Dim C (mm)	Color & No. of Stripes
14008235	1.8	3 white
476709	2.1	1 orange
476710	2.4	2 orange
476711	2.7	3 orange
476712	3.0	1 blue
476713	3.3	2 blue
476714	3.6	3 blue
476715	3.9	1 white
476716	4.2	2 white

CLUTCH

REMOVAL AND INSTALLATION

1. Remove the transaxle.
2. Mark the pressure plate assembly and flywheel so that they can be assembled in the same position. They were balanced as an assembly at the factory.

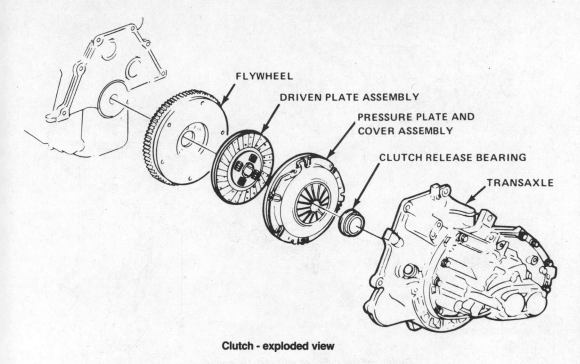

Clutch - exploded view

3. Loosen the attaching bolts one turn at a time until spring tension is relieved.

4. Support the pressure plate and remove the bolts. Remove the pressure plate and clutch disc. Do not disassemble the pressure plate assembly; replace it if it is defective.

5. Inspect the flywheel, clutch disc, pressure plate, throwout bearing and the clutch fork and pivot shaft assembly for wear. Replace the parts as required. If the flywheel shows any signs of overheating, or if it badly grooved or scored, it should be replaced.

6. Clean the pressure plate and flywheel mating surfaces thoroughly. Place the clutch disc and pressure plate into the installed position, and support with a dummy shaft or clutch aligning tool. The clutch plate is aligned with the damper springs offset towards the transaxle. One side of the factory supplied clutch disc is stamped "Flywheel Side".

7. Install the pressure plate-to-flywheel bolts and tighten them gradually in a criss-cross pattern.

8. Lubricate the outside groove and the inside recess of the release bearing with high temperature grease. Wipe off any excess. Install the release bearing.

Clutch Master Cylinder
REMOVAL

1. Disconnect the cylinder pushrod at the clutch pedal.

2. Disconnect the hydraulic line at the master cylinder.

3. Remove the nuts attaching the cylinder to the cowl, then remove the cylinder.

INSTALLATION

1. Position the cylinder pushrod through the cowl and loosely install the cylinder-to-cowl nuts.

2. Connect the cylinder pushrod to the clutch pedal with the spring clip.

3. Tighten the cylinder-to-cowl nuts to 13 ft. lbs.

4. Connect the hydraulic line to the master cylinder and torque it to 13 ft. lbs.

5. Fill the clutch master cylinder with the recommended fluid, and bleed the system.

Clutch Slave Cylinder

NOTE: *Prior to any vehicle service that requires removal of the slave cylinder, the master cylinder pushrod must be disconnected from the clutch pedal. If it is not disconnected, permanent damage to the slave cylinder will occur if the clutch pedal is depressed while the slave cylinder is disconnected.*

REMOVAL

1. Disconnect the hydraulic line at the slave cylinder.

2. Remove the slave cylinder-to-bracket bolts, and remove the slave cylinder.

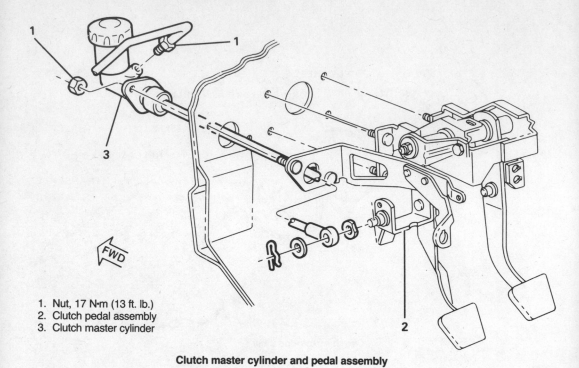

1. Nut, 17 N·m (13 ft. lb.)
2. Clutch pedal assembly
3. Clutch master cylinder

Clutch master cylinder and pedal assembly

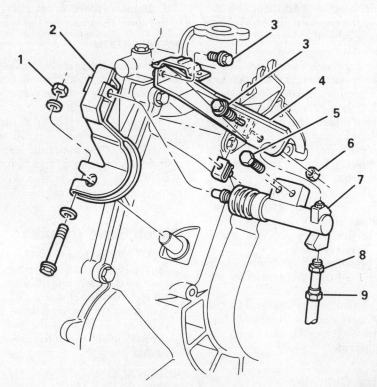

1. Nut, 38 N·m (28 ft. lb.)
2. Clutch lever
3. Bolt—50 N·m (32 ft. lb.)

4. Bracket
5. Bolt—27 N·m (20 ft. lb.)
6. Nut—22 N·m (16 ft. lb.)

7. Slave cylinder
8. Nut—17 N·m (13 ft. lb.)
9. Pipe & hose assembly

Clutch slave cylinder mounting

INSTALLATION

1. Place the slave cylinder at the mounting bracket and position the cylinder pushrod into the clutch release lever.
2. Install the slave cylinder-to-bracket nuts and tighten them to 16 ft. lbs.
3. Install the hydraulic line to the slave cylinder and tighten it to 13 ft. lbs.
4. Fill the clutch master cylinder with the recommended fluid and bleed the system.

Bleeding the Clutch System

NOTE: *It is extremely important that cleanliness be maintained throughout the bleeding operation.*

1. Fill the reservoir directly from an unused can of Delco Supreme No. 11 brake fluid or an equivalent brand fluid conforming to DOT 3 specifications.

NOTE: *Never use fluid which has been bled from a system to fill the reservoir as it may be aerated or contain moisture, or possibly be contaminated.*

Also, during the bleeding operation, never let the fluid level in the reservoir fall to a point where air may be admitted to the hydraulic system.

2. Unscrew the bleed screw at the slave cylinder enough (usually a half turn) to allow fluid to be pumped out.
3. Push the pedal all the way down one full stroke, followed by three sort rapid strokes.
4. Allow the pedal to return quickly to its stop by removing your foot from the pedal.
5. Repeat the above procedure until all air is dispelled at the bleedscrew.
6. Close the bleed screw immediately after the last downward stroke of the pedal, when air bubbles no longer appear.

AUTOMATIC TRANSAXLE

NOTE: *For automatic transaxle oil pan, filter, and fluid removal and installation procedures, please refer to Fluids and Lubricants in Chapter One.*

For removal and installation of the automatic transaxle assembly please refer to Transaxles above.

MANUAL LINKAGE ADJUSTMENT

The transaxle manual linkage must be adjusted so that the indicator quadrant and stops correspond with the transaxle detent. If the linkage is not adjusted properly, an internal leak could occur which could cause a clutch or band slip.

CAUTION: *If a manual linkage adjustment is made with the selector lever in the PARK position, the parking pawl should freely engage the reaction internal gear to prevent the car from rolling. Transmission, vehicle or personal injury may occur if adjustment is not properly made.*

TRANSMISSION CONTROL CABLE ADJUSTMENT

1. Place the shift lever in the N (neutral) position.

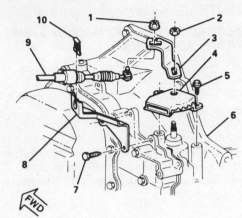

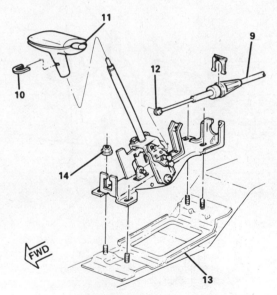

1. Nut/cable assy.
2. Nut/shifting lever
3. Lever/shifting
4. Switch/neutral start and back-up
5. Bolt/neutral start switch (2)
6. Transaxle
7. Bolt/bracket
8. Bracket
9. Cable assy.
10. Retainer assy.
11. T handle
12. Snap securely onto pin
13. Gear shift support
14. Nut 23 N·m (17 ft. lb.)

Transaxle controls, cable attachment and neutral switch

2. Place the transmission lever in the N (neutral) position. Obtain the neutral position by rotating the transmission lever clockwise from PARK through R into N (neutral).

3. Insert the threaded pin (part of the shift cable assembly) upward through the slotted hole in the lever and hand start the nut. The lever must be held out of PARK when torquing the nut. Torque the nut to 15-25 ft. lbs.

NOTE: *Do not use impact type tools.*

NEUTRAL SAFETY AND BACKUP LAMP SWITCH ADJUSTMENT

1. Place the transmission shifter in the NEUTRAL position.

2. Loosen the bolts attaching the switch to the transmission case.

3. Insert a 2.34mm dia. gauge pin (or rounded shank of a 3/32 in. drill bit) into the service adjustment hole. Rotate the switch until the gauge pin drops to a depth of 9mm.

4. Tighten the attaching bolts and remove the gauge pin.

THROTTLE VALVE CABLE ADJUSTMENT

1. After installation of the cable to the transmission, engine bracket, and throttle lever, check to ensure that the cable slider is in the zero or fully adjusted position. If not, please refer to the readjustment procedure, below.

2. Rotate the throttle lever to the "full travel stop" position.

3. The slider must move (ratchet) toward the idler lever when the idler lever is rotated to the full travel stop position.

READJUSTMENT PROCEDURE

In case adjustment is necessary because of inadvertent adjustment before or during assembly, perform the following:

1. Depress and hold the metal readjust tab.

2. Move the slider back through the fitting in the direction away from the throttle lever until the slider stops against the fitting.

3. Release the metal readjust tab.

4. Rotate the throttle lever to the "full travel stop" position.

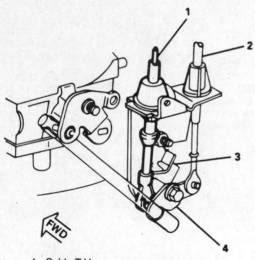

1. Cable T.V.
2. Cable accelerator
3. Lever throttle idler "at full travel stop"
4. Lever throttle idler

TV cable adjustment

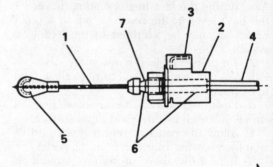

READJUSTMENT DIRECTION

1. To throttle idler
2. Fitting
3. Tab readjustment
4. Cable
5. Terminal
6. Slider
7. Slider against fitting zero or readjust position

TV cable readjustment

FRONT SUSPENSION

Springs/Lower Control Arm

REMOVAL

1. Raise the vehicle and safely support it with jackstands under the crossmember.

2. Remove the front wheels.

3. Disconnect the stabilizer bar from the lower control arm.

4. Disconnect the tie rod from the steering knuckle.

5. Disconnect the shock absorber at the lower control arm.

6. Support the lower control arm with a jack.

7. Remove the nut from the lower ball joint, then use tool J-26407 or its equivalent to press the ball joint out of the knuckle.

8. Swing the knuckle and hub out of the way.

9. Loosen the lower control arm pivot bolts.

10. Install a chain through the coil spring as a safety precaution.

CAUTION: *The coil spring is under load and could result in personal injury if it is released too quickly. Be sure to install a chain and slowly lower the jack.*

11. Slowly lower the jack and remove the spring.

12. Remove the pivot bolts at the chassis and the crossmember and remove the lower control arm.

NOTE: *Removal of the pivot bolt at the crossmember may require the loosing or removal of the steering assembly mounting bolts.*

INSTALLATION

1. Install the lower control arm and pivot bolts at the crossmember and body. Tighten slightly, but do not torque the bolts.

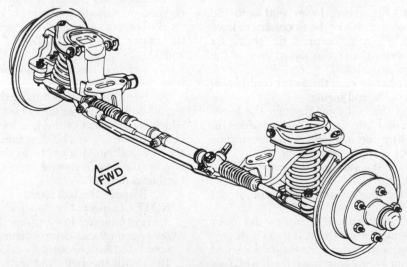

FWD

Front suspension

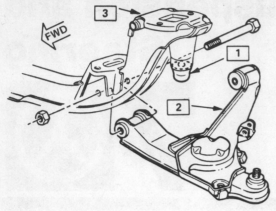

1. Bumper
2. Arm asm. frt. lower cont.
3. Frt. crossmember asm.

Lower control arm

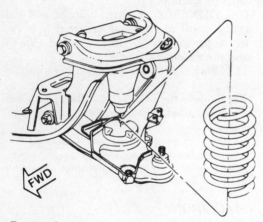

Front spring

2. Position the spring into the upper pocket. Align the spring bottom with the lower control arm pocket.

3. Install the spring lower end onto the lower control arm. It may be necessary to have an assistant help you compress the spring far enough to slide it over the raised area of the lower control arm seat.

4. Use a jack to raise the lower control arm and compress the coil spring.

5. Install the ball joint through the lower control arm and into the steering knuckle. Install the nut on the ball joint stud, and torque it to 55 ft. lbs. Install a new cotter pin.

6. Connect the stabilizer bar and torque the bolt to 16 ft. lbs.

7. Connect the tie rod and torque it to 29 ft. lbs.

8. Install the shock absorber on the lower control arm and torque the bolt to 35 ft. lbs.

9. If the bolts were removed or loosened at the steering assembly, replace them with new bolts and torque them to 21 ft. lbs.

10. With the car on the ground and the suspension system in its normal standing height, torque the bolt between the lower control arm and the body to 62 ft. lbs. and the lower control arm-to-crossmember nut to 52 ft. lbs.

11. The alignment should be checked and set as necessary.

Shock Absorber
REMOVAL AND INSTALLATION

1. Raise the vehicle and support it safely.
2. Remove the wheel and tire assembly.
3. Remove the two upper retaining bolts.
4. Remove the nut and bolt from the lower end of the shock absorber and remove the shock absorber from the vehicle.
5. To install, place the lower portion of the shock into position and hand tighten the nut and bolt.
6. Extend the shock up into the shock absorber support and torque both bolts to 20 ft. lbs.
7. Torque the lower nut and bolt to 20 ft. lbs.
8. Replace the wheel and tire assembly.

Ball Joints
REMOVAL AND INSTALLATION
Upper

1. Raise the vehicle and support it safely.
2. Remove the tire and wheel assembly.
3. Support the lower control arm with a floor jack.
4. Remove the upper ball stud nut, then install the nut finger tight.
5. Install tool J-26407 or equivalent with the cup end over the lower ball stud nut.
6. Turn the threaded end of the tool until the upper ball stud is free of the steering knuckle.
7. Remove the tool and remove the nut from the ball stud.
8. Remove the two nuts and bolts attaching the ball joint to the upper control arm. Note which way the flat of the ball joint is pointing before removing it. The direction of the flat on the new ball joint should be in the same direction as the one removed unless a change in camber is desired.
9. Remove the ball joint.
NOTE: *Inspect the tapered hole in the steering knuckle. Remove any dirt and if any out-of-roundness, deformation, or damage is noted, the knuckle must be replaced.*
10. Install the bolts and nuts attaching the ball joint to the upper control arm and torque

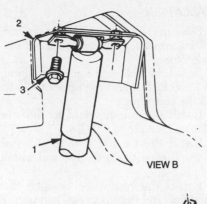

VIEW B

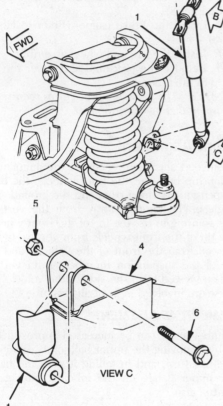

VIEW C

1. Shock absorber
2. Support shock absorber
3. Bolt
4. Control arm
5. Nut
6. Bolt

Shock absorber assembly

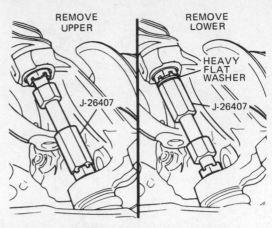

Removal of the ball joints from the knuckle

Lower

The lower ball joint is welded to the lower control arm and cannot be serviced separately. Replacement of the entire lower control arm will be necessary if the lower ball joint requires replacement. Refer to the Front Spring/Lower Control Arm Removal and Installation procedure.

Upper Control Arm

REMOVAL

1. Raise the vehicle and support it on jack-stands.
2. Remove the tire and wheel assembly.
3. Remove the rivet holding the brake line clip to the upper control arm.
4. Support the lower control arm with a floor jack.
5. Remove the upper ball joint from the steering knuckle, as described earlier.
6. Remove the control arm pivot bolt and remove the control arm from the vehicle.
7. Transfer the ball joint if not damaged or worn.

INSTALLATION

NOTE: *Washers and shims must be installed as removed unless a change in geometry is desired.*

1. Install the upper control arm and pivot bolt on the vehicle. The inner pivot bolt must be installed with the bolt head toward the front.
2. Install the pivot bolt nut.
3. Position the control arm in a horizontal plane and torque the nut to 66 ft. lbs.

NOTE: *The bolt may turn when torqued to minimum if the nut is not backed up with a wrench. This does not mean the joint is loose.*

4. Install the ball joint on the upper control arm and to the steering knuckle, as described

---

them to 28 ft. lbs., then mate the upper control arm ball stud to the steering knuckle.

11. Install the ball stud nut and torque it to 35 ft. lbs., then turn it $\frac{1}{16}$ of a turn to align it with the cotter pin hole, and install the cotter pin.

12. Install the tire and wheel assembly and lower the vehicle.

NOTE: *The toe adjustment must be checked and adjusted as necessary.*

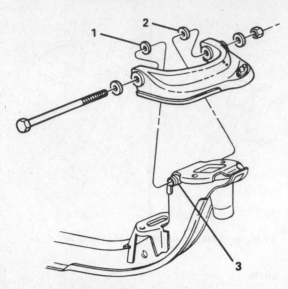

1. Front washer
2. Rear washer
3. Upper control arm support bracket

Upper control arm and shim arrangement

earlier. Install the nut and torque it to 35 ft. lbs. Install a new cotter pin.

5. Install the wheel and tire and lower the vehicle to the floor.

Steering Knuckle

REMOVAL

1. Raise the vehicle on and support it on jackstands under the front crossmember. Support the lower control arm with a floor jack.

CAUTION: *This keeps the coil spring compressed. Use care to support the control arm adequately, or personal injury could result.*

2. Remove the tire and wheel assembly.

3. Remove the disc brake caliper. See Chapter 8. Secure the caliper to the suspension using wire. Do not allow the caliper to hang by the brake hose. Insert a piece of wood between the shoes to hold the piston in the caliper bore. (The block of wood should be about the same thickness as the brake disc.).

4. Remove the hub and disc.

5. Remove the splash shield.

6. Remove both ball stud nuts.

7. Remove the tie rod end from the steering knuckle.

8. Using tool J-26407 or its equivalent, press the upper ball stud from the steering knuckle.

9. Reverse tool J-26407 to the other ball stud nut and press the lower ball stud from the steering knuckle.

10. Remove the ball stud nuts and remove the steering knuckle.

INSTALLATION

1. Place the steering knuckle in position and insert the upper and lower ball studs into the knuckle bosses.

2. Install the ball stud nuts and tighten the lower to 55 ft. lbs. and the upper to 35 ft. lbs. Install the cotter pins.

3. Install the splash shield to the steering knuckle and torque to 7 ft. lbs.

4. Install the tie rod end to the steering knuckle. Torque to 29 ft. lbs. and install the cotter pin.

5. Repack the front wheel bearings then install the hub and disc, bearings and nut. (Refer to Chapter 8).

6. Install the brake caliper.(Refer to Chapter 8).

7. Install the tire and wheel assembly.

8. Remove the jackstand and lower the vehicle to the ground.

NOTE: *The following procedures require the use of alignment equipment.*

Front Alignment

Front end alignment refers to the angular relationship between the front wheels, the front suspension attaching parts and the ground. The angle of the knuckle away from the vertical, the pointing in or "toe-in" of the front wheels, the tilt of the front wheels from vertical (when viewed from the front of the vehicle) and the tilt of the suspension members from vertical (when viewed from the side of the vehicle), all these are involved in front alignment.

CAMBER ADJUSTMENT

Camber angle can be increased approximately 1° by removing the upper ball joint, rotating it one-half turn, and installing it with the flat of the upper flange on the inboard side of the control arm.

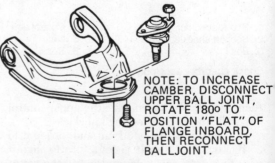

NOTE: TO INCREASE CAMBER, DISCONNECT UPPER BALL JOINT, ROTATE 180° TO POSITION "FLAT" OF FLANGE INBOARD, THEN RECONNECT BALLJOINT.

Front camber adjustment

CASTER ADJUSTMENT

Caster angle can be changed by 1° by changing the position of the washers located between the

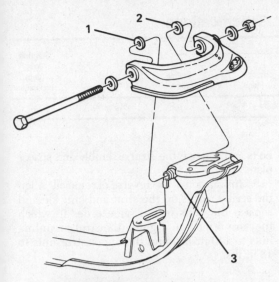

1. Front washer
2. Rear washer
3. Upper control arm support bracket

Front caster adjustment

legs of the upper control arm. Placing the thinner washer in front will increase caster, while placing it at the back will reduce caster.

NOTE: *A kit is available containing two washers, one of 3mm thickness and one of 9mm thickness. Whenever adjusting caster, it is important to always use two washers totaling 12mm thickness, with one washer at each end of locating tube.*

TOE-IN ADJUSTMENT

Toe-in is adjusted by loosening the jam nuts on the toe link rods then rotating the toe link rods to adjust the toe to specifications.

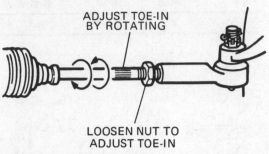

ADJUST TOE-IN
BY ROTATING

LOOSEN NUT TO
ADJUST TOE-IN

Front and rear toe-in adjustment

REAR SUSPENSION

MacPherson Strut
REMOVAL AND INSTALLATION

1. Remove the engine compartment cover.
2. Remove the three upper strut nuts and washers.
3. Loosen the wheel lug nuts.
4. Raise the vehicle and support it on jackstands under the frame members. Support the rear control arm with a floor jack.
5. Remove the wheel and tire.
6. Remove the brake line clip.

1. Strut asm.
2. Toe link rods
3. Spring
4. Rear control arm
5. Drive axles

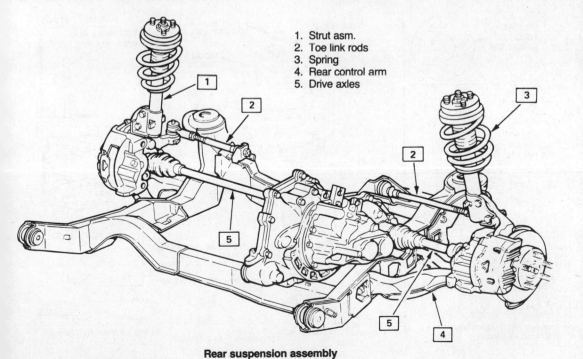

Rear suspension assembly

Wheel Alignment Specifications

Year	Model	Caster		Camber		Toe-In (in.)	Steering Axis (deg) Inclination
		Range (deg)	Pref Setting (deg)	Range (deg)	Pref Setting (deg)		
'84–'85	All	3N-7P	3½P	⁵⁄₁₆N–1⁵⁄₁₆P	³⁄₁₆P	¹⁄₁₆ ± ¹⁄₃₂	—

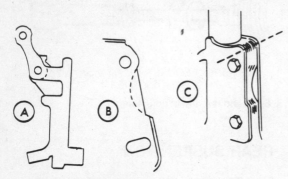

Scribing strut and knuckle

7. Scribe the strut and knuckle.

a. Using a sharp tool, scribe the knuckle along the lower outboard strut radius, as in view A.

b. Scribe the strut flange, on the inboard side, along the curve of the knuckle, as in view B.

c. Make a chisel mark across the strut/knuckle interface, as shown in view C.

8. Remove the two strut mounting nuts and bolts and remove the strut assembly and spacer plate.

9. Installation is the reverse of removal. Align the scribe marks on the strut and knuckle and replace the bolts in the same order in which they are removed. Tighten the strut mounting nuts to 140 ft. lbs. and the upper strut nuts to 18 ft. lbs.

Coil Spring
REMOVAL

NOTE: *A strut compressor, special tool No. J-26584 or its equivalent must be used to disassemble and assemble the strut damper. Care must be used not to damage the special coating on the coil springs or damage could occur to the coils.*

1. Clamp the strut compressor in a vise.

2. Place the strut assembly in the bottom adapter of the compressor and install tool No. J-26584-89 (make sure the adapter captures the spring and the locating pins are engaged).

3. Rotate the strut assembly to align the top

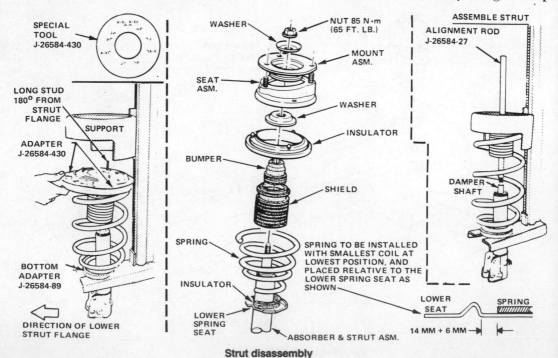

Strut disassembly

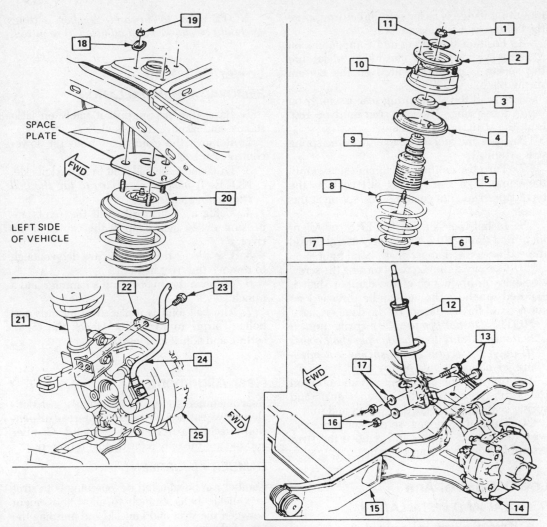

1. Mounting nut
2. Mount assy.
3. Seat washer
4. Upper spring insulator
5. Shield
6. Lower spring insulator
7. Lower spring seat
8. Spring
9. Bumper
10. Seat assy.
11. Upper mount washer
12. Strut assy.
13. Strut mounting bolts
14. Knuckle and hub assy.
15. Cradle assy.
16. Strut mounting nuts
17. Strut lower washers
18. Strut upper washers
19. Strut upper nuts
20. Rear strut mount assy.
21. Strut assy.
22. Brake line clip
23. Brake line clip bolt
24. Rear brake hose
25. Caliper assy.

Removal and installation of the strut assembly

mounting assembly lip with the strut compressor support notch.

4. Insert tool No. 26584-430 top adapter on the top spring seal. Position the top adapters so that the long stud is at high location to the strut flange.

5. Using a ratchet with a 1 inch socket, turn the compressor forcing screw clockwise until the top support flange contacts the tool No. tool J-26584-430 top adapter. Continue turning the screw compressing the strut screw.

6. Place tool No. J-26584-430 top adapter over the spring seat assembly.

7. Turn the strut compressor forcing the screw counterclockwise until the strut spring tension is relieved. Remove the top adapter, bottom adapter, then remove the strut.

INSTALLATION

1. Clamp the strut compressor body in a vise.

2. Place the strut assembly in the bottom adapter of the compressor and install tool No. J-26584-89 (make sure the adapter captures the spring and the locating pins are engaged).

3. Rotate the strut assembly until the

mounting flange is facing out, directly opposite the compressor forcing screw.

4. Position the spring and components on the strut as shown in the illustration. Make sure the spring is properly seated on the bottom spring plate.

5. Install the strut spring seat assembly on top of the spring. The long stud must be 180° from the strut mounting flange.

6. Place the tool top adapter over the spring seat assembly.

7. Turn the compressor forcing screw until the compressor top support just contacts the top adapters (do not compress the spring at this time).

8. Install tool No. J-26584-27 Strut Alignment Rod through the top spring seat and thread the rod onto the damper shaft, hand tight.

9. Compress the screw by turning the screw clockwise until enough of the damper shaft is exposed to where the nut can be threaded securely, and thread the nut on the damper shaft.

NOTE: *Do not compress the spring until it bottoms. Be sure that the damper shaft comes through the center of the spring seat opening, or damage could occur.*

10. Remove the alignment rod and position the strut mount over the damper shaft and spring seat studs. Install the washer and nut.

11. Turn the forcing screw counterclockwise to back off support and remove the strut assembly from the compressor.

Lower Control Arm

REMOVAL AND INSTALLATION

1. Raise the car and support it safely on jackstands.

2. Remove the ball joint clamping bolt.

3. Separate the knuckle from the ball joint.

4. Remove the lower control arm pivot bolts at the frame and remove the control arm.

5. Installation is the reverse of removal.

NOTE: *The toe-in and camber settings should be checked and adjusted as required.*

Lower Ball Joint

REMOVAL AND INSTALLATION

1. Raise the car, support it safely on jackstands, and remove the wheel.

2. Remove the clamp bolt from the lower control arm ball stud.

3. Disconnect the ball joint from the knuckle. NOTE: *It may be necessary to tap the ball stud with a mallet.*

4. Using a ⅛ in. drill, drill the rivets approximately ¼ inch deep in the center of the rivet.

5. Use a ½ in. drill and drill just deep enough to remove the rivet head.

6. Remove the rivets using a hammer and a punch.

7. The ball joint is replaced using nuts and bolts. Torque to 13 ft. lbs. Check the toe-in setting and adjust as necessary.

Rear Alignment

Rear alignment refers to the angular relationship between the rear wheels, the rear suspension attaching parts and the ground. Camber and toe are the only adjustments required.

CAMBER ADJUSTMENT

Camber can be adjusted by loosening both strut to knuckle bolts enough to allow movement between the strut and knuckle and grasping the top of the tire and moving it inboard or outboard until the correct camber is obtained.

TOE ADJUSTMENT

Toe-in is adjusted by loosening the jam nuts on the toe link rods then rotating the toe link rods to adjust the toe to specifications.

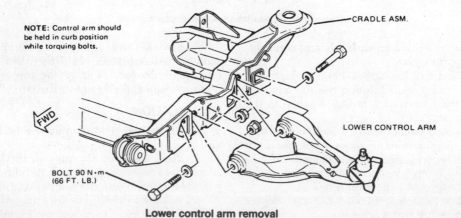

NOTE: Control arm should be held in curb position while torquing bolts.

CRADLE ASM.

FWD

LOWER CONTROL ARM

BOLT 90 N·m (66 FT. LB.)

Lower control arm removal

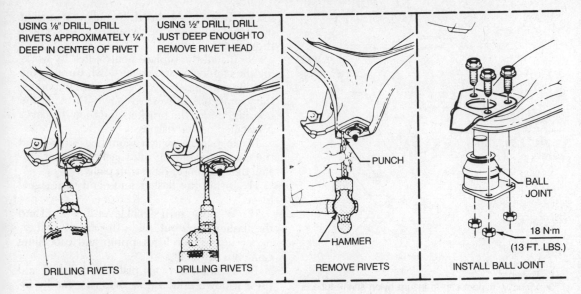

USING ⅛" DRILL, DRILL RIVETS APPROXIMATELY ¼" DEEP IN CENTER OF RIVET

DRILLING RIVETS

USING ½" DRILL, DRILL JUST DEEP ENOUGH TO REMOVE RIVET HEAD

DRILLING RIVETS

PUNCH

HAMMER

REMOVE RIVETS

BALL JOINT

18 N·m
(13 FT. LBS.)

INSTALL BALL JOINT

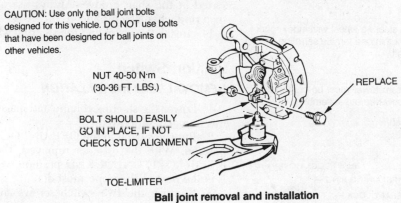

CAUTION: Use only the ball joint bolts designed for this vehicle. DO NOT use bolts that have been designed for ball joints on other vehicles.

NUT 40-50 N·m
(30-36 FT. LBS.)

REPLACE

BOLT SHOULD EASILY GO IN PLACE, IF NOT CHECK STUD ALIGNMENT

TOE-LIMITER

Ball joint removal and installation

STEERING

Steering Wheel

REMOVAL AND INSTALLATION

1. Pry off the center cap and remove the retainer clip and nut.

2. Remove the steering wheel using a steering wheel puller.

3. When installing, align the index mark on the steering wheel with the index mark on the steering shaft. Torque the retaining nut to 35 ft. lbs.

CAUTION: *The cancelling cam tower must be centered in the slot of the lock plate cover before assembling the wheel.*

Turn Signal Switch

REMOVAL AND INSTALLATION

1. Remove the steering wheel and trim cover.

2. Pry the cover from the steering column.

3. Position a U-shaped lockplate compressing tool on the end of the steering shaft and compress the lockplate by turning the shaft nut clockwise. Pry the wire snap ring out of the shaft groove.

4. Remove the tool and lift the lockplate off the shaft.

5. Slip the cancelling cam, upper bearing preload spring, and thrust washer off the shaft.

6. Remove the turn signal lever. Remove the hazard flasher button retaining screw and remove the button spring and knob.

7. Pull the switch connector out of the mast jacket and tape the upper part to facilitate switch removal. Attach a long piece of wire to the turn signal switch connector. When installing the turn signal switch, feed this wire through the column first, and then use this wire to pull the switch connector into position. On tilt wheels, place the turn signal and shifter housing in the low position and remove the harness cover.

8. Remove the three switch mounting

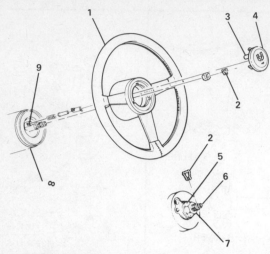

1. Wheel assembly
2. Retainer
3. Visually inspect cap to insure nylon shrink tube is secured to cap
4. Cap assembly
5. Align index mark on steering wheel with index mark on steering shaft within one female serration
6. Steering column shaft
7. 48 N·m (35 ft. lbs.)
8. Steering column
9. Caution: canceling cam tower must be centered in slot of lock plate cover before assembling wheel

Steering wheel removal

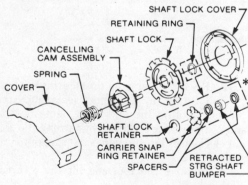

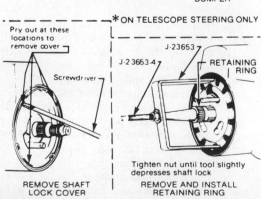

These parts must be removed to remove the turn signal switch

screws. Remove the switch by pulling it straight up while guiding the wiring harness cover through the column.

9. Install the replacement switch by working the connector and cover down through the housing and under the bracket. On tilt models, the connector is worked down through the housing, under the bracket, and then the cover is installed on the harness.

10. Install the switch mounting screws and the connector on the mast jacket bracket. Install the column-to-dash trim plate.

11. Install the flasher knob and turn signal lever.

12. With the turn signal lever in neutral and the flasher knob out, slide the thrust washer, upper bearing preload spring, and cancelling cam onto the shaft.

13. Position the lock plate on the shaft and press it down until a new snap ring can be inserted in the shaft groove. Always use a new snap ring when assembling.

14. Install the cover and the steering wheel.

Ignition Switch
REMOVAL AND INSTALLATION

1. Lower the steering column and make sure it is properly supported.

2. Put the switch in the OFF UNLOCKED position. With the cylinder removed, the rod is in the OFF UNLOCKED position when it is in the next to the uppermost detent.

3. Remove the two switch screws and remove the switch assembly.

4. Before installing, place the new switch in the OFF UNLOCKED position and make sure the lock cylinder and actuating rod are in the OFF UNLOCKED position. (second detent from the top).

5. Install the activating rod into the switch and assemble the switch on the column. Tighten the mounting screws. Use only the specified screws, since over length screws could impair the collapsibilty of the column.

6. Reinstall the steering column.

Ignition Lock Cylinder
REMOVAL AND INSTALLATION

1. Remove the steering wheel.
2. Turn the lock to the RUN position.
3. Remove the lock plate, turn signal switch or combination switch, and the key warning buzzer switch. The warning buzzer switch can be fished out with a bent paper clip.
4. Remove the lock cylinder retaining screw and lock cylinder.

CAUTION: *If the screw is dropped on re-*

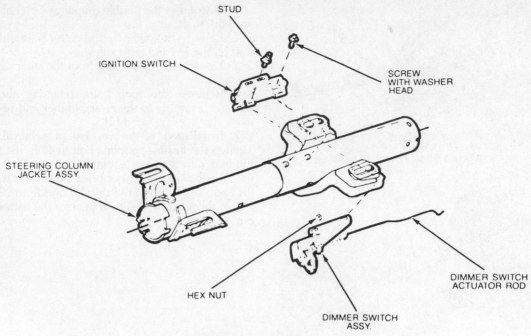

Ignition switch removal

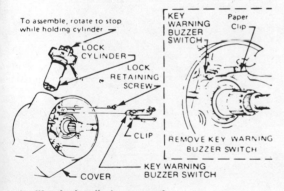

Ignition lock cylinder removal

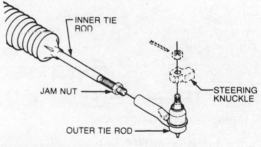

Outer tie-rod end

moval, it could fall into the column, requiring complete disassembly to retrieve the screw.

5. Rotate the cylinder clockwise to align the cylinder key with the keyway in the housing.

6. Push the lock all the way in.

7. Install the screw and tighten to 15 in. lbs.

8. The rest of installation is the reverse of removal. Turn the lock to RUN to install the key warning buzzer switch, which is simply pushed down into place.

Outer Tie Rod
REMOVAL AND INSTALLATION

1. Loosen the jam nut and remove the tie rod from the steering knuckle.

NOTE: *GM recommends a special tool for this procedure. Tool No.J-24319 or BT-7101.*

2. Count the number of threads showing on the tie rod, inboard of the jam nut. This number will be a reference for installing the new tie rod end. Remove the outer tie rod.

3. Install the outer tie rod in the reverse order of removal. Do not tighten the jam nut at this time.

4. Adjust the toe-in by turning the inner tie rod.

5. Make sure the boot is not twisted then torque the jam nut to 50 ft. lbs.

Rack and Pinion Assembly
REMOVAL AND INSTALLATION

1. Raise the vehicle and support it safely.

2. Disconnect both front crossmember braces.

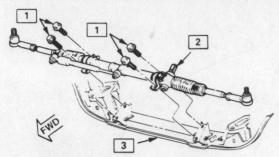

STEERING GEAR TO CROSS MEMBER

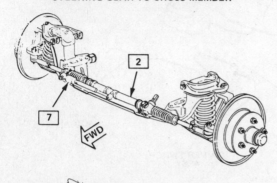

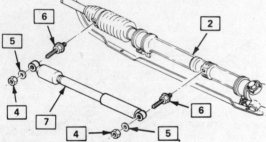

STEERING LINKAGE DAMPER ASM.

1. Bolt 29 N·m (21 ft. lbs.)
2. Steering assembly
3. Cross member
4. Nut 43 N·m (32 ft. lbs.)
5. Washer
6. Stud assembly 48 N·m (36 ft. lbs.)
7. Damper, steering link

Rack and pinion assembly

3. Disconnect the flexible coupling pinch bolt from the shaft.

4. Remove the outer tie rod cotter pins and nuts on the left and right sides.

5. Disconnect the tie rods from the steering knuckle.

6. Remove the four bolts retaining the steering assembly to the crossmember and remove the steering assembly.

7. Installation is the reverse of removal. Tighten the flexible coupling bolt to 46 ft. lbs., the four new steering assembly bolts to 21 ft. lbs., the four crossmember brace bolts to 20 ft. lbs., and the tie rod nut at each knuckle to 29 ft. lbs. followed by a ⅙ turn to align the cotter pin.

HYDRAULIC SYSTEM

Master Cylinder
REMOVAL AND INSTALLATION

1. Place a number of cloths or a container under the master cylinder to catch the brake fluid. Disconnect the brake tubes from the master cylinder, using a flare nut wrench if one is available. Cap the open ends of the tubes.

NOTE: *Brake fluid dissolves paint. Wipe up any spilled fluid immediately, then flush the area with clear water.*

2. Remove the two nuts attaching the master cylinder to the booster or firewall, then remove the master cylinder.

3. To install, position the master cylinder and install the retaining bolts. Torque to 22-30 ft. lbs..

4. Reconnect the fluid tubes and bleed the brake system.

OVERHAUL

1. Remove the reservoir cover and diaphragm and discard any fluid in the reservoir.

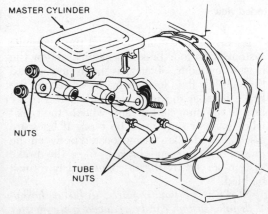

MASTER CYLINDER

NUTS

TUBE
NUTS

Master cylinder mounting

2. Depress the primary piston and remove the lock ring.

3. Direct compressed air into the outlet at the blind end of the bore, and plug the other outlet to remove the primary and secondary pistons.

4. Remove the spring retainer and seals from the secondary piston.

5. Clamp the master cylinder in a vise and use an appropriate prybar to remove the reservoir.

NOTE: *Do not clamp on the master cylinder body. Do not attempt to remove the quick take-up valve from the body. The valve is not serviceable separately.*

6. Remove the reservoir grommets.

7. Inspect the master cylinder bore for corrosion. If the bore is corroded, replace the master cylinder. Do not use any abrasives on the bore.

8. Lubricate the new reservoir grommets with silicone brake lube and press them into the master cylinder body. Make sure the grommets are properly seated.

9. Lay the reservoir upside down on a flat, hard surface. Press the master cylinder body onto the reservoir using a rocking motion.

10. Lubricate new seals with clean brake fluid and install them on the secondary piston. Install the spring retainer.

11. Install the spring and secondary piston assembly into the cylinder.

12. Lubricate the primary piston seals with clean brake fluid. Install the primary piston, depress, and install the lock ring.

13. Fit the diaphragm in the reservoir cover and install on the reservoir.

Combination Valve
REMOVAL AND INSTALLATION

NOTE: *The combination valve is not repairable and must be serviced as a complete assembly.*

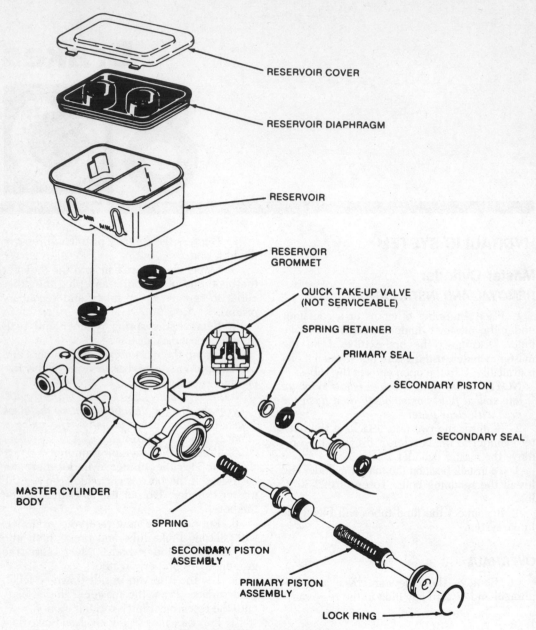

RESERVOIR COVER

RESERVOIR DIAPHRAGM

RESERVOIR

RESERVOIR GROMMET

QUICK TAKE-UP VALVE (NOT SERVICEABLE)

SPRING RETAINER

PRIMARY SEAL

SECONDARY PISTON

SECONDARY SEAL

MASTER CYLINDER BODY

SPRING

SECONDARY PISTON ASSEMBLY

PRIMARY PISTON ASSEMBLY

LOCK RING

Master cylinder - exploded view

1. Disconnect the hydraulic lines at the combination valve and plug the lines to prevent loss of fluid and entrance of dirt.

2. Disconnect the warning switch wiring harness from the valve switch terminal.

3. Remove the combination valve.

4. Installation is the reverse of removal.

5. Bleed the entire brake system.

CAUTION: *Do not move the car until a firm brake pedal is obtained.*

BLEEDING THE BRAKE SYSTEM

It is necessary to bleed the brake system any time air is introduced into the hydraulic system.

It may be necessary to bleed the hydraulic system at all four brakes positions, and/or the master cylinder, if air has been introduced through low fluid level or by disconnecting the brake lines at the master cylinder. If a brake line is disconnected at any wheel, then that wheel caliper only need be bled. If lines are disconnected at any fitting located between the master cylinder and brakes, then the brake system served by the disconnected line must be bled.

NOTE: *The time required to bleed the hydraulic system can be reduced if the master cylinder is filled with fluid and as much air as possible is expelled before the cylinder is*

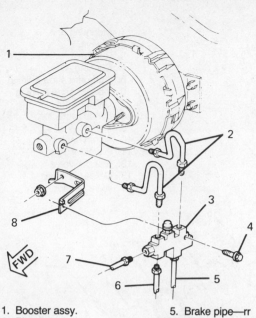

1. Booster assy.
2. Pipe assy.
3. Valve assy.
4. Bolt

5. Brake pipe—rr
6. Pipe assy.—r.h.
7. Pipe assy.—l.h.
8. Bracket

Combination valve to master cylinder mounting

installed on the vehicle. Power brakes require removing the vacuum reserve by applying the brakes several times with the engine off.

1. Fill the master cylinder reservoirs with brake fluid and keep them at least half full of fluid during the bleeding operation.

2. If the master cylinder is known or suspected to have air in the bore, then it must be bled before any caliper in the following matter.

a. Disconnect the forward brake line connection at the master cylinder.

b. Fill the master cylinder bore until fluid begins to flow from the forward line connector port.

c. Connect the forward brake line to the master cylinder and tighten it.

d. Have an assistant depress the brake pedal slowly one time and hold it down. Loosen the forward brake line connection at the master cylinder to purge air from the bore. Tighten the connection and then release the brake pedal slowly. Wait 15 seconds. Repeat the sequence including the 15 minute wait, until air is removed from the bore. Use care as brake fluid dissolves paint.

e. After all air has been removed at the forward connection, bleed the master cylinder at the rear (cowl) connection in the same manner as the front in step d above.

f. If it is known that the calipers do not contain any air, then it will not be necessary to bleed them.

3. Individual calipers are bled only after all air is removed from the master cylinder. Place a proper size box end wrench over the bleeder valve. Attach a transparent tube over the valve and allow the tube to hang submerged in brake fluid in a transparent container. Depress the brake pedal slowly one time and hold. Loosen the bleeder valve to purge the air from the cylinder. Tighten the bleeder screw and slowly release the pedal. Wait 15 seconds and repeat the above sequence including the 15 second wait until all air is removed.

NOTE: *It may be necessary to repeat the sequence 10 or more times until all air is removed from the system. Rapid pumping of the brake pedal pushes the master cylinder secondary piston down the bore in a manner that mkaes it difficult to bleed the rear side of the system.*

4. If it is necessary to bleed all of the calipers, the following sequence should be followed: right rear; left rear; right front; left front.

NOTE: *Check the brake pedal for sponginess and the brake warning light for indication of unbalanced pressure. To correct either of these two conditions repeat the entire bleeding procedure.*

FRONT BRAKES

Pads

INSPECTION

The pad thickness should be inspected every time that the wheels are removed. Pad thickness can be checked by looking down through the inspection hole in the top of the caliper. If the thickness of the pad is worn to within 0.030

Lining inspection

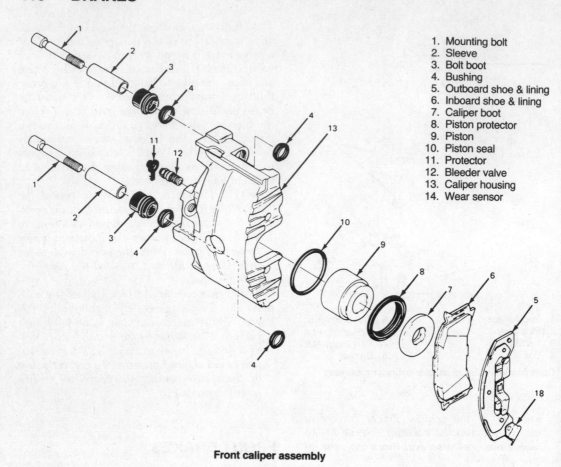

1. Mounting bolt
2. Sleeve
3. Bolt boot
4. Bushing
5. Outboard shoe & lining
6. Inboard shoe & lining
7. Caliper boot
8. Piston protector
9. Piston
10. Piston seal
11. Protector
12. Bleeder valve
13. Caliper housing
14. Wear sensor

Front caliper assembly

in. (0.76mm) of the rivet at either end of the pad, all the pads should be replaced. A thermal material is sandwiched between the lining and backing. Don't include this material when determining the lining thickness. This is the factory recommended measurement. Your state's automobile inspection laws may be different.

NOTE: *Always replace all pads on both front wheels at the same time. Failure to do so will result in uneven braking action and premature wear.*

REMOVAL AND INSTALLATION

1. Siphon ⅔ of the brake fluid from the master cylinder reservoir.

2. Loosen the wheel lug nuts and raise the car. Support the car safely then remove the wheel.

3. Remove the two boots and mounting bolts using a No. 50 Torx wrench.

4. Position 4-inch adjustable pliers over the inboard surface of the caliper housing and caliper support bracket.

5. Squeeze the pliers to compress the piston back into the caliper bore and provide clearance between the linings and rotor.

6. Remove the caliper from the rotor and

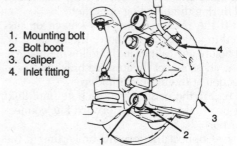

1. Mounting bolt
2. Bolt boot
3. Caliper
4. Inlet fitting

Caliper mounting

suspend with a wire hook from the suspension. Do not allow the caliper to hang by the hose.

7. Remove the shoe and lining assemblies from the caliper. To remove the outboard shoe and lining use a suitable tool to disengage the buttons on the shoe from the holes in the caliper.

8. Remove the sleeves from the mounting bolt holes.

9. Remove the busings from the grooves in the mounting bolt holes.

10. Bottom the piston in the in the caliper bore before installing new linings.

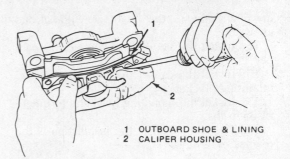

1 OUTBOARD SHOE & LINING
2 CALIPER HOUSING

Removing the outboard shoe

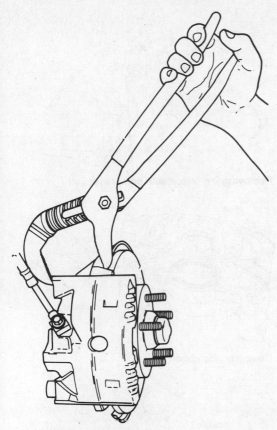

Compressing the piston

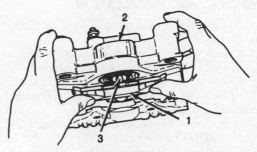

1. INBOARD SHOE & LINING
2. CALIPER HOUSING
3. SHOE RETAINING SPRING

Installing the inboard lining

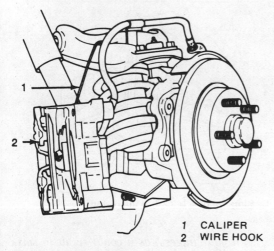

1 CALIPER
2 WIRE HOOK

Suspending the caliper

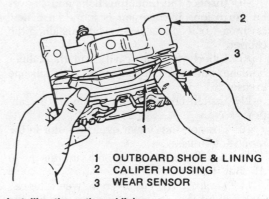

1 OUTBOARD SHOE & LINING
2 CALIPER HOUSING
3 WEAR SENSOR

Installing the outboard lining

11. Use new bushings and sleeves and lubricate with a silcone lubricant.

12. Install the inboard shoe and lining as shown in the illustration.

13. Install the outboard shoe and lining with the wear sensor at the leading edge of the shoe during forward wheel rotation.

14. Liberly fill both cavities in the caliper

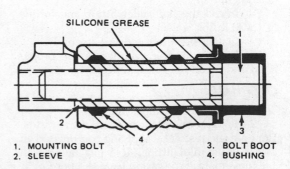

1. MOUNTING BOLT   3. BOLT BOOT
2. SLEEVE   4. BUSHING

Lubricating the caliper cavity

housing between the bushings with silcone grease.

15. Install the sleeves and boots in the caliper.

16. Install the caliper over the rotor in the mounting bracket.

17. Install the mounting bolts and torque to 21-35 ft. lbs.

18. The remainder of the installation is the reverse of removal.

Caliper

REMOVAL AND INSTALLATION

1. Remove ⅔ of the brake fluid from the master cylinder.

2. Jack up the vehicle and support it safely.

3. Remove the wheel and tire assembly.

4. Install two lug nuts to retain the rotor.

5. Remove the bolt attaching the fluid inlet fitting to the caliper.

6. Remove the boots and mounting bolts using a No. 50 Torx wrench.

7. Position a 4-inch adjustable pliers over the inboard surface of the caliper housing and caliper support bracket.

8. Squeeze the pliers to compress the piston back into the caliper bore and provide clearance between the linings and rotor.

9. Inspect the mounting bolts and sleeves for corrosion. If corrosion is found, use new bushings, bolts and sleeves when installing the caliper.

10. Liberly fill both cavities in the caliper housing between the bushings with silicone grease.

11. Install the sleeves and boots in the caliper.

12. Position the caliper over the rotor in the mounting bracket.

13. Install the mounting bolts and torque to 21-35 ft. lbs.

14. Measure the clearance between the caliper and bracket stops and if necessary file the ends of the bracket stops to provide the proper clearance.

15. Install the fluid inlet fitting and torque to 18-30 ft. lbs.

16. Install the wheel and tire assembly.

17. Fill the master cylinder to the proper level and bleed the brake system.

OVERHAUL

1. Remove the caliper and pads.

2. Place some cloths in front of the piston. Remove the piston by applying compressed air to the fluid inlet fitting. Use just enough air pressure to ease the piston from the bore. CAUTION: *Do not try to catch the piston*

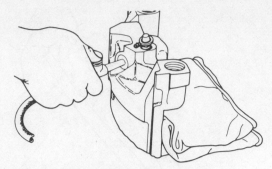

Removing the piston with compressed air

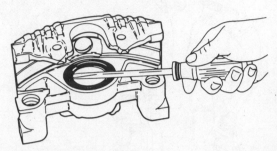

Removing the piston boot

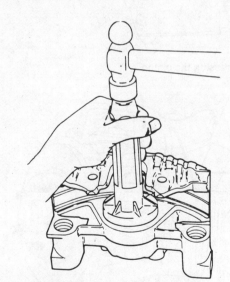

Seating the new boot into the piston

with your fingers, as it could result in serious injury.

3. Remove the piston boot using a suitable prying tool, working carefully so that the piston bore is not scratched.

4. Remove the bleeder screw.

5. Inspect the piston for scoring, nicks, corrosion, wear, etc., and replace the piston if any defects are found.

6. Remove the piston seal from the caliper bore groove using a piece of wood or plastic. Do not use a metal tool as damage to the bore

could result. Very light wear can be cleaned up with a crocus cloth. Use finger pressure to rub the crocus cloth around the circumference of the bore (do not slide it in and out). More extensive wear or corrosion warrants replacement of the part.

7. Clean any parts which are to be reused, in denatured alcohol. Dry them with compressed air or allow them to air dry. Do not wipe the parts dry with a cloth, which will leave behind bits of lint.

8. Lubricate the new seal, provided in the repair kit, with clean brake fluid. Install the seal in its groove, making sure it is fully seated and not twisted.

9. Install the new dust boot on the piston. Lubricate the bore of the caliper with clean brake fluid and insert the piston into its bore. Position the boot in the caliper housing and seat with a seal driver, G.M. tool no. J-2907.

10. Install the bleeder screw, tightening to 80-140 ft. lbs. Do not overtighten.

11. Install the pads , install the caliper and bleed the brake system.

Wheel Hub/Disc and Bearings

NOTE: *This procedure also includes repacking and adjustment of the wheel bearings.*

REMOVAL

1. Raise the vehicle and support it safely with jackstands.

2. Remove the wheel and tire assembly.

3. Remove the brake caliper from the knuckle.

4. Remove the dust cap, cotter pin, spindle nut and washer and remove the hub and bearing.

NOTE: *Do not allow the bearing to fall out of the hub when removing the hub from the spindle.*

5. Remove the outer bearing with your fingers, then remove the inner bearing by prying out the grease seal. Discard the seal.

6. Wash all parts thorough in cleaning solvent.

7. If needed, drive out the old race from the hub with a brass drift inserted behind the race in the notches in the hub.

8. Lubricate the new race with a light film of grease.

9. Start the race squarely into the hub and carefully seat the race using an appropriate tool.

NOTE: *Check the bearings for cracks or pitting. Check the races for scoring or pitting. If it is necessary to replace either the outer or inner bearing, it will be necessary to replace the race for that bearing.*

INSTALLATION

1. Clean off any grease in the hub and spindle and thoroughly clean out any grease in the bearings, using a small brush, with no loose bristles, and cleaning solvent.

2. Use a high temperature front wheel bearing grease.

NOTE: *Do not mix different kinds of greases, as mixing may change the grease properties and result in poor performance.*

3. Apply a thin film of grease to the spindle at the inner and outer bearing seat, shoulder, and seal seat.

4. Put a small quanity of grease inboard of each bearing race in the hub.

5. Fill the bearing cone and roller assemblies 100% full of grease. It is extremely important to work the grease thoroughly into the bearings between the rollers, cone and the cage.

6. Place the inner bearing cone and roller assembly into the hub. Then, using your finger, put an additional quanity of grease outboard of the bearing.

7. Install a new grease seal using a flat plate until the seal is flush with the hub. Lubricate the seal lip with a thin layer of grease.

8. Carefully install the hub and rotor assembly.

9. Place the outer bearing cone and roller assembly in the outer bearing race. Install the washer and nut. Draw up the spindle nut. Do not overtighten.

10. Install the brake caliper then install the wheel and tire.

11. Tighten the spindle nut to 12 ft. lbs. while turning the wheel assembly forward by hand to fully seat the bearings.

12. Back off the nut to the just-loose position. Tighten the spindle nut by hand, then loosen until either hole in the spindle lines up with a slot in the nut (Not more than ½ flat). Install a new cotter pin and bend the ends of the cotter pin against the nut. Cut off any extra length to ensure that the ends will not interfere with the dust cap.

13. Lower the vehicle to the floor.

REAR BRAKES

Pads

INSPECTION

Inspection of the rear disc brakes is the same as for the front disc brakes. Please refer to that section.

REMOVAL

1. Remove ⅔ of the brake fluid from the master cylinder assembly.

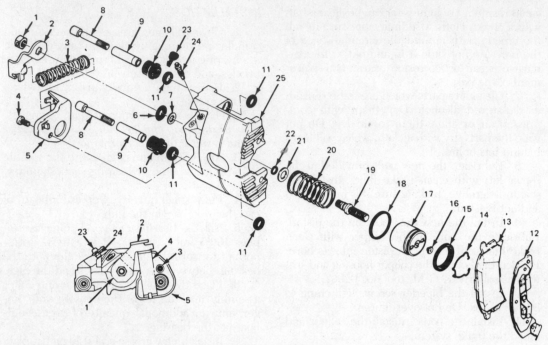

Rear caliper exploded view

2. Jack up the vehicle and support it safely with jackstands.

3. Remove the wheel and tire assembly then install two lug nuts to retain the rotor.

4. Loosen the tension on the parking brake cable at the equalizer.

   a. Remove the cable and spring from the lever.

   b. Remove the lock nut while holding the lever.

   c. Remove the lever, lever seal and anti-friction washer.

5. Remove the caliper mounting bolts with a No. 50 Torx® wrench.

6. Position 4-inch adjustable pliers over the inboard surface of the caliper housing and outboard surface of the mounting bracket.

7. Squeeze the pliers to compress the piston back into the caliper bore and provide clearance between the lining and the rotor.

8. Remove the caliper from the rotor and mounting bracket and support it to prevent strain on the brake hose.

9. Use a suitable tool and disengage the shoe

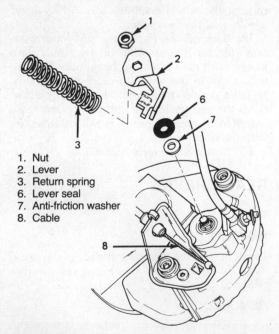

1. Nut
2. Lever
3. Return spring
6. Lever seal
7. Anti-friction washer
8. Cable

Parking brake lever attachment

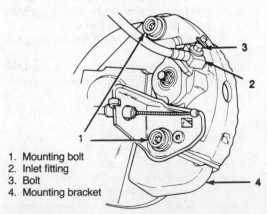

1. Mounting bolt
2. Inlet fitting
3. Bolt
4. Mounting bracket

Caliper mounting

buttons from the holes in the caliper and remove the shoe and lining assemblies.

10. Remove the sleeves from the mounting bolt holes.

11. Remove the boots and bushings from the caliper.

12. Remove the flexible two-way check valve from the end of the piston, using a suitable tool.

INSTALLATION

1. Bottom the piston in the cylinder bore.

2. Use new bushings, boots and sleeves in the mounting bolt holes and lubricate these parts with a silicone grease.

3. Use a new two-way check valve and press into the end of the piston.

4. Install the inboard shoe and lining into the caliper and make sure that the D-shaped tabs on the shoe will engage with the D-shape notches in the piston. Also make sure the wear sensor is at the leading edge of the shoe during forward wheel rotation. Slide the edge of the inboard metal shoe under the edge of the dampening spring and snap the shoe into position against the piston.

NOTE: *If the D-shaped tabs and notches do not line up, the piston will have to be turned. Pontiac recommends the use of Tool No. J-7624 or its equivalent to turn the piston.*

5. Install the outboard shoe and lining and make sure the ends of the spring on the outboard shoe snap into the caliper recesses.

6. Position the caliper over the rotor mounting bracket and tighten the mounting bolts to 30–45 ft. lbs.

7. Install the parking brake cable lever anti-friction washer and lever seal and lubricate the lever seal with silicone brake lube.

8. Install the lever on the actuator screw with the lever pointing in the direction shown in the illustration.

9. Make sure the lever stays properly in-

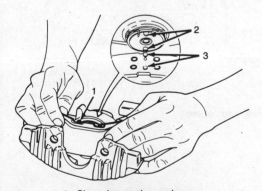

1. Shoe dampening spring
2. D-shaped notch in piston
3. D-shaped tab on shoe

Inboard shoe and retainer

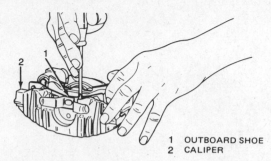

1 OUTBOARD SHOE
2 CALIPER

Outboard shoe spring

stalled on the actuator screw then torque the nut to 30–40 ft. lbs.

10. Rotate the lever back against the stop on the caliper and install the spring.

11. Install the parking brake cable . Tighten the cable at the equalizer until the lever starts to move off the stop on the caliper. Loosen the adjustment until the lever moves back against the stop.

12. Install the wheel and tire assembly.

13. Fill the master cylinder and check the operation of the brake pedal.

Caliper
REMOVAL

1. Follow Steps 1,2,3 and 4 of the pad removal procedure.

2. Remove the bolt holding the brake hose to the caliper then follow Steps 5-8 of the of the pad removal procedure.

INSTALLATION

1. Refer to the pad installation procedure to install the caliper.

2. Liberally fill both cavities in the caliper housing, between the bushings, with silicone grease.

3. Torque the mounting bolts to 30–45 ft. lbs.

4. When installing the brake hose fitting use two new copper washers, then torque the bolt to 30 ft. lbs.

5. Bleed the brake system. Refer to the bleeding procedure outlined earlier.

PARKING BRAKE
Cable
REMOVAL AND INSTALLATION
Front

1. Jack up the vehicle and support it safely with jackstands.

2. Loosen the adjusting nut at the equalizer and separate the cables.

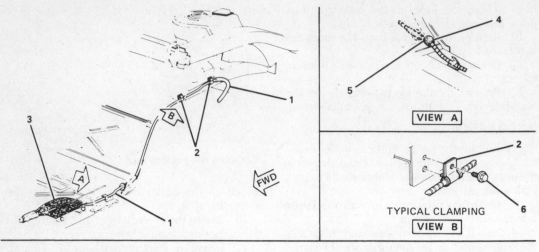

VIEW A

TYPICAL CLAMPING
VIEW B

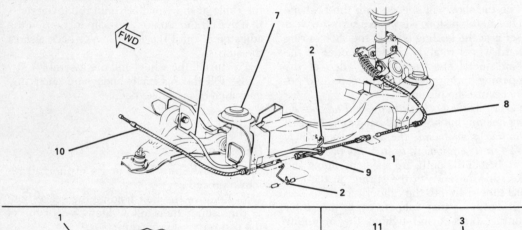

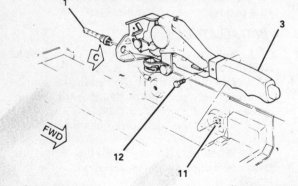

VIEW C

1. Cable assy., front
2. Clip
3. Lever assy.
4. Grommet (cable assy., front)

5. Hose in floor pan
6. Bolt
7. Frame assy.
8. Cable assy., rh

9. Equalizer
10. Cable assy., lh
11. Weld nut
12. Bolt/screw

Parking brake lever assembly and cables

Brake Specifications
(All specifications in inches (in.) unless noted)

Year	Model	Wheel Lug Nut Torque (ft. lbs.)	Brake Disc			Master Cyl. Bore	Wheel Cyl. or Caliper Bore	
			Original Thickness	Minimum Thickness	Maximum Run-out		F	R
'84–'85	All	100	—	.390	.004	1.00	—	—

NOTE: Minimum lining thickness is $\frac{1}{32}$ in. of lining thickness remaining above rivet head (riveted linings) or $\frac{2}{32}$ in. of lining remaining over backing plate (bonded linings). Minimum lining thickness may differ due to variation in local inspection codes.

3. Remove the clip from the cable.

4. Remove the two retaining clip bolts in the left wheel well.

5. Lower the vehicle then unsnap the clip holding the parking brake boot to the lever.

6. Remove the seat belt bolt and carpeting finishing molding.

7. Remove the shoulder harness retaining bolt.

8. Remove the quarter trim finishing molding.

9. Pull the carpet back and note how the cable is routed.

10. Remove the cable from the parking brake lever and push it through the body.

11. Installation is the reverse of removal.

Rear

1. Jack up the vehicle and support it safely with jackstands.

2. Loosen the adjusting nut at the equalizer and separate the cables.

3. Remove the cables at the calipers.

4. Disconnect the cables at the cradle. Pontiac recommends using tool No. J-34065 for this step.

5. Installation is the reverse of removal. Adjust the parking brake.

Parking Brake Adjustment

Adjustment of the parking brake is necessary anytime the rear brake cables have been disconnected or if the hydraulic system operates with good reserve, but the parking brake hand lever travel is more than 9 ratchet clicks.

1. Place the parking barke hand lever in the fully released position.

2. Raise the rear wheels off the floor and support it safely with jackstands.

3. Apply lubricant to the groove in the equalizer nut.

4. Hold the brake cable stud from turning and tighten the equalizer nut until cable slack is removed.

NOTE: *Make sure the caliper levers are against the stops on the caliper housing after tightening the equalizer nut. If the levers are off the stops, loosen the cable until the levers do return to the stops.*

5. Operate the parking brake lever several times to check the adjustment. If the parking brake shoes and cable are properly adjusted, the parking brake handle will move five to eight notches when a force is applied perpendicularly at the mid-point of the handle grip.

NOTE: *The levers must be on the caliper stops after completion of adjustment. If necessary, back off the parking brake adjuster to keep the levers on the stops.*

Troubleshooting

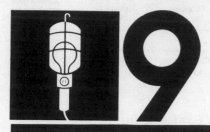

9

This section is designed to aid in the quick, accurate diagnosis of automotive problems. While automotive repairs can be made by many people, accurate troubleshooting is a rare skill for the amateur and professional alike.

In its simplest state, troubleshooting is an exercise in logic. It is essential to realize that an automobile is really composed of a series of systems. Some of these systems are interrelated; others are not. Automobiles operate within a framework of logical rules and physical laws, and the key to troubleshooting is a good understanding of all the automotive systems.

This section breaks the car or truck down into its component systems, allowing the problem to be isolated. The charts and diagnostic road maps list the most common problems and the most probable causes of trouble. Obviously it would be impossible to list every possible problem that could happen along with every possible cause, but it will locate MOST problems and eliminate a lot of unnecessary guesswork. The systematic format will locate problems within a given system, but, because many automotive systems are interrelated, the solution to your particular problem may be found in a number of systems on the car or truck.

USING THE TROUBLESHOOTING CHARTS

This book contains all of the specific information that the average do-it-yourself mechanic needs to repair and maintain his or her car or truck. The troubleshooting charts are designed to be used in conjunction with the specific procedures and information in the text. For instance, troubleshooting a point-type ignition system is fairly standard for all models, but you may be directed to the text to find procedures for troubleshooting an individual type of electronic ignition. You will also have to refer to the specification charts throughout the book for specifications applicable to your car or truck.

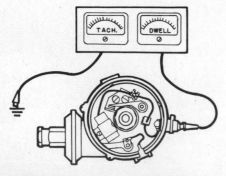

Tach-dwell hooked-up to distributor

TOOLS AND EQUIPMENT

The tools illustrated in Chapter 1 (plus two more diagnostic pieces) will be adequate to troubleshoot most problems. The two other tools needed are a voltmeter and an ohmmeter. These can be purchased separately or in combination, known as a VOM meter.

In the event that other tools are required, they will be noted in the procedures.

Troubleshooting Engine Problems

See Chapters 2, 3, 4 for more information and service procedures.

Index to Systems

System	To Test	Group
Battery	Engine need not be running	1
Starting system	Engine need not be running	2
Primary electrical system	Engine need not be running	3
Secondary electrical system	Engine need not be running	4
Fuel system	Engine need not be running	5
Engine compression	Engine need not be running	6
Engine vacuum	Engine must be running	7
Secondary electrical system	Engine must be running	8
Valve train	Engine must be running	9
Exhaust system	Engine must be running	10
Cooling system	Engine must be running	11
Engine lubrication	Engine must be running	12

Index to Problems

Problem: Symptom	Begin at Specific Diagnosis, Number
Engine Won't Start:	
Starter doesn't turn	1.1, 2.1
Starter turns, engine doesn't	2.1
Starter turns engine very slowly	1.1, 2.4
Starter turns engine normally	3.1, 4.1
Starter turns engine very quickly	6.1
Engine fires intermittently	4.1
Engine fires consistently	5.1, 6.1
Engine Runs Poorly:	
Hard starting	3.1, 4.1, 5.1, 8.1
Rough idle	4.1, 5.1, 8.1
Stalling	3.1, 4.1, 5.1, 8.1
Engine dies at high speeds	4.1, 5.1
Hesitation (on acceleration from standing stop)	5.1, 8.1
Poor pickup	4.1, 5.1, 8.1
Lack of power	3.1, 4.1, 5.1, 8.1
Backfire through the carburetor	4.1, 8.1, 9.1
Backfire through the exhaust	4.1, 8.1, 9.1
Blue exhaust gases	6.1, 7.1
Black exhaust gases	5.1
Running on (after the ignition is shut off)	3.1, 8.1
Susceptible to moisture	4.1
Engine misfires under load	4.1, 7.1, 8.4, 9.1
Engine misfires at speed	4.1, 8.4
Engine misfires at idle	3.1, 4.1, 5.1, 7.1, 8.4

Sample Section

Test and Procedure	Results and Indications	Proceed to
4.1—Check for spark: Hold each spark plug wire approximately ¼″ from ground with gloves or a heavy, dry rag. Crank the engine and observe the spark.	If no spark is evident:	4.2
	If spark is good in some cases:	4.3
	If spark is good in all cases:	4.6

Specific Diagnosis

This section is arranged so that following each test, instructions are given to proceed to another, until a problem is diagnosed.

Section 1—Battery

Test and Procedure	Results and Indications	Proceed to
1.1—Inspect the battery visually for case condition (corrosion, cracks) and water level.	If case is cracked, replace battery:	1.4
	If the case is intact, remove corrosion with a solution of baking soda and water (**CAUTION**: *do not get the solution into the battery*), and fill with water:	1.2

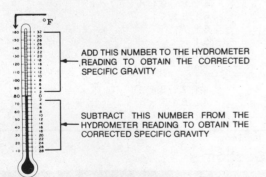

DIRT ON TOP OF BATTERY   PLUGGED VENT
CORROSION
LOOSE CABLE OR POSTS
CRACKS
LOW WATER LEVEL

Inspect the battery case

Test and Procedure	Results and Indications	Proceed to
1.2—Check the battery cable connections: Insert a screwdriver between the battery post and the cable clamp. Turn the headlights on high beam, and observe them as the screwdriver is gently twisted to ensure good metal to metal contact.	If the lights brighten, remove and clean the clamp and post; coat the post with petroleum jelly, install and tighten the clamp:	1.4
	If no improvement is noted:	1.3

TESTING BATTERY CABLE CONNECTIONS USING A SCREWDRIVER

Test and Procedure	Results and Indications	Proceed to
1.3—Test the state of charge of the battery using an individual cell tester or hydrometer.	If indicated, charge the battery. **NOTE:** *If no obvious reason exists for the low state of charge (i.e., battery age, prolonged storage)*, proceed to:	1.4

°F

ADD THIS NUMBER TO THE HYDROMETER READING TO OBTAIN THE CORRECTED SPECIFIC GRAVITY

SUBTRACT THIS NUMBER FROM THE HYDROMETER READING TO OBTAIN THE CORRECTED SPECIFIC GRAVITY

Specific Gravity (@ 80° F.)

Minimum	Battery Charge
1.260	100% Charged
1.230	75% Charged
1.200	50% Charged
1.170	25% Charged
1.140	Very Little Power Left
1.110	Completely Discharged

The effects of temperature on battery specific gravity (left) and amount of battery charge in relation to specific gravity (right)

Test and Procedure	Results and Indications	Proceed to
1.4—Visually inspect battery cables for cracking, bad connection to ground, or bad connection to starter.	If necessary, tighten connections or replace the cables:	2.1

Section 2—Starting System
See Chapter 3 for service procedures

Test and Procedure	Results and Indications	Proceed to
Note: Tests in Group 2 are performed with coil high tension lead disconnected to prevent accidental starting.		
2.1—Test the starter motor and solenoid: Connect a jumper from the battery post of the solenoid (or relay) to the starter post of the solenoid (or relay).	If starter turns the engine normally:	2.2
	If the starter buzzes, or turns the engine very slowly:	2.4
	If no response, replace the solenoid (or relay).	3.1
	If the starter turns, but the engine doesn't, ensure that the flywheel ring gear is intact. If the gear is undamaged, replace the starter drive.	3.1
2.2—Determine whether ignition override switches are functioning properly (clutch start switch, neutral safety switch), by connecting a jumper across the switch(es), and turning the ignition switch to "start".	If starter operates, adjust or replace switch:	3.1
	If the starter doesn't operate:	2.3
2.3—Check the ignition switch "start" position: Connect a 12V test lamp or voltmeter between the starter post of the solenoid (or relay) and ground. Turn the ignition switch to the "start" position, and jiggle the key.	If the lamp doesn't light or the meter needle doesn't move when the switch is turned, check the ignition switch for loose connections, cracked insulation, or broken wires. Repair or replace as necessary:	3.1
	If the lamp flickers or needle moves when the key is jiggled, replace the ignition switch.	3.3

Checking the ignition switch "start" position

STARTER RELAY (IF EQUIPPED)

Test and Procedure	Results and Indications	Proceed to
2.4—Remove and bench test the starter, according to specifications in the engine electrical section.	If the starter does not meet specifications, repair or replace as needed:	3.1
	If the starter is operating properly:	2.5
2.5—Determine whether the engine can turn freely: Remove the spark plugs, and check for water in the cylinders. Check for water on the dipstick, or oil in the radiator. Attempt to turn the engine using an 18" flex drive and socket on the crankshaft pulley nut or bolt.	If the engine will turn freely only with the spark plugs out, and hydrostatic lock (water in the cylinders) is ruled out, check valve timing:	9.2
	If engine will not turn freely, and it is known that the clutch and transmission are free, the engine must be disassembled for further evaluation:	Chapter 3

Section 3—Primary Electrical System

Test and Procedure	Results and Indications	Proceed to
3.1—Check the ignition switch "on" position: Connect a jumper wire between the distributor side of the coil and ground, and a 12V test lamp between the switch side of the coil and ground. Remove the high tension lead from the coil. Turn the ignition switch on and jiggle the key.	If the lamp lights:	**3.2**
	If the lamp flickers when the key is jiggled, replace the ignition switch:	**3.3**
	If the lamp doesn't light, check for loose or open connections. If none are found, remove the ignition switch and check for continuity. If the switch is faulty, replace it:	**3.3**

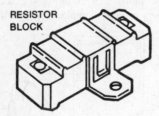

Checking the ignition switch "on" position

3.2—Check the ballast resistor or resistance wire for an open circuit, using an ohmmeter. See Chapter 3 for specific tests.	Replace the resistor or resistance wire if the resistance is zero. **NOTE:** *Some ignition systems have no ballast resistor.*	**3.3**

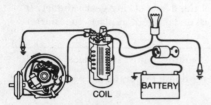

Two types of resistors

3.3—On point-type ignition systems, visually inspect the breaker points for burning, pitting or excessive wear. Gray coloring of the point contact surfaces is normal. Rotate the crankshaft until the contact heel rests on a high point of the distributor cam and adjust the point gap to specifications. On electronic ignition models, remove the distributor cap and visually inspect the armature. Ensure that the armature pin is in place, and that the armature is on tight and rotates when the engine is cranked. Make sure there are no cracks, chips or rounded edges on the armature.	If the breaker points are intact, clean the contact surfaces with fine emery cloth, and adjust the point gap to specifications. If the points are worn, replace them. On electronic systems, replace any parts which appear defective. If condition persists:	**3.4**

Test and Procedure	Results and Indications	Proceed to
3.4—On point-type ignition systems, connect a dwell-meter between the distributor primary lead and ground. Crank the engine and observe the point dwell angle. On electronic ignition systems, conduct a stator (magnetic pickup assembly) test. See Chapter 3.	On point-type systems, adjust the dwell angle if necessary. **NOTE:** *Increasing the point gap decreases the dwell angle and vice-versa.*	**3.6**
	If the dwell meter shows little or no reading;	**3.5**
	On electronic ignition systems, if the stator is bad, replace the stator. If the stator is good, proceed to the other tests in Chapter 3.	

Dwell is a function of point gap

3.5—On the point-type ignition systems, check the condenser for short: connect an ohmmeter across the condenser body and the pigtail lead.	If any reading other than infinite is noted, replace the condenser	**3.6**

Checking the condenser for short

3.6—Test the coil primary resistance: On point-type ignition systems, connect an ohmmeter across the coil primary terminals, and read the resistance on the low scale. Note whether an external ballast resistor or resistance wire is used. On electronic ignition systems, test the coil primary resistance as in Chapter 3.	Point-type ignition coils utilizing ballast resistors or resistance wires should have approximately 1.0 ohms resistance. Coils with internal resistors should have approximately 4.0 ohms resistance. If values far from the above are noted, replace the coil.	**4.1**

Check the coil primary resistance

Section 4—Secondary Electrical System
See Chapters 2–3 for service procedures

Test and Procedure	Results and Indications	Proceed to
4.1—Check for spark: Hold each spark plug wire approximately ¼″ from ground with gloves or a heavy, dry rag. Crank the engine, and observe the spark.	If no spark is evident:	**4.2**
	If spark is good in some cylinders:	**4.3**
	If spark is good in all cylinders:	**4.6**

Check for spark at the plugs

4.2—Check for spark at the coil high tension lead: Remove the coil high tension lead from the distributor and position it approximately ¼″ from ground. Crank the engine and observe spark. **CAUTION: *This test should not be performed on engines equipped with electronic ignition.***	If the spark is good and consistent:	**4.3**
	If the spark is good but intermittent, test the primary electrical system starting at 3.3:	**3.3**
	If the spark is weak or non-existent, replace the coil high tension lead, clean and tighten all connections and retest. If no improvement is noted:	**4.4**
4.3—Visually inspect the distributor cap and rotor for burned or corroded contacts, cracks, carbon tracks, or moisture. Also check the fit of the rotor on the distributor shaft (where applicable).	If moisture is present, dry thoroughly, and retest per 4.1:	**4.1**
	If burned or excessively corroded contacts, cracks, or carbon tracks are noted, replace the defective part(s) and retest per 4.1:	**4.1**
	If the rotor and cap appear intact, or are only slightly corroded, clean the contacts thoroughly (including the cap towers and spark plug wire ends) and retest per 4.1:	
	If the spark is good in all cases:	**4.6**
	If the spark is poor in all cases:	**4.5**

CORRODED OR LOOSE WIRE

EXCESSIVE WEAR OF BUTTON

HIGH RESISTANCE CARBON

ROTOR TIP BURNED AWAY

Inspect the distributor cap and rotor

CHILTON'S
AUTO BODY REPAIR TIPS

Tools and Materials • Step-by-Step Illustrated Procedures
How To Repair Dents, Scratches and Rust Holes
Spray Painting and Refinishing Tips

With a little practice, basic body repair procedures can be mastered by any do-it-yourself mechanic. The step-by-step repairs shown here can be applied to almost any type of auto body repair.

TOOLS & MATERIALS

You may already have basic tools, such as hammers and electric drills. Other tools unique to body repair — body hammers, grinding attachments, sanding blocks, dent puller, half-round plastic file and plastic spreaders — are relatively inexpensive and can be obtained wherever auto parts or auto body repair parts are sold. Portable air compressors and paint spray guns can be purchased or rented.

Auto Body Repair Kits

The best and most often used products are available to the do-it-yourselfer in kit form, from major manufacturers of auto body repair products. The same manufacturers also merchandise the individual products for use by pros.

Kits are available to make a wide variety of repairs, including holes, dents and scratches and fiberglass, and offer the advantage of buying the materials you'll need for the job. There is little waste or chance of materials going bad from not being used. Many kits may also contain basic body-working tools such as body files, sanding blocks and spreaders. Check the contents of the kit before buying your tools.

BODY REPAIR TIPS

Safety

Many of the products associated with auto body repair and refinishing contain toxic chemicals. Read all labels before opening containers and store them in a safe place and manner.
- Wear eye protection (safety goggles) when using power tools or when performing any operation that involves

the removal of any type of material.
- Wear lung protection (disposable mask or respirator) when grinding, sanding or painting.

Sanding

1 Sand off paint before using a dent puller. When using a non-adhesive sanding disc, cover the back of the disc with an overlapping layer or two of masking tape and trim the edges. The disc will last considerably longer.

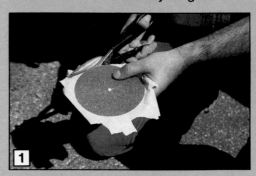

2 Use the circular motion of the sanding disc to grind *into* the edge of the repair. Grinding or sanding away from the jagged edge will only tear the sandpaper.

3 Use the palm of your hand flat on the panel to detect high and low spots. Do not use your fingertips. Slide your hand slowly back and forth.

WORKING WITH BODY FILLER

Mixing The Filler

Cleanliness and proper mixing and application are extremely important. Use a clean piece of plastic or glass or a disposable artist's palette to mix body filler.

1 Allow plenty of time and follow directions. No useful purpose will be served by adding more hardener to make it cure (set-up) faster. Less hardener means more curing time, but the mixture dries harder; more hardener means less curing time but a softer mixture.

2 Both the hardener and the filler should be thoroughly kneaded or stirred before mixing. Hardener should be a solid paste and dispense like thin toothpaste. Body filler should be smooth, and free of lumps or thick spots.

Getting the proper amount of hardener in the filler is the trickiest part of preparing the filler. Use the same amount of hardener in cold or warm weather. For contour filler (thick coats), a bead of hardener twice the diameter of the filler is about right. There's about a 15% margin on either side, but, if in doubt use less hardener.

3 Mix the body filler and hardener by wiping across the mixing surface, picking the mixture up and wiping it again. Colder weather requires longer mixing times. Do not mix in a circular motion; this will trap air bubbles which will become holes in the cured filler.

Applying The Filler

1 For best results, filler should not be applied over 1/4″ thick.

Apply the filler in several coats. Build it up to above the level of the repair surface so that it can be sanded or grated down.

The first coat of filler must be pressed on with a firm wiping motion.

Apply the filler in one direction only. Working the filler back and forth will either pull it off the metal or trap air bubbles.

REPAIRING DENTS

Before you start, take a few minutes to study the damaged area. Try to visualize the shape of the panel before it was damaged. If the damage is on the left fender, look at the right fender and use it as a guide. If there is access to the panel from behind, you can reshape it with a body hammer. If not, you'll have to use a dent puller. Go slowly and work the metal a little at a time. Get the panel as straight as possible before applying filler.

1 This dent is typical of one that can be pulled out or hammered out from behind. Remove the headlight cover, headlight assembly and turn signal housing.

2 Drill a series of holes ½ the size of the end of the dent puller along the stress line. Make some trial pulls and assess the results. If necessary, drill more holes and try again. Do not hurry.

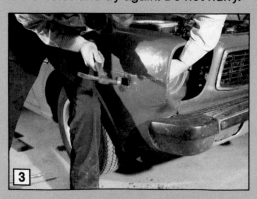

3 If possible, use a body hammer and block to shape the metal back to its original contours. Get the metal back as close to its original shape as possible. Don't depend on body filler to fill dents.

4 Using an 80-grit grinding disc on an electric drill, grind the paint from the surrounding area down to bare metal. Use a new grinding pad to prevent heat buildup that will warp metal.

5 The area should look like this when you're finished grinding. Knock the drill holes in and tape over small openings to keep plastic filler out.

6 Mix the body filler (see Body Repair Tips). Spread the body filler evenly over the entire area (see Body Repair Tips). Be sure to cover the area completely.

7 Let the body filler dry until the surface can just be scratched with your fingernail. Knock the high spots from the body filler with a body file ("Cheesegrater"). Check frequently with the palm of your hand for high and low spots.

8 Check to be sure that trim pieces that will be installed later will fit exactly. Sand the area with 40-grit paper.

9 If you wind up with low spots, you may have to apply another layer of filler.

10 Knock the high spots off with 40-grit paper. When you are satisfied with the contours of the repair, apply a thin coat of filler to cover pin holes and scratches.

11 Block sand the area with 40-grit paper to a smooth finish. Pay particular attention to body lines and ridges that must be well-defined.

12 Sand the area with 400 paper and then finish with a scuff pad. The finished repair is ready for priming and painting (see Painting Tips).

Materials and photos courtesy of Ritt Jones Auto Body, Prospect Park, PA.

REPAIRING RUST HOLES

There are many ways to repair rust holes. The fiberglass cloth kit shown here is one of the most cost efficient for the owner because it provides a strong repair that resists cracking and moisture and is relatively easy to use. It can be used on large and small holes (with or without backing) and can be applied over contoured areas. Remember, however, that short of replacing an entire panel, no repair is a guarantee that the rust will not return.

1 Remove any trim that will be in the way. Clean away all loose debris. Cut away all the rusted metal. But be sure to leave enough metal to retain the contour or body shape.

2 Grind away all traces of rust with a 24-grit grinding disc. Be sure to grind back 3-4 inches from the edge of the hole down to bare metal and be sure all traces of paint, primer and rust are removed.

3 Block sand the area with 80 or 100 grit sandpaper to get a clear, shiny surface and feathered paint edge. Tap the edges of the hole inward with a ball peen hammer.

4 If you are going to use release film, cut a piece about 2-3″ larger than the area you have sanded. Place the film over the repair and mark the sanded area on the film. Avoid any unnecessary wrinkling of the film.

5 Cut 2 pieces of fiberglass matte to match the shape of the repair. One piece should be about 1″ smaller than the sanded area and the second piece should be 1″ smaller than the first. Mix enough filler and hardener to saturate the fiberglass material (see Body Repair Tips).

6 Lay the release sheet on a flat surface and spread an even layer of filler, large enough to cover the repair. Lay the smaller piece of fiberglass cloth in the center of the sheet and spread another layer of filler over the fiberglass cloth. Repeat the operation for the larger piece of cloth.

7 Place the repair material over the repair area, with the release film facing outward. Use a spreader and work from the center outward to smooth the material, following the body contours. Be sure to remove all air bubbles.

8 Wait until the repair has dried tack-free and peel off the release sheet. The ideal working temperature is 60°-90° F. Cooler or warmer temperatures or high humidity may require additional curing time. Wait longer, if in doubt.

9 Sand and feather-edge the entire area. The initial sanding can be done with a sanding disc on an electric drill if care is used. Finish the sanding with a block sander. Low spots can be filled with body filler; this may require several applications.

10 When the filler can just be scratched with a fingernail, knock the high spots down with a body file and smooth the entire area with 80-grit. Feather the filled areas into the surrounding areas.

11 When the area is sanded smooth, mix some topcoat and hardener and apply it directly with a spreader. This will give a smooth finish and prevent the glass matte from showing through the paint.

12 Block sand the topcoat smooth with finishing sandpaper (200 grit), and 400 grit. The repair is ready for masking, priming and painting (see Painting Tips).

Materials and photos courtesy Marson Corporation, Chelsea, Massachusetts

PAINTING TIPS

Preparation

1 SANDING — Use a 400 or 600 grit wet or dry sandpaper. Wet-sand the area with a ¼ sheet of sandpaper soaked in clean water. Keep the paper wet while sanding. Sand the area until the repaired area tapers into the original finish.

2 CLEANING — Wash the area to be painted thoroughly with water and a clean rag. Rinse it thoroughly and wipe the surface dry until you're sure it's completely free of dirt, dust, fingerprints, wax, detergent or other foreign matter.

3 MASKING — Protect any areas you don't want to overspray by covering them with masking tape and newspaper. Be careful not get fingerprints on the area to be painted.

4 PRIMING — All exposed metal should be primed before painting. Primer protects the metal and provides an excellent surface for paint adhesion. When the primer is dry, wet-sand the area again with 600 grit wet-sandpaper. Clean the area again after sanding.

Painting Techniques

Paint applied from either a spray gun or a spray can (for small areas) will provide good results. Experiment on an old piece of metal to get the right combination before you begin painting.

SPRAYING VISCOSITY (SPRAY GUN ONLY) — Paint should be thinned to spraying viscosity according to the directions on the can. Use only the recommended thinner or reducer and the same amount of reduction regardless of temperature.

AIR PRESSURE (SPRAY GUN ONLY) — This is extremely important. Be sure you are using the proper recommended pressure.

TEMPERATURE — The surface to be painted should be approximately the same temperature as the surrounding air. Applying warm paint to a cold surface, or vice versa, will completely upset the paint characteristics.

THICKNESS — Spray with smooth strokes. In general, the thicker the coat of paint, the longer the drying time. Apply several thin coats about 30 seconds apart. The paint should remain wet long enough to flow out and no longer; heavier coats will only produce sags or wrinkles. Spray a light (fog) coat, followed by heavier color coats.

DISTANCE — The ideal spraying distance is 8″-12″ from the gun or can to the surface. Shorter distances will produce ripples, while greater distances will result in orange peel, dry film and poor color match and loss of material due to overspray.

OVERLAPPING — The gun or can should be kept at right angles to the surface at all times. Work to a wet edge at an even speed, using a 50% overlap and direct the center of the spray at the lower or nearest edge of the previous stroke.

RUBBING OUT (BLENDING) FRESH PAINT — Let the paint dry thoroughly. Runs or imperfections can be sanded out, primed and repainted.

Don't be in too big a hurry to remove the masking. This only produces paint ridges. When the finish has dried for at least a week, apply a small amount of fine grade rubbing compound with a clean, wet cloth. Use lots of water and blend the new paint with the surrounding area.

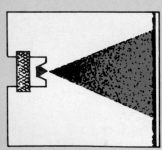

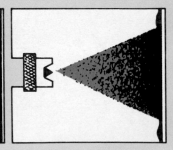

WRONG

CORRECT

WRONG

Thin coat. Stroke too fast, not enough overlap, gun too far away.

Medium coat. Proper distance, good stroke, proper overlap.

Heavy coat. Stroke too slow, too much overlap, gun too close.

Test and Procedure	Results and Indications	Proceed to
4.4—Check the coil secondary resistance: On point-type systems connect an ohmmeter across the distributor side of the coil and the coil tower. Read the resistance on the high scale of the ohmmeter. On electronic ignition systems, see Chapter 3 for specific tests.	The resistance of a satisfactory coil should be between 4,000 and 10,000 ohms. If resistance is considerably higher (i.e., 40,000 ohms) replace the coil and retest per 4.1. **NOTE:** *This does not apply to high performance coils.*	

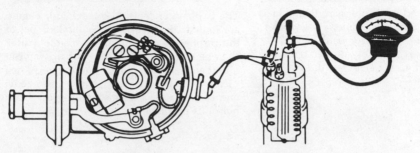

Testing the coil secondary resistance

Test and Procedure	Results and Indications	Proceed to
4.5—Visually inspect the spark plug wires for cracking or brittleness. Ensure that no two wires are positioned so as to cause induction firing (adjacent and parallel). Remove each wire, one by one, and check resistance with an ohmmeter.	Replace any cracked or brittle wires. If any of the wires are defective, replace the entire set. Replace any wires with excessive resistance (over $8000\,\Omega$ per foot for suppression wire), and separate any wires that might cause induction firing.	4.6

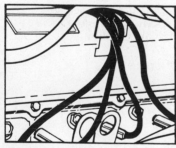

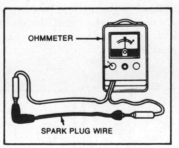

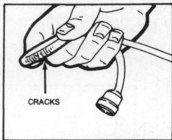

Misfiring can be the result of spark plug leads to adjacent, consecutively firing cylinders running parallel and too close together

On point-type ignition systems, check the spark plug wires as shown. On electronic ignitions, do not remove the wire from the distributor cap terminal; instead, test through the cap

Spark plug wires can be checked visually by bending them in a loop over your finger. This will reveal any cracks, burned or broken insulation. Any wire with cracked insulation should be replaced

Test and Procedure	Results and Indications	Proceed to
4.6—Remove the spark plugs, noting the cylinders from which they were removed, and evaluate according to the color photos in the middle of this book.	See following.	**See following.**

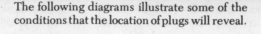

Test and Procedure	Results and Indications	Proceed to

4.7—Examine the location of all the plugs.

The following diagrams illustrate some of the conditions that the location of plugs will reveal.

4.8

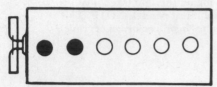

Two adjacent plugs are fouled in a 6-cylinder engine, 4-cylinder engine or either bank of a V-8. This is probably due to a blown head gasket between the two cylinders

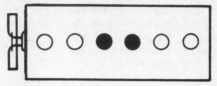

The two center plugs in a 6-cylinder engine are fouled. Raw fuel may be "boiled" out of the carburetor into the intake manifold after the engine is shut-off. Stop-start driving can also foul the center plugs, due to overly rich mixture. Proper float level, a new float needle and seat or use of an insulating spacer may help this problem

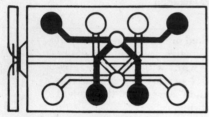

An unbalanced carburetor is indicated. Following the fuel flow on this particular design shows that the cylinders fed by the right-hand barrel are fouled from overly rich mixture, while the cylinders fed by the left-hand barrel are normal

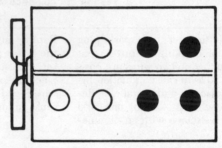

If the four rear plugs are overheated, a cooling system problem is suggested. A thorough cleaning of the cooling system may restore coolant circulation and cure the problem

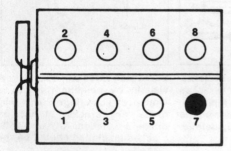

Finding one plug overheated may indicate an intake manifold leak near the affected cylinder. If the overheated plug is the second of two adjacent, consecutively firing plugs, it could be the result of ignition cross-firing. Separating the leads to these two plugs will eliminate cross-fire

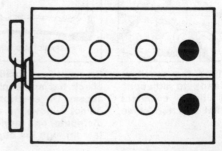

Occasionally, the two rear plugs in large, lightly used V-8's will become oil fouled. High oil consumption and smoky exhaust may also be noticed. It is probably due to plugged oil drain holes in the rear of the cylinder head, causing oil to be sucked in around the valve stems. This usually occurs in the rear cylinders first, because the engine slants that way

Test and Procedure	Results and Indications	Proceed to
4.8—Determine the static ignition timing. Using the crankshaft pulley timing marks as a guide, locate top dead center on the compression stroke of the number one cylinder.	The rotor should be pointing toward the No. 1 tower in the distributor cap, and, on electronic ignitions, the armature spoke for that cylinder should be lined up with the stator.	4.8
4.9—Check coil polarity: Connect a voltmeter negative lead to the coil high tension lead, and the positive lead to ground (**NOTE:** *Reverse the hook-up for positive ground systems*). Crank the engine momentarily. **Checking coil polarity**	If the voltmeter reads up-scale, the polarity is correct: If the voltmeter reads down-scale, reverse the coil polarity (switch the primary leads):	5.1 5.1

Section 5—Fuel System
See Chapter 4 for service procedures

Test and Procedure	Results and Indications	Proceed to
5.1—Determine that the air filter is functioning efficiently: Hold paper elements up to a strong light, and attempt to see light through the filter.	Clean permanent air filters in solvent (or manufacturer's recommendation), and allow to dry. Replace paper elements through which light cannot be seen:	5.2
5.2—Determine whether a flooding condition exists: Flooding is identified by a strong gasoline odor, and excessive gasoline present in the throttle bore(s) of the carburetor. **If the engine floods repeatedly, check the choke butterfly flap**	If flooding is not evident: If flooding is evident, permit the gasoline to dry for a few moments and restart. If flooding doesn't recur: If flooding is persistent:	5.3 5.7 5.5
5.3—Check that fuel is reaching the carburetor: Detach the fuel line at the carburetor inlet. Hold the end of the line in a cup (not styrofoam), and crank the engine. **Check the fuel pump by disconnecting the output line (fuel pump-to-carburetor) at the carburetor and operating the starter briefly**	If fuel flows smoothly: If fuel doesn't flow (**NOTE:** *Make sure that there is fuel in the tank*), or flows erratically:	5.7 5.4

Test and Procedure	Results and Indications	Proceed to
5.4—Test the fuel pump: Disconnect all fuel lines from the fuel pump. Hold a finger over the input fitting, crank the engine (with electric pump, turn the ignition or pump on); and feel for suction.	If suction is evident, blow out the fuel line to the tank with low pressure compressed air until bubbling is heard from the fuel filler neck. Also blow out the carburetor fuel line (both ends disconnected):	5.7
	If no suction is evident, replace or repair the fuel pump: **NOTE:** *Repeated oil fouling of the spark plugs, or a no-start condition, could be the result of a ruptured vacuum booster pump diaphragm, through which oil or gasoline is being drawn into the intake manifold (where applicable).*	5.7
5.5—Occasionally, small specks of dirt will clog the small jets and orifices in the carburetor. With the engine cold, hold a flat piece of wood or similar material over the carburetor, where possible, and crank the engine.	If the engine starts, but runs roughly the engine is probably not run enough. If the engine won't start:	5.9
5.6—Check the needle and seat: Tap the carburetor in the area of the needle and seat.	If flooding stops, a gasoline additive (e.g., Gumout) will often cure the problem:	5.7
	If flooding continues, check the fuel pump for excessive pressure at the carburetor (according to specifications). If the pressure is normal, the needle and seat must be removed and checked, and/or the float level adjusted:	5.7
5.7—Test the accelerator pump by looking into the throttle bores while operating the throttle.	If the accelerator pump appears to be operating normally:	5.8
	If the accelerator pump is not operating, the pump must be reconditioned. Where possible, service the pump with the carburetor(s) installed on the engine. If necessary, remove the carburetor. Prior to removal:	5.8

Check for gas at the carburetor by looking down the carburetor throat while someone moves the accelerator

Test and Procedure	Results and Indications	Proceed to
5.8—Determine whether the carburetor main fuel system is functioning: Spray a commercial starting fluid into the carburetor while attempting to start the engine.	If the engine starts, runs for a few seconds, and dies:	5.9
	If the engine doesn't start:	6.1

Test and Procedure	Results and Indications	Proceed to
5.9—Uncommon fuel system malfunctions: See below:	If the problem is solved:	6.1
	If the problem remains, remove and recondition the carburetor.	

Condition	Indication	Test	Prevailing Weather Conditions	Remedy
Vapor lock	Engine will not restart shortly after running.	Cool the components of the fuel system until the engine starts. Vapor lock can be cured faster by draping a wet cloth over a mechanical fuel pump.	Hot to very hot	Ensure that the exhaust manifold heat control valve is operating. Check with the vehicle manufacturer for the recommended solution to vapor lock on the model in question.
Carburetor icing	Engine will not idle, stalls at low speeds.	Visually inspect the throttle plate area of the throttle bores for frost.	High humidity, 32–40° F.	Ensure that the exhaust manifold heat control valve is operating, and that the intake manifold heat riser is not blocked.
Water in the fuel	Engine sputters and stalls; may not start.	Pump a small amount of fuel into a glass jar. Allow to stand, and inspect for droplets or a layer of water.	High humidity, extreme temperature changes.	For droplets, use one or two cans of commercial gas line anti-freeze. For a layer of water, the tank must be drained, and the fuel lines blown out with compressed air.

Section 6—Engine Compression
See Chapter 3 for service procedures

6.1—Test engine compression: Remove all spark plugs. Block the throttle wide open. Insert a compression gauge into a spark plug port, crank the engine to obtain the maximum reading, and record.	If compression is within limits on all cylinders:	7.1
	If gauge reading is extremely low on all cylinders:	6.2
	If gauge reading is low on one or two cylinders: (If gauge readings are identical and low on two or more adjacent cylinders, the head gasket must be replaced.)	6.2

Checking compression

6.2—Test engine compression (wet): Squirt approximately 30 cc. of engine oil into each cylinder, and retest per 6.1.	If the readings improve, worn or cracked rings or broken pistons are indicated:	See Chapter 3
	If the readings do not improve, burned or excessively carboned valves or a jumped timing chain are indicated:	
	NOTE: *A jumped timing chain is often indicated by difficult cranking.*	7.1

Section 7—Engine Vacuum
See Chapter 3 for service procedures

Test and Procedure	Results and Indications	Proceed to
7.1—Attach a vacuum gauge to the intake manifold beyond the throttle plate. Start the engine, and observe the action of the needle over the range of engine speeds.	See below.	**See below**

INDICATION: normal engine in good condition

Proceed to: 8.1

Normal engine
Gauge reading: steady, from 17–22 in./Hg.

INDICATION: sticking valves or ignition miss

Proceed to: 9.1, 8.3

Sticking valves
Gauge reading: intermittent fluctuation at idle

INDICATION: late ignition or valve timing, low compression, stuck throttle valve, leaking carburetor or manifold gasket

Proceed to: 6.1

Incorrect valve timing
Gauge reading: low (10–15 in./Hg) but steady

INDICATION: improper carburetor adjustment or minor intake leak.

Proceed to: 7.2

Carburetor requires adjustment
Gauge reading: drifting needle

INDICATION: ignition miss, blown cylinder head gasket, leaking valve or weak valve spring

Proceed to: 8.3, 6.1

Blown head gasket
Gauge reading: needle fluctuates as engine speed increases

INDICATION: burnt valve or faulty valve clearance. Needle will fall when defective valve operates

Proceed to: 9.1

Burnt or leaking valves
Gauge reading: steady needle, but drops regularly

INDICATION: choked muffler, excessive back pressure in system

Proceed to: 10.1

Clogged exhaust system
Gauge reading: gradual drop in reading at idle

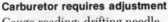

INDICATION: worn valve guides

Proceed to: 9.1

Worn valve guides
Gauge reading: needle vibrates excessively at idle, but steadies as engine speed increases

White pointer = steady gauge hand   Black pointer = fluctuating gauge hand

Test and Procedure	Results and Indications	Proceed to
7.2—Attach a vacuum gauge per 7.1, and test for an intake manifold leak. Squirt a small amount of oil around the intake manifold gaskets, carburetor gaskets, plugs and fittings. Observe the action of the vacuum gauge.	If the reading improves, replace the indicated gasket, or seal the indicated fitting or plug: If the reading remains low:	**8.1** **7.3**
7.3—Test all vacuum hoses and accessories for leaks as described in 7.2. Also check the carburetor body (dashpots, automatic choke mechanism, throttle shafts) for leaks in the same manner.	If the reading improves, service or replace the offending part(s): If the reading remains low:	**8.1** **6.1**

Section 8—Secondary Electrical System
See Chapter 2 for service procedures

Test and Procedure	Results and Indications	Proceed to
8.1—Remove the distributor cap and check to make sure that the rotor turns when the engine is cranked. Visually inspect the distributor components.	Clean, tighten or replace any components which appear defective.	**8.2**
8.2—Connect a timing light (per manufacturer's recommendation) and check the dynamic ignition timing. Disconnect and plug the vacuum hose(s) to the distributor if specified, start the engine, and observe the timing marks at the specified engine speed.	If the timing is not correct, adjust to specifications by rotating the distributor in the engine: (Advance timing by rotating distributor opposite normal direction of rotor rotation, retard timing by rotating distributor in same direction as rotor rotation.)	**8.3**
8.3—Check the operation of the distributor advance mechanism(s): To test the mechanical advance, disconnect the vacuum lines from the distributor advance unit and observe the timing marks with a timing light as the engine speed is increased from idle. If the mark moves smoothly, without hesitation, it may be assumed that the mechanical advance is functioning properly. To test vacuum advance and/or retard systems, alternately crimp and release the vacuum line, and observe the timing mark for movement. If movement is noted, the system is operating.	If the systems are functioning: If the systems are not functioning, remove the distributor, and test on a distributor tester:	**8.4** **8.4**
8.4—Locate an ignition miss: With the engine running, remove each spark plug wire, one at a time, until one is found that doesn't cause the engine to roughen and slow down.	When the missing cylinder is identified:	**4.1**

Section 9—Valve Train
See Chapter 3 for service procedures

Test and Procedure	Results and Indications	Proceed to
9.1—Evaluate the valve train: Remove the valve cover, and ensure that the valves are adjusted to specifications. A mechanic's stethoscope may be used to aid in the diagnosis of the valve train. By pushing the probe on or near push rods or rockers, valve noise often can be isolated. A timing light also may be used to diagnose valve problems. Connect the light according to manufacturer's recommendations, and start the engine. Vary the firing moment of the light by increasing the engine speed (and therefore the ignition advance), and moving the trigger from cylinder to cylinder. Observe the movement of each valve.	Sticking valves or erratic valve train motion can be observed with the timing light. The cylinder head must be disassembled for repairs.	**See Chapter 3**
9.2—Check the valve timing: Locate top dead center of the No. 1 piston, and install a degree wheel or tape on the crankshaft pulley or damper with zero corresponding to an index mark on the engine. Rotate the crankshaft in its direction of rotation, and observe the opening of the No. 1 cylinder intake valve. The opening should correspond with the correct mark on the degree wheel according to specifications.	If the timing is not correct, the timing cover must be removed for further investigation.	**See Chapter 3**

Section 10—Exhaust System

Test and Procedure	Results and Indications	Proceed to
10.1—Determine whether the exhaust manifold heat control valve is operating: Operate the valve by hand to determine whether it is free to move. If the valve is free, run the engine to operating temperature and observe the action of the valve, to ensure that it is opening.	If the valve sticks, spray it with a suitable solvent, open and close the valve to free it, and retest. If the valve functions properly: If the valve does not free, or does not operate, replace the valve:	**10.2** **10.2**
10.2—Ensure that there are no exhaust restrictions: Visually inspect the exhaust system for kinks, dents, or crushing. Also note that gases are flowing freely from the tailpipe at all engine speeds, indicating no restriction in the muffler or resonator.	Replace any damaged portion of the system:	**11.1**

Section 11—Cooling System
See Chapter 3 for service procedures

Test and Procedure	Results and Indications	Proceed to
11.1—Visually inspect the fan belt for glazing, cracks, and fraying, and replace if necessary. Tighten the belt so that the longest span has approximately ½″ play at its midpoint under thumb pressure (see Chapter 1).	Replace or tighten the fan belt as necessary:	11.2

Checking belt tension

Test and Procedure	Results and Indications	Proceed to
11.2—Check the fluid level of the cooling system.	If full or slightly low, fill as necessary:	11.5
	If extremely low:	11.3
11.3—Visually inspect the external portions of the cooling system (radiator, radiator hoses, thermostat elbow, water pump seals, heater hoses, etc.) for leaks. If none are found, pressurize the cooling system to 14–15 psi.	If cooling system holds the pressure:	11.5
	If cooling system loses pressure rapidly, reinspect external parts of the system for leaks under pressure. If none are found, check dipstick for coolant in crankcase. If no coolant is present, but pressure loss continues:	11.4
	If coolant is evident in crankcase, remove cylinder head(s), and check gasket(s). If gaskets are intact, block and cylinder head(s) should be checked for cracks or holes.	
	If the gasket(s) is blown, replace, and purge the crankcase of coolant:	12.6
	NOTE: *Occasionally, due to atmospheric and driving conditions, condensation of water can occur in the crankcase. This causes the oil to appear milky white. To remedy, run the engine until hot, and change the oil and oil filter.*	
11.4—Check for combustion leaks into the cooling system: Pressurize the cooling system as above. Start the engine, and observe the pressure gauge. If the needle fluctuates, remove each spark plug wire, one at a time, noting which cylinder(s) reduce or eliminate the fluctuation.	Cylinders which reduce or eliminate the fluctuation, when the spark plug wire is removed, are leaking into the cooling system. Replace the head gasket on the affected cylinder bank(s).	

Pressurizing the cooling system

Test and Procedure	Results and Indications	Proceed to
11.5—Check the radiator pressure cap: Attach a radiator pressure tester to the radiator cap (wet the seal prior to installation). Quickly pump up the pressure, noting the point at which the cap releases.	If the cap releases within ± 1 psi of the specified rating, it is operating properly:	**11.6**
	If the cap releases at more than ± 1 psi of the specified rating, it should be replaced:	**11.6**

Checking radiator pressure cap

Test and Procedure	Results and Indications	Proceed to
11.6—Test the thermostat: Start the engine cold, remove the radiator cap, and insert a thermometer into the radiator. Allow the engine to idle. After a short while, there will be a sudden, rapid increase in coolant temperature. The temperature at which this sharp rise stops is the thermostat opening temperature.	If the thermostat opens at or about the specified temperature:	**11.7**
	If the temperature doesn't increase: (If the temperature increases slowly and gradually, replace the thermostat.)	**11.7**
11.7—Check the water pump: Remove the thermostat elbow and the thermostat, disconnect the coil high tension lead (to prevent starting), and crank the engine momentarily.	If coolant flows, replace the thermostat and retest per 11.6:	**11.6**
	If coolant doesn't flow, reverse flush the cooling system to alleviate any blockage that might exist. If system is not blocked, and coolant will not flow, replace the water pump.	

Section 12—Lubrication
See Chapter 3 for service procedures

Test and Procedure	Results and Indications	Proceed to
12.1—Check the oil pressure gauge or warning light: If the gauge shows low pressure, or the light is on for no obvious reason, remove the oil pressure sender. Install an accurate oil pressure gauge and run the engine momentarily.	If oil pressure builds normally, run engine for a few moments to determine that it is functioning normally, and replace the sender.	—
	If the pressure remains low:	**12.2**
	If the pressure surges:	**12.3**
	If the oil pressure is zero:	**12.3**
12.2—Visually inspect the oil: If the oil is watery or very thin, milky, or foamy, replace the oil and oil filter.	If the oil is normal:	**12.3**
	If after replacing oil the pressure remains low:	**12.3**
	If after replacing oil the pressure becomes normal:	—

Test and Procedure	Results and Indications	Proceed to
12.3—Inspect the oil pressure relief valve and spring, to ensure that it is not sticking or stuck. Remove and thoroughly clean the valve, spring, and the valve body.	If the oil pressure improves: If no improvement is noted:	— **12.4**
12.4—Check to ensure that the oil pump is not cavitating (sucking air instead of oil): See that the crankcase is neither over nor underfull, and that the pickup in the sump is in the proper position and free from sludge.	Fill or drain the crankcase to the proper capacity, and clean the pickup screen in solvent if necessary. If no improvement is noted:	**12.5**
12.5—Inspect the oil pump drive and the oil pump:	If the pump drive or the oil pump appear to be defective, service as necessary and retest per 12.1: If the pump drive and pump appear to be operating normally, the engine should be disassembled to determine where blockage exists:	**12.1** **See Chapter 3**
12.6—Purge the engine of ethylene glycol coolant: Completely drain the crankcase and the oil filter. Obtain a commercial butyl cellosolve base solvent, designated for this purpose, and follow the instructions precisely. Following this, install a new oil filter and refill the crankcase with the proper weight oil. The next oil and filter change should follow shortly thereafter (1000 miles).		

TROUBLESHOOTING EMISSION CONTROL SYSTEMS

See Chapter 4 for procedures applicable to individual emission control systems used on specific combinations of engine/transmission/model.

TROUBLESHOOTING THE CARBURETOR
See Chapter 4 for service procedures

Carburetor problems cannot be effectively isolated unless all other engine systems (particularly ignition and emission) are functioning properly and the engine is properly tuned.

Condition	Possible Cause
Engine cranks, but does not start	1. Improper starting procedure 2. No fuel in tank 3. Clogged fuel line or filter 4. Defective fuel pump 5. Choke valve not closing properly 6. Engine flooded 7. Choke valve not unloading 8. Throttle linkage not making full travel 9. Stuck needle or float 10. Leaking float needle or seat 11. Improper float adjustment
Engine stalls	1. Improperly adjusted idle speed or mixture **Engine hot** 2. Improperly adjusted dashpot 3. Defective or improperly adjusted solenoid 4. Incorrect fuel level in fuel bowl 5. Fuel pump pressure too high 6. Leaking float needle seat 7. Secondary throttle valve stuck open 8. Air or fuel leaks 9. Idle air bleeds plugged or missing 10. Idle passages plugged **Engine Cold** 11. Incorrectly adjusted choke 12. Improperly adjusted fast idle speed 13. Air leaks 14. Plugged idle or idle air passages 15. Stuck choke valve or binding linkage 16. Stuck secondary throttle valves 17. Engine flooding—high fuel level 18. Leaking or misaligned float
Engine hesitates on acceleration	1. Clogged fuel filter 2. Leaking fuel pump diaphragm 3. Low fuel pump pressure 4. Secondary throttle valves stuck, bent or misadjusted 5. Sticking or binding air valve 6. Defective accelerator pump 7. Vacuum leaks 8. Clogged air filter 9. Incorrect choke adjustment (engine cold)
Engine feels sluggish or flat on acceleration	1. Improperly adjusted idle speed or mixture 2. Clogged fuel filter 3. Defective accelerator pump 4. Dirty, plugged or incorrect main metering jets 5. Bent or sticking main metering rods 6. Sticking throttle valves 7. Stuck heat riser 8. Binding or stuck air valve 9. Dirty, plugged or incorrect secondary jets 10. Bent or sticking secondary metering rods. 11. Throttle body or manifold heat passages plugged 12. Improperly adjusted choke or choke vacuum break.
Carburetor floods	1. Defective fuel pump. Pressure too high. 2. Stuck choke valve 3. Dirty, worn or damaged float or needle valve/seat 4. Incorrect float/fuel level 5. Leaking float bowl

Condition	Possible Cause
Engine idles roughly and stalls	1. Incorrect idle speed 2. Clogged fuel filter 3. Dirt in fuel system or carburetor 4. Loose carburetor screws or attaching bolts 5. Broken carburetor gaskets 6. Air leaks 7. Dirty carburetor 8. Worn idle mixture needles 9. Throttle valves stuck open 10. Incorrectly adjusted float or fuel level 11. Clogged air filter
Engine runs unevenly or surges	1. Defective fuel pump 2. Dirty or clogged fuel filter 3. Plugged, loose or incorrect main metering jets or rods 4. Air leaks 5. Bent or sticking main metering rods 6. Stuck power piston 7. Incorrect float adjustment 8. Incorrect idle speed or mixture 9. Dirty or plugged idle system passages 10. Hard, brittle or broken gaskets 11. Loose attaching or mounting screws 12. Stuck or misaligned secondary throttle valves
Poor fuel economy	1. Poor driving habits 2. Stuck choke valve 3. Binding choke linkage 4. Stuck heat riser 5. Incorrect idle mixture 6. Defective accelerator pump 7. Air leaks 8. Plugged, loose or incorrect main metering jets 9. Improperly adjusted float or fuel level 10. Bent, misaligned or fuel-clogged float 11. Leaking float needle seat 12. Fuel leak 13. Accelerator pump discharge ball not seating properly 14. Incorrect main jets
Engine lacks high speed performance or power	1. Incorrect throttle linkage adjustment 2. Stuck or binding power piston 3. Defective accelerator pump 4. Air leaks 5. Incorrect float setting or fuel level 6. Dirty, plugged, worn or incorrect main metering jets or rods 7. Binding or sticking air valve 8. Brittle or cracked gaskets 9. Bent, incorrect or improperly adjusted secondary metering rods 10. Clogged fuel filter 11. Clogged air filter 12. Defective fuel pump

TROUBLESHOOTING FUEL INJECTION PROBLEMS

Each fuel injection system has its own unique components and test procedures, for which it is impossible to generalize. Refer to Chapter 4 of this Repair & Tune-Up Guide for specif test and repair procedures, if the vehic! equipped with fuel injection.

TROUBLESHOOTING ELECTRICAL PROBLEMS

See Chapter 5 for service procedures

For any electrical system to operate, it must make a complete circuit. This simply means that the power flow from the battery must make a complete circle. When an electrical component is operating, power flows from the battery to the component, passes through the component causing it to perform its function (lighting a light bulb), and then returns to the battery through the ground of the circuit. This ground is usually (but not always) the metal part of the car or truck on which the electrical component is mounted.

Perhaps the easiest way to visualize this is to think of connecting a light bulb with two wires attached to it to the battery. If one of the two wires attached to the light bulb were attached to the negative post of the battery and the other were attached to the positive post of the battery, you would have a complete circuit. Current from the battery would flow to the light bulb, causing it to light, and return to the negative post of the battery.

The normal automotive circuit differs from this simple example in two ways. First, instead of having a return wire from the bulb to the battery, the light bulb returns the current to the battery through the chassis of the vehicle. Since the negative battery cable is attached to the chassis and the chassis is made of electrically conductive metal, the chassis of the vehicle can serve as a ground wire to complete the circuit. Secondly, most automotive circuits contain switches to turn components on and off as required.

Every complete circuit from a power source must include a component which is using the power from the power source. If you were to disconnect the light bulb from the wires and touch the two wires together (don't do this) the power supply wire to the component would be grounded before the normal ground connection for the circuit.

Because grounding a wire from a power source makes a complete circuit—less the required component to use the power—this phenomenon is called a short circuit. Common causes are: broken insulation (exposing the metal wire to a metal part of the car or truck), or a shorted switch.

Some electrical components which require large amount of current to operate also have lay in their circuit. Since these circuits a large amount of current, the thickness

of the wire in the circuit (gauge size) is also greater. If this large wire were connected from the component to the control switch on the instrument panel, and then back to the component, a voltage drop would occur in the circuit. To prevent this potential drop in voltage, an electromagnetic switch (relay) is used. The large wires in the circuit are connected from the battery to one side of the relay, and from the opposite side of the relay to the component. The relay is normally open, preventing current from passing through the circuit. An additional, smaller, wire is connected from the relay to the control switch for the circuit. When the control switch is turned on, it grounds the smaller wire from the relay and completes the circuit. This closes the relay and allows current to flow from the battery to the component. The horn, headlight, and starter circuits are three which use relays.

It is possible for larger surges of current to pass through the electrical system of your car or truck. If this surge of current were to reach an electrical component, it could burn it out. To prevent this, fuses, circuit breakers or fusible links are connected into the current supply wires of most of the major electrical systems. When an electrical current of excessive power passes through the component's fuse, the fuse blows out and breaks the circuit, saving the component from destruction.

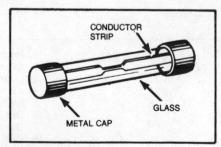

Typical automotive fuse

A circuit breaker is basically a self-repairing fuse. The circuit breaker opens the circuit the same way a fuse does. However, when either the short is removed from the circuit or the surge subsides, the circuit breaker resets itself and does not have to be replaced as a fuse does.

A fuse link is a wire that acts as a fuse. It is normally connected between the starter relay and the main wiring harness. This connection is usually under the hood. The fuse link (if installed) protects all the

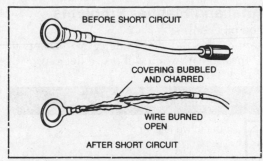

BEFORE SHORT CIRCUIT

COVERING BUBBLED
AND CHARRED

WIRE BURNED
OPEN

AFTER SHORT CIRCUIT

Most fusible links show a charred, melted insulation when they burn out

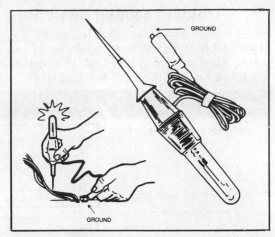

GROUND

GROUND

The test light will show the presence of current when touched to a hot wire and grounded at the other end

chassis electrical components, and is the probable cause of trouble when none of the electrical components function, unless the battery is disconnected or dead.

Electrical problems generally fall into one of three areas:

1. The component that is not functioning is not receiving current.

2. The component itself is not functioning.

3. The component is not properly grounded.

The electrical system can be checked with a test light and a jumper wire. A test light is a device that looks like a pointed screwdriver with a wire attached to it and has a light bulb in its handle. A jumper wire is a piece of insulated wire with an alligator clip attached to each end.

If a component is not working, you must follow a systematic plan to determine which of the three causes is the villain.

1. Turn on the switch that controls the inoperable component.

2. Disconnect the power supply wire from the component.

3. Attach the ground wire on the test light to a good metal ground.

4. Touch the probe end of the test light to the end of the power supply wire that was disconnected from the component. If the component is receiving current, the test light will go on.

NOTE: *Some components work only when the ignition switch is turned on.*

If the test light does not go on, then the problem is in the circuit between the battery and the component. This includes all the switches, fuses, and relays in the system. Follow the wire that runs back to the battery. The problem is an open circuit between the

battery and the component. If the fuse is blown and, when replaced, immediately blows again, there is a short circuit in the system which must be located and repaired. If there is a switch in the system, bypass it with a jumper wire. This is done by connecting one end of the jumper wire to the power supply wire into the switch and the other end of the jumper wire to the wire coming out of the switch. If the test light lights with the jumper wire installed, the switch or whatever _____ _____ _____ _____

_____

for the
the power ,

5. If the bulb _____ _____ s on, then the current is gettin _____ _____ ponent that is not working. This el _____ es the first of the three possible causes. Connect the power supply wire and connect a jumper wire from the component to a good metal ground. Do this with the switch which controls the component turned on, and also the ignition switch turned on if it is required for the component to work. If the component works with the jumper wire installed, then it has a bad ground. This is usually caused by the metal area on which the component mounts to the chassis being coated with some type of foreign matter.

6. If neither test located the source of the trouble, then the component itself is defective. Remember that for any electrical system to work, all connections must be clean and tight.

Troubleshooting Basic Turn Signal and Flasher Problems
See Chapter 5 for service procedures

Most problems in the turn signals or flasher system can be reduced to defective flashers or bulbs, which are easily replaced. Occasionally, the turn signal switch will prove defective.

F = Front   R = Rear   ● = Lights off   ○ = Lights on

Condition		Possible Cause
Turn signals light, but do not flash	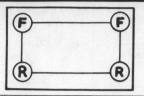	Defective flasher
No turn signals light on either side	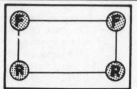	Blown fuse. Replace if defective. Defective flasher. Check by substitution. Open circuit, short circuit or poor ground.
Both turn signals on one side don't work	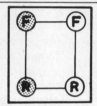	Bad bulbs. Bad ground in both (or either) housings.
One turn signal light on one side doesn't work	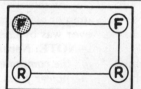	Defective bulb. Corrosion in socket. Clean contacts. Poor ground at socket.
Turn signal flashes too fast or too slowly	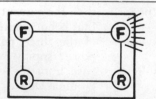	Check any bulb on the side flashing too fast. A heavy-duty bulb is probably installed in place of a regular bulb. Check the bulb flashing too slowly. A standard bulb was probably installed in place of a heavy-duty bulb. Loose connections or corrosion at the bulb socket.
Indicator lights don't work in either direction		Check if the turn signals are working. Check the dash indicator lights. Check the flasher by substitution.
One indicator light doesn't light		On systems with one dash indicator: See if the lights work on the same side. Often the filaments have been reversed in systems combining stoplights with taillights and turn signals. Check the flasher by substitution. On systems with two indicators: Check the bulbs on the same side. Check the indicator light bulb. Check the flasher by substitution.

Troubleshooting Lighting Problems

See Chapter 5 for service procedures

Condition	Possible Cause
One or more lights don't work, but others do	1. Defective bulb(s) 2. Blown fuse(s) 3. Dirty fuse clips or light sockets 4. Poor ground circuit
Lights burn out quickly	1. Incorrect voltage regulator setting or defective regulator 2. Poor battery/alternator connections
Lights go dim	1. Low/discharged battery 2. Alternator not charging 3. Corroded sockets or connections 4. Low voltage output
Lights flicker	1. Loose connection 2. Poor ground. (Run ground wire from light housing to frame) 3. Circuit breaker operating (short circuit)
Lights "flare"—Some flare is normal on acceleration—If excessive, see "Lights Burn Out Quickly"	High voltage setting
Lights glare—approaching drivers are blinded	1. Lights adjusted too high 2. Rear springs or shocks sagging 3. Rear tires soft

Troubleshooting Dash Gauge Problems

Most problems can be traced to a defective sending unit or faulty wiring. Occasionally, the gauge itself is at fault. See Chapter 5 for service procedures.

Condition	Possible Cause
COOLANT TEMPERATURE GAUGE	
Gauge reads erratically or not at all	1. Loose or dirty connections 2. Defective sending unit. 3. Defective gauge. To test a bi-metal gauge, remove the wire from the sending unit. Ground the wire for an instant. If the gauge registers, replace the sending unit. To test a magnetic gauge, disconnect the wire at the sending unit. With ignition ON gauge should register COLD. Ground the wire; gauge should register HOT.
AMMETER GAUGE—TURN HEADLIGHTS ON (DO NOT START ENGINE). NOTE REACTION	
Ammeter shows charge Ammeter shows discharge Ammeter does not move	1. Connections reversed on gauge 2. Ammeter is OK 3. Loose connections or faulty wiring 4. Defective gauge

Condition	Possible Cause

OIL PRESSURE GAUGE

Gauge does not register or is inaccurate	1. On mechanical gauge, Bourdon tube may be bent or kinked. 2. Low oil pressure. Remove sending unit. Idle the engine briefly. If no oil flows from sending unit hole, problem is in engine. 3. Defective gauge. Remove the wire from the sending unit and ground it for an instant with the ignition ON. A good gauge will go to the top of the scale. 4. Defective wiring. Check the wiring to the gauge. If it's OK and the gauge doesn't register when grounded, replace the gauge. 5. Defective sending unit.

ALL GAUGES

All gauges do not operate All gauges read low or erratically All gauges pegged	1. Blown fuse 2. Defective instrument regulator 3. Defective or dirty instrument voltage regulator 4. Loss of ground between instrument voltage regulator and frame 5. Defective instrument regulator

WARNING LIGHTS

Light(s) do not come on when ignition is ON, but engine is not started Light comes on with engine running	1. Defective bulb 2. Defective wire 3. Defective sending unit. Disconnect the wire from the sending unit and ground it. Replace the sending unit if the light comes on with the ignition ON. 4. Problem in individual system 5. Defective sending unit

Troubleshooting Clutch Problems

It is false economy to replace individual clutch components. The pressure plate, clutch plate and throwout bearing should be replaced as a set, and the flywheel face inspected, whenever the clutch is overhauled. See Chapter 6 for service procedures.

Condition	Possible Cause
Clutch chatter	1. Grease on driven plate (disc) facing 2. Binding clutch linkage or cable 3. Loose, damaged facings on driven plate (disc) 4. Engine mounts loose 5. Incorrect height adjustment of pressure plate release levers 6. Clutch housing or housing to transmission adapter misalignment 7. Loose driven plate hub
Clutch grabbing	1. Oil, grease on driven plate (disc) facing 2. Broken pressure plate 3. Warped or binding driven plate. Driven plate binding on clutch shaft
Clutch slips	1. Lack of lubrication in clutch linkage or cable (linkage or cable binds, causes incomplete engagement) 2. Incorrect pedal, or linkage adjustment 3. Broken pressure plate springs 4. Weak pressure plate springs 5. Grease on driven plate facings (disc)

Troubleshooting Clutch Problems (cont.)

Condition	Possible Cause
Incomplete clutch release	1. Incorrect pedal or linkage adjustment or linkage or cable binding 2. Incorrect height adjustment on pressure plate release levers 3. Loose, broken facings on driven plate (disc) 4. Bent, dished, warped driven plate caused by overheating
Grinding, whirring grating noise when pedal is depressed	1. Worn or defective throwout bearing 2. Starter drive teeth contacting flywheel ring gear teeth. Look for milled or polished teeth on ring gear.
Squeal, howl, trumpeting noise when pedal is being released (occurs during first inch to inch and one-half of pedal travel)	Pilot bushing worn or lack of lubricant. If bushing appears OK, polish bushing with emery cloth, soak lube wick in oil, lube bushing with oil, apply film of chassis grease to clutch shaft pilot hub, reassemble. NOTE: Bushing wear may be due to misalignment of clutch housing or housing to transmission adapter
Vibration or clutch pedal pulsation with clutch disengaged (pedal fully depressed)	1. Worn or defective engine transmission mounts 2. Flywheel run out. (Flywheel run out at face not to exceed 0.005") 3. Damaged or defective clutch components

Troubleshooting Manual Transmission Problems
See Chapter 6 for service procedures

Condition	Possible Cause
Transmission jumps out of gear	1. Misalignment of transmission case or clutch housing. 2. Worn pilot bearing in crankshaft. 3. Bent transmission shaft. 4. Worn high speed sliding gear. 5. Worn teeth or end-play in clutch shaft. 6. Insufficient spring tension on shifter rail plunger. 7. Bent or loose shifter fork. 8. Gears not engaging completely. 9. Loose or worn bearings on clutch shaft or mainshaft. 10. Worn gear teeth. 11. Worn or damaged detent balls.
Transmission sticks in gear	1. Clutch not releasing fully. 2. Burred or battered teeth on clutch shaft, or sliding sleeve. 3. Burred or battered transmission mainshaft. 4. Frozen synchronizing clutch. 5. Stuck shifter rail plunger. 6. Gearshift lever twisting and binding shifter rail. 7. Battered teeth on high speed sliding gear or on sleeve. 8. Improper lubrication, or lack of lubrication. 9. Corroded transmission parts. 10. Defective mainshaft pilot bearing. 11. Locked gear bearings will give same effect as stuck in gear.
Transmission gears will not synchronize	1. Binding pilot bearing on mainshaft, will synchronize in high gear only. 2. Clutch not releasing fully. 3. Detent spring weak or broken. 4. Weak or broken springs under balls in sliding gear sleeve. 5. Binding bearing on clutch shaft, or binding countershaft. 6. Binding pilot bearing in crankshaft. 7. Badly worn gear teeth. 8. Improper lubrication. 9. Constant mesh gear not turning freely on transmission mainshaft. Will synchronize in that gear only.

Condition	Possible Cause
Gears spinning when shifting into gear from neutral	1. Clutch not releasing fully. 2. In some cases an extremely light lubricant in transmission will cause gears to continue to spin for a short time after clutch is released. 3. Binding pilot bearing in crankshaft.
Transmission noisy in all gears	1. Insufficient lubricant, or improper lubricant. 2. Worn countergear bearings. 3. Worn or damaged main drive gear or countergear. 4. Damaged main drive gear or mainshaft bearings. 5. Worn or damaged countergear anti-lash plate.
Transmission noisy in neutral only	1. Damaged main drive gear bearing. 2. Damaged or loose mainshaft pilot bearing. 3. Worn or damaged countergear anti-lash plate. 4. Worn countergear bearings.
Transmission noisy in one gear only	1. Damaged or worn constant mesh gears. 2. Worn or damaged countergear bearings. 3. Damaged or worn synchronizer.
Transmission noisy in reverse only	1. Worn or damaged reverse idler gear or idler bushing. 2. Worn or damaged mainshaft reverse gear. 3. Worn or damaged reverse countergear. 4. Damaged shift mechanism.

TROUBLESHOOTING AUTOMATIC TRANSMISSION PROBLEMS

Keeping alert to changes in the operating characteristics of the transmission (changing shift points, noises, etc.) can prevent small problems from becoming large ones. If the problem cannot be traced to loose bolts, fluid level, misadjusted linkage, clogged filters or similar problems, you should probably seek professional service.

Transmission Fluid Indications

The appearance and odor of the transmission fluid can give valuable clues to the overall condition of the transmission. Always note the appearance of the fluid when you check the fluid level or change the fluid. Rub a small amount of fluid between your fingers to feel for grit and smell the fluid on the dipstick.

If the fluid appears:	It indicates:
Clear and red colored	Normal operation
Discolored (extremely dark red or brownish) or smells burned	Band or clutch pack failure, usually caused by an overheated transmission. Hauling very heavy loads with insufficient power or failure to change the fluid often result in overheating. Do not confuse this appearance with newer fluids that have a darker red color and a strong odor (though not a burned odor).
Foamy or aerated (light in color and full of bubbles)	1. The level is too high (gear train is churning oil) 2. An internal air leak (air is mixing with the fluid). Have the transmission checked professionally.
Solid residue in the fluid	Defective bands, clutch pack or bearings. Bits of band material or metal abrasives are clinging to the dipstick. Have the transmission checked professionally.
Varnish coating on the dipstick	The transmission fluid is overheating

TROUBLESHOOTING DRIVE AXLE PROBLEMS

First, determine when the noise is most noticeable.

Drive Noise: Produced under vehicle acceleration.

Coast Noise: Produced while coasting with a closed throttle.

Float Noise: Occurs while maintaining constant speed (just enough to keep speed constant) on a level road.

External Noise Elimination

It is advisable to make a thorough road test to determine whether the noise originates in the rear axle or whether it originates from the tires, engine, transmission, wheel bearings or road surface. Noise originating from other places cannot be corrected by servicing the rear axle.

ROAD NOISE

Brick or rough surfaced concrete roads produce noises that seem to come from the rear axle. Road noise is usually identical in Drive or Coast and driving on a different type of road will tell whether the road is the problem.

TIRE NOISE

Tire noise can be mistaken as rear axle noise, even though the tires on the front are at fault. Snow tread and mud tread tires or tires worn unevenly will frequently cause vibrations which seem to originate elsewhere; *temporarily, and for test purposes only,* inflate the tires to 40–50 lbs. This will significantly alter the noise produced by the tires, but will not alter noise from the rear axle. Noises from the rear axle will normally cease at speeds below 30 mph on coast, while tire noise will continue at lower tone as speed is decreased. The rear axle noise will usually change from drive conditions to coast conditions, while tire noise will not. Do not forget to lower the tire pressure to normal after the test is complete.

ENGINE/TRANSMISSION NOISE

Determine at what speed the noise is most pronounced, then stop in a quiet place. With the transmission in Neutral, run the engine through speeds corresponding to road speeds where the noise was noticed. Noises produced with the vehicle standing still are coming from the engine or transmission.

FRONT WHEEL BEARINGS

Front wheel bearing noises, sometimes confused with rear axle noises, will not change when comparing drive and coast conditions. While holding the speed steady, lightly apply the footbrake. This will often cause wheel bearing noise to lessen, as some of the weight is taken off the bearing. Front wheel bearings are easily checked by jacking up the wheels and spinning the wheels. Shaking the wheels will also determine if the wheel bearings are excessively loose.

REAR AXLE NOISES

Eliminating other possible sources can narrow the cause to the rear axle, which normally produces noise from worn gears or bearings. Gear noises tend to peak in a narrow speed range, while bearing noises will usually vary in pitch with engine speeds.

Noise Diagnosis

The Noise Is:	Most Probably Produced By:
1. Identical under Drive or Coast	Road surface, tires or front wheel bearings
2. Different depending on road surface	Road surface or tires
3. Lower as speed is lowered	Tires
4. Similar when standing or moving	Engine or transmission
5. A vibration	Unbalanced tires, rear wheel bearing, unbalanced driveshaft or worn U-joint
6. A knock or click about every two tire revolutions	Rear wheel bearing
7. Most pronounced on turns	Damaged differential gears
8. A steady low-pitched whirring or scraping, starting at low speeds	Damaged or worn pinion bearing
9. A chattering vibration on turns	Wrong differential lubricant or worn clutch plates (limited slip rear axle)
10. Noticed only in Drive, Coast or Float conditions	Worn ring gear and/or pinion gear

Troubleshooting Steering & Suspension Problems

Condition	Possible Cause
Hard steering (wheel is hard to turn)	1. Improper tire pressure 2. Loose or glazed pump drive belt 3. Low or incorrect fluid 4. Loose, bent or poorly lubricated front end parts 5. Improper front end alignment (excessive caster) 6. Bind in steering column or linkage 7. Kinked hydraulic hose 8. Air in hydraulic system 9. Low pump output or leaks in system 10. Obstruction in lines 11. Pump valves sticking or out of adjustment 12. Incorrect wheel alignment
Loose steering (too much play in steering wheel)	1. Loose wheel bearings 2. Faulty shocks 3. Worn linkage or suspension components 4. Loose steering gear mounting or linkage points 5. Steering mechanism worn or improperly adjusted 6. Valve spool improperly adjusted 7. Worn ball joints, tie-rod ends, etc.
Veers or wanders (pulls to one side with hands off steering wheel)	1. Improper tire pressure 2. Improper front end alignment 3. Dragging or improperly adjusted brakes 4. Bent frame 5. Improper rear end alignment 6. Faulty shocks or springs 7. Loose or bent front end components 8. Play in Pitman arm 9. Steering gear mountings loose 10. Loose wheel bearings 11. Binding Pitman arm 12. Spool valve sticking or improperly adjusted 13. Worn ball joints
Wheel oscillation or vibration transmitted through steering wheel	1. Low or uneven tire pressure 2. Loose wheel bearings 3. Improper front end alignment 4. Bent spindle 5. Worn, bent or broken front end components 6. Tires out of round or out of balance 7. Excessive lateral runout in disc brake rotor 8. Loose or bent shock absorber or strut
Noises (see also "Troubleshooting Drive Axle Problems")	1. Loose belts 2. Low fluid, air in system 3. Foreign matter in system 4. Improper lubrication 5. Interference or chafing in linkage 6. Steering gear mountings loose 7. Incorrect adjustment or wear in gear box 8. Faulty valves or wear in pump 9. Kinked hydraulic lines 10. Worn wheel bearings
Poor return of steering	1. Over-inflated tires 2. Improperly aligned front end (excessive caster) 3. Binding in steering column 4. No lubrication in front end 5. Steering gear adjusted too tight
Uneven tire wear (see "How To Read Tire Wear")	1. Incorrect tire pressure 2. Improperly aligned front end 3. Tires out-of-balance 4. Bent or worn suspension parts

HOW TO READ TIRE WEAR

The way your tires wear is a good indicator of other parts of the suspension. Abnormal wear patterns are often caused by the need for simple tire maintenance, or for front end alignment.

Excessive wear at the center of the tread indicates that the air pressure in the tire is consistently too high. The tire is riding on the center of the tread and wearing it prematurely. Occasionally, this wear pattern can result from outrageously wide tires on narrow rims. The cure for this is to replace either the tires or the wheels.

This type of wear usually results from consistent under-inflation. When a tire is under-inflated, there is too much contact with the road by the outer treads, which wear prematurely. When this type of wear occurs, and the tire pressure is known to be consistently correct, a bent or worn steering component or the need for wheel alignment could be indicated.

Feathering is a condition when the edge of each tread rib develops a slightly rounded edge on one side and a sharp edge on the other. By running your hand over the tire, you can usually feel the sharper edges before you'll be able to see them. The most common causes of feathering are incorrect toe-in setting or deteriorated bushings in the front suspension.

When an inner or outer rib wears faster than the rest of the tire, the need for wheel alignment is indicated. There is excessive camber in the front suspension, causing the wheel to lean too much putting excessive load on one side of the tire. Misalignment could also be due to sagging springs, worn ball joints, or worn control arm bushings. Be sure the vehicle is loaded the way it's normally driven when you have the wheels aligned.

Cups or scalloped dips appearing around the edge of the tread almost always indicate worn (sometimes bent) suspension parts. Adjustment of wheel alignment alone will seldom cure the problem. Any worn component that connects the wheel to the suspension can cause this type of wear. Occasionally, wheels that are out of balance will wear like this, but wheel imbalance usually shows up as bald spots between the outside edges and center of the tread.

Second-rib wear is usually found only in radial tires, and appears where the steel belts end in relation to the tread. It can be kept to a minimum by paying careful attention to tire pressure and frequently rotating the tires. This is often considered normal wear but excessive amounts indicate that the tires are too wide for the wheels.

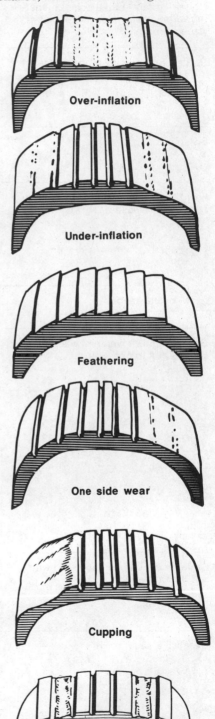

Over-inflation

Under-inflation

Feathering

One side wear

Cupping

Second-rib wear

Troubleshooting Disc Brake Problems

Condition	Possible Cause
Noise—groan—brake noise emanating when slowly releasing brakes (creep-groan)	Not detrimental to function of disc brakes—no corrective action required. (This noise may be eliminated by slightly increasing or decreasing brake pedal efforts.)
Rattle—brake noise or rattle emanating at low speeds on rough roads, (front wheels only).	1. Shoe anti-rattle spring missing or not properly positioned. 2. Excessive clearance between shoe and caliper. 3. Soft or broken caliper seals. 4. Deformed or misaligned disc. 5. Loose caliper.
Scraping	1. Mounting bolts too long. 2. Loose wheel bearings. 3. Bent, loose, or misaligned splash shield.
Front brakes heat up during driving and fail to release	1. Operator riding brake pedal. 2. Stop light switch improperly adjusted. 3. Sticking pedal linkage. 4. Frozen or seized piston. 5. Residual pressure valve in master cylinder. 6. Power brake malfunction. 7. Proportioning valve malfunction.
Leaky brake caliper	1. Damaged or worn caliper piston seal. 2. Scores or corrosion on surface of cylinder bore.
Grabbing or uneven brake action— Brakes pull to one side	1. Causes listed under "Brakes Pull". 2. Power brake malfunction. 3. Low fluid level in master cylinder. 4. Air in hydraulic system. 5. Brake fluid, oil or grease on linings. 6. Unmatched linings. 7. Distorted brake pads. 8. Frozen or seized pistons. 9. Incorrect tire pressure. 10. Front end out of alignment. 11. Broken rear spring. 12. Brake caliper pistons sticking. 13. Restricted hose or line. 14. Caliper not in proper alignment to braking disc. 15. Stuck or malfunctioning metering valve. 16. Soft or broken caliper seals. 17. Loose caliper.
Brake pedal can be depressed without braking effect	1. Air in hydraulic system or improper bleeding procedure. 2. Leak past primary cup in master cylinder. 3. Leak in system. 4. Rear brakes out of adjustment. 5. Bleeder screw open.
Excessive pedal travel	1. Air, leak, or insufficient fluid in system or caliper. 2. Warped or excessively tapered shoe and lining assembly. 3. Excessive disc runout. 4. Rear brake adjustment required. 5. Loose wheel bearing adjustment. 6. Damaged caliper piston seal. 7. Improper brake fluid (boil). 8. Power brake malfunction. 9. Weak or soft hoses.

Troubleshooting Disc Brake Problems (cont.)

Condition	Possible Cause
Brake roughness or chatter (pedal pumping)	1. Excessive thickness variation of braking disc. 2. Excessive lateral runout of braking disc. 3. Rear brake drums out-of-round. 4. Excessive front bearing clearance.
Excessive pedal effort	1. Brake fluid, oil or grease on linings. 2. Incorrect lining. 3. Frozen or seized pistons. 4. Power brake malfunction. 5. Kinked or collapsed hose or line. 6. Stuck metering valve. 7. Scored caliper or master cylinder bore. 8. Seized caliper pistons.
Brake pedal fades (pedal travel increases with foot on brake)	1. Rough master cylinder or caliper bore. 2. Loose or broken hydraulic lines/connections. 3. Air in hydraulic system. 4. Fluid level low. 5. Weak or soft hoses. 6. Inferior quality brake shoes or fluid. 7. Worn master cylinder piston cups or seals.

Troubleshooting Drum Brakes

Condition	Possible Cause
Pedal goes to floor	1. Fluid low in reservoir. 2. Air in hydraulic system. 3. Improperly adjusted brake. 4. Leaking wheel cylinders. 5. Loose or broken brake lines. 6. Leaking or worn master cylinder. 7. Excessively worn brake lining.
Spongy brake pedal	1. Air in hydraulic system. 2. Improper brake fluid (low boiling point). 3. Excessively worn or cracked brake drums. 4. Broken pedal pivot bushing.
Brakes pulling	1. Contaminated lining. 2. Front end out of alignment. 3. Incorrect brake adjustment. 4. Unmatched brake lining. 5. Brake drums out of round. 6. Brake shoes distorted. 7. Restricted brake hose or line. 8. Broken rear spring. 9. Worn brake linings. 10. Uneven lining wear. 11. Glazed brake lining. 12. Excessive brake lining dust. 13. Heat spotted brake drums. 14. Weak brake return springs. 15. Faulty automatic adjusters. 16. Low or incorrect tire pressure.

Condition	Possible Cause
Squealing brakes	1. Glazed brake lining. 2. Saturated brake lining. 3. Weak or broken brake shoe retaining spring. 4. Broken or weak brake shoe return spring. 5. Incorrect brake lining. 6. Distorted brake shoes. 7. Bent support plate. 8. Dust in brakes or scored brake drums. 9. Linings worn below limit. 10. Uneven brake lining wear. 11. Heat spotted brake drums.
Chirping brakes	1. Out of round drum or eccentric axle flange pilot.
Dragging brakes	1. Incorrect wheel or parking brake adjustment. 2. Parking brakes engaged or improperly adjusted. 3. Weak or broken brake shoe return spring. 4. Brake pedal binding. 5. Master cylinder cup sticking. 6. Obstructed master cylinder relief port. 7. Saturated brake lining. 8. Bent or out of round brake drum. 9. Contaminated or improper brake fluid. 10. Sticking wheel cylinder pistons. 11. Driver riding brake pedal. 12. Defective proportioning valve. 13. Insufficient brake shoe lubricant.
Hard pedal	1. Brake booster inoperative. 2. Incorrect brake lining. 3. Restricted brake line or hose. 4. Frozen brake pedal linkage. 5. Stuck wheel cylinder. 6. Binding pedal linkage. 7. Faulty proportioning valve.
Wheel locks	1. Contaminated brake lining. 2. Loose or torn brake lining. 3. Wheel cylinder cups sticking. 4. Incorrect wheel bearing adjustment. 5. Faulty proportioning valve.
Brakes fade (high speed)	1. Incorrect lining. 2. Overheated brake drums. 3. Incorrect brake fluid (low boiling temperature). 4. Saturated brake lining. 5. Leak in hydraulic system. 6. Faulty automatic adjusters.
Pedal pulsates	1. Bent or out of round brake drum.
Brake chatter and shoe knock	1. Out of round brake drum. 2. Loose support plate. 3. Bent support plate. 4. Distorted brake shoes. 5. Machine grooves in contact face of brake drum (Shoe Knock). 6. Contaminated brake lining. 7. Missing or loose components. 8. Incorrect lining material. 9. Out-of-round brake drums. 10. Heat spotted or scored brake drums. 11. Out-of-balance wheels.

Troubleshooting Drum Brakes (cont.)

Condition	Possible Cause
Brakes do not self adjust	1. Adjuster screw frozen in thread. 2. Adjuster screw corroded at thrust washer. 3. Adjuster lever does not engage star wheel. 4. Adjuster installed on wrong wheel.
Brake light glows	1. Leak in the hydraulic system. 2. Air in the system. 3. Improperly adjusted master cylinder pushrod. 4. Uneven lining wear. 5. Failure to center combination valve or proportioning valve.

Mechanic's Data

General Conversion Table

Multiply By	To Convert	To	
LENGTH			
2.54	Inches	Centimeters	.3937
25.4	Inches	Millimeters	.03937
30.48	Feet	Centimeters	.0328
.304	Feet	Meters	3.28
.914	Yards	Meters	1.094
1.609	Miles	Kilometers	.621
VOLUME			
.473	Pints	Liters	2.11
.946	Quarts	Liters	1.06
3.785	Gallons	Liters	.264
.016	Cubic inches	Liters	61.02
16.39	Cubic inches	Cubic cms.	.061
28.3	Cubic feet	Liters	.0353
MASS (Weight)			
28.35	Ounces	Grams	.035
.4536	Pounds	Kilograms	2.20
—	To obtain	From	Multiply by

Multiply By	To Convert	To	
AREA			
.645	Square inches	Square cms.	.155
.836	Square yds.	Square meters	1.196
FORCE			
4.448	Pounds	Newtons	.225
.138	Ft./lbs.	Kilogram/meters	7.23
1.36	Ft./lbs.	Newton-meters	.737
.112	In./lbs.	Newton-meters	8.844
PRESSURE			
.068	Psi	Atmospheres	14.7
6.89	Psi	Kilopascals	.145
OTHER			
1.104	Horsepower (DIN)	Horsepower (SAE)	.9861
.746	Horsepower (SAE)	Kilowatts (KW)	1.34
1.60	Mph	Km/h	.625
.425	Mpg	Km/1	2.35
—	To obtain	From	Multiply by

Tap Drill Sizes

National Coarse or U.S.S.

Screw & Tap Size	Threads Per Inch	Use Drill Number
No. 5	40	.39
No. 6	32	.36
No. 8	32	.29
No. 10	24	.25
No. 12	24	.17
$\frac{1}{4}$	20	8
$\frac{5}{16}$	18	F
$\frac{3}{8}$	16	$\frac{5}{16}$
$\frac{7}{16}$	14	U
$\frac{1}{2}$	13	$\frac{27}{64}$
$\frac{9}{16}$	12	$\frac{31}{64}$
$\frac{5}{8}$	11	$\frac{17}{32}$
$\frac{3}{4}$	10	$\frac{21}{32}$
$\frac{7}{8}$	9	$\frac{49}{64}$

National Coarse or U.S.S.

Screw & Tap Size	Threads Per Inch	Use Drill Number
1	8	$\frac{7}{8}$
$1\frac{1}{8}$	7	$\frac{63}{64}$
$1\frac{1}{4}$	7	$1\frac{7}{64}$
$1\frac{1}{2}$	6	$1\frac{11}{32}$

National Fine or S.A.E.

Screw & Tap Size	Threads Per Inch	Use Drill Number
No. 5	44	.37
No. 6	40	.33
No. 8	36	.29
No. 10	32	.21

National Fine or S.A.E.

Screw & Tap Size	Threads Per Inch	Use Drill Number
No. 12	28	.15
$\frac{1}{4}$	28	3
$\frac{6}{16}$	24	1
$\frac{3}{8}$	24	Q
$\frac{7}{16}$	20	W
$\frac{1}{2}$	20	$\frac{29}{64}$
$\frac{9}{16}$	18	$\frac{33}{64}$
$\frac{5}{8}$	18	$\frac{37}{64}$
$\frac{3}{4}$	16	$\frac{11}{16}$
$\frac{7}{8}$	14	$\frac{13}{16}$
$1\frac{1}{8}$	12	$1\frac{3}{64}$
$1\frac{1}{4}$	12	$1\frac{11}{64}$
$1\frac{1}{2}$	12	$1\frac{27}{64}$

Drill Sizes In Decimal Equivalents

Inch	Decimal	Wire	mm	Inch	Decimal	Wire	mm	Inch	Decimal	Wire & Letter	mm	Inch	Decimal	Letter	mm	Inch	Decimal	mm
1/64	.0156		.39		.0730	49			.1614		4.1		.2717		6.9		.4331	11.0
	.0157		.4		.0748		1.9		.1654		4.2		.2720	I		7/16	.4375	11.11
	.0160	78			.0760	48			.1660	19			.2756		7.0		.4528	11.5
	.0165		.42		.0768		1.95		.1673		4.25		.2770	J		29/64	.4531	11.51
	.0173		.44	5/64	.0781		1.98		.1693		4.3		.2795		7.1	15/32	.4688	11.90
	.0177		.45		.0785	47			.1695	18			.2810	K			.4724	12.0
	.0180	77			.0787		2.0	11/64	.1719		4.36	9/32	.2812		7.14	31/64	.4844	12.30
	.0181		.46		.0807		2.05		.1730	17			.2835		7.2		.4921	12.5
	.0189		.48		.0810	46			.1732		4.4		.2854		7.25	1/2	.5000	12.70
	.0197		.5		.0820	45			.1770	16			.2874		7.3		.5118	13.0
	.0200	76			.0827		2.1		.1772		4.5		.2900	L		33/64	.5156	13.09
	.0210	75			.0846		2.15		.1800	15			.2913		7.4	17/32	.5312	13.49
	.0217		.55		.0860	44			.1811		4.6		.2950	M			.5315	13.5
	.0225	74			.0866		2.2		.1820	14			.2953		7.5	35/64	.5469	13.89
	.0236		.6		.0886		2.25		.1850	13		19/64	.2969		7.54		.5512	14.0
	.0240	73			.0890	43			.1850		4.7		.2992		7.6	9/16	.5625	14.28
	.0250	72			.0906		2.3		.1870		4.75		.3020	N			.5709	14.5
	.0256		.65		.0925		2.35	3/16	.1875		4.76		.3031		7.7	37/64	.5781	14.68
	.0260	71			.0935	42			.1890		4.8		.3051		7.75		.5906	15.0
	.0276		.7	3/32	.0938		2.38		.1890	12			.3071		7.8	19/32	.5938	15.08
	.0280	70			.0945		2.4		.1910	11			.3110		7.9	39/64	.6094	15.47
	.0292	69			.0960	41			.1929		4.9	5/16	.3125		7.93		.6102	15.5
	.0295		.75		.0965		2.45		.1935	10			.3150		8.0	5/8	.6250	15.87
	.0310	68			.0980	40			.1960	9			.3160	O			.6299	16.0
1/32	.0312		.79		.0981		2.5		.1969		5.0		.3189		8.1	41/64	.6406	16.27
	.0315		.8		.0995	39			.1990	8			.3228		8.2		.6496	16.5
	.0320	67			.1015	38			.2008		5.1		.3230	P		21/32	.6562	16.66
	.0330	66			.1024		2.6		.2010	7			.3248		8.25		.6693	17.0
	.0335		.85		.1040	37		13/64	.2031		5.16		.3268		8.3	43/64	.6719	17.06
	.0350	65			.1063		2.7		.2040	6		21/64	.3281		8.33	11/16	.6875	17.46
	.0354		.9		.1065	36			.2047		5.2		.3307		8.4		.6890	17.5
	.0360	64			.1083		2.75		.2055	5			.3320	Q		45/64	.7031	17.85
	.0370	63		7/64	.1094		2.77		.2067		5.25		.3346		8.5		.7087	18.0
	.0374		.95		.1100	35			.2087		5.3		.3386		8.6	23/32	.7188	18.25
	.0380	62			.1102		2.8		.2090	4			.3390	R			.7283	18.5
	.0390	61			.1110	34			.2126		5.4		.3425		8.7	47/64	.7344	18.65
	.0394		1.0		.1130	33			.2130	3		11/32	.3438		8.73		.7480	19.0
	.0400	60			.1142		2.9		.2165		5.5		.3445		8.75	3/4	.7500	19.05
	.0410	59			.1160	32		7/32	.2188		5.55		.3465		8.8	49/64	.7656	19.44
	.0413		1.05		.1181		3.0		.2205		5.6		.3480	S			.7677	19.5
	.0420	58			.1200	31			.2210	2			.3504		8.9	25/32	.7812	19.84
	.0430	57			.1220		3.1		.2244		5.7		.3543		9.0		.7874	20.0
	.0433		1.1	1/8	.1250		3.17		.2264		5.75		.3580	T		51/64	.7969	20.24
	.0453		1.15		.1260		3.2		.2280	1			.3583		9.1		.8071	20.5
3/64	.0465	56			.1280		3.25		.2283		5.8	23/64	.3594		9.12	13/16	.8125	20.63
	.0469		1.19		.1285	30			.2323		5.9		.3622		9.2		.8268	21.0
	.0472		1.2		.1299		3.3		.2340	A			.3642		9.25	53/64	.8281	21.03
	.0492		1.25		.1339		3.4	15/64	.2344		5.95		.3661		9.3	27/32	.8438	21.43
	.0512		1.3		.1360	29			.2362		6.0		.3680	U			.8465	21.5
	.0520	55			.1378		3.5		.2380	B			.3701		9.4	55/64	.8594	21.82
	.0531		1.35		.1405	28			.2402		6.1		.3740		9.5		.8661	22.0
	.0550	54		9/64	.1406		3.57		.2420	C		3/8	.3750		9.52	7/8	.8750	22.22
	.0551		1.4		.1417		3.6		.2441		6.2		.3770	V			.8858	22.5
	.0571		1.45		.1440	27			.2460	D			.3780		9.6	57/64	.8906	22.62
	.0591		1.5		.1457		3.7		.2461		6.25		.3819		9.7		.9055	23.0
	.0595	53			.1470	26			.2480		6.3		.3839		9.75	29/32	.9062	23.01
	.0610		1.55		.1476		3.75	1/4	.2500	E	6.35		.3858		9.8	59/64	.9219	23.41
1/16	.0625		1.59		.1495	25			.2520		6.		.3860	W			.9252	23.5
	.0630		1.6		.1496		3.8		.2559		6.5		.3898		9.9	15/16	.9375	23.81
	.0635	52			.1520	24			.2570	F		25/64	.3906		9.92		.9449	24.0
	.0650		1.65		.1535		3.9		.2598		6.6		.3937		10.0	61/64	.9531	24.2
	.0669		1.7		.1540	23			.2610	G			.3970	X			.9646	24.5
	.0670	51		5/32	.1562		3.96		.2638		6.7		.4040	Y		31/32	.9688	24.6
	.0689		1.75		.1570	22		17/64	.2656		6.74	13/32	.4062		10.31		.9843	25.0
	.0700	50			.1575		4.0		.2657		6.75		.4130	Z		63/64	.9844	25.0
	.0709		1.8		.1590	21			.2660	H			.4134		10.5	1	1.0000	25.4
	.0728		1.85		.1610	20			.2677		6.8	27/64	.4219		10.71			

Index